Counterfact

Counterfact

Fake News and Misinformation in the Digital Information Age

Andrew Weiss

ROWMAN & LITTLEFIELD
Lanham • Boulder • New York • London

Published by Rowman & Littlefield
An imprint of The Rowman & Littlefield Publishing Group, Inc.
4501 Forbes Boulevard, Suite 200, Lanham, Maryland 20706
www.rowman.com

86-90 Paul Street, London EC2A 4NE

British Library Cataloguing in Publication Information Available

Library of Congress Cataloging-in-Publication Data

Names: Weiss, Andrew, 1971- author.
Title: Counterfact : fake news and misinformation in the digital information age /
    Andrew Weiss.
Description: Lanham : Rowman and Littlefield, 2024. | Includes bibliographical
    references and index.
Identifiers: LCCN 2023050642 (print) | LCCN 2023050643 (ebook) | ISBN
    9781538177372 (cloth) | ISBN 9781538177389 (paperback) | ISBN
    9781538177396 (ebook)
Subjects: LCSH: Fake news—Social aspects. | Disinformation—Social aspects. | Digital
    media—Social aspects. | Media literacy—Social aspects.
Classification: LCC PN4784.F27 .W35 2024 (print) | LCC PN4784.F27 (ebook) | DDC
    070.4/3–dc23/eng/20231219
LC record available at https://lccn.loc.gov/2023050642
LC ebook record available at https://lccn.loc.gov/2023050643

To Akiko, Mia, Stella, and Winnie

Contents

List of Figures

Acknowledgments

Special acknowledgment to the editorial staff at Rowman & Littlefield for their help in shaping and developing this book, especially Charles Harmon for being an incredibly supportive and positive editor. Among colleagues at CSUN, many thanks to library dean Mark Stover for his general support of research and scholarship and to Ahmed Alwan and Eric Garcia, my longtime research collaborators in fake news and misinformation, much of which informs the fake news model outlined in this book. Finally, a special acknowledgment to Akiko for her patience as I write yet another book, much of it after hours during evenings, weekends, vacations, and holidays.

Preface

Buck Rogers in the 25th Century was my favorite show on TV when I was about eight or nine. I remember just a few things about it now but recall being so in love with the show that I told my mother I wanted to "go there" when I was older. It seemed like the logical thing to say as they were showing me exactly what the future was going to look like! She looked at me funny and said, "you know it's not real, right?" I hesitated and finally said, "Uh . . . yeah?" To my mind, though, it definitely *felt* real. It sure seemed like what the future was going to look like. Of course, that was all an illusion. Looking at online video clips of the show now, it's obviously closer to the reality of 1980 than even the second decade of the twenty-first century, let alone the year 2491. It's aged badly, to say the least.

Perhaps some of the show's impact on me stemmed from the opening credits sequence, which showed Buck Rogers launching into space in the near future of 1987. The narrator's serious voice-over and the use of video footage taken from real NASA rocket launches seemed convincing to this nine-year-old. It didn't occur to me that stock documentary video footage could be taken and reworked into a completely new narrative, which in this case was the far-fetched return of Buck Rogers found cryogenically frozen in deep space! Factor in the little knowledge I had of recent space exploration—I knew about the Apollo moon landings, but the fiction of *Star Wars* loomed larger—and I was ripe for falling for a false idea that appeared on the surface to be plausible. It really only took a quizzical look from my mother to set me straight, but the fantasy would be hard to shake for a while. I recall the palpable disappointment of learning it was just fiction.

My example isn't much different than many others who have fallen for an illusion or were tricked by something that seemed real. It seems to be a very human thing to do. Our narratives, false or not, give us meaning and serve to point us in the directions we want to go. Forty years later, we still don't yet have flying cars, hyperdrives, or high-functioning robot servants, but other technological advances have taken us much farther than we ever could have imagined.

It may be surprising for some readers to learn that despite the recent notoriety around fake news and misinformation, it is not something new. We find that the more things change, the more they stay the same when it comes to dealing with falsehoods. Indeed, we are confronted with early examples of fake news that still remain relevant to us today and that have taken on even wider meanings in the internet age. This includes similar preoccupations with trust and the fear of being lied to, or how we are focused on similar desires for knowledge for our own personal growth through learning. But we can be harmed by these same desires as well.

Underpinning this book, then, are themes and behaviors that hearken back to previous eras and earlier cultures. Similarly, throughout this book we will come to examine the issues fundamental for all students and seekers of information who thirst for knowledge and understanding. We come to realize that we can often lose our way in our search for this information and knowledge. In fact, this happens more easily than many of us would care to admit. Even the most dedicated of us—students, academics, librarians, working professionals—can easily fall prey to errors and deception. This book examines some of the reasons why this occurs by looking at not only the actors who drive and develop fake news and misinformation but also the personal individual traits inherent to all of us that may make us, from time to time, gullible marks to those who would deceive us.

FOUNDATIONAL MYTHS AND LEGENDS

A look at our present, however, and our dreams about the future (both near and far off) requires a look into the past. In a mass media–driven society, libraries have become powerful symbols not only of the collective accumulation of knowledge itself but also of the beneficial promise that universal knowledge would bestow upon our cultures and the powerful influence that projects to outsiders. In the liberal world order, this provides hope and potential for all who seek it out. It is ironically through the loss or weakening of libraries, when they are destroyed and damaged, vandalized by the "unenlightened," or debased and censored in times of fear and upheaval, that their fragile value becomes most realized and their contents prioritized for protection. Sometimes this comes too late, especially in times when libraries' enduring presence and influence are taken for granted or devalued. The dream of universal knowledge lived on through centuries with the image of the Library of Alexandria, the burned and lost collection of the Classical world's most prized knowledge and culture. Through the lost dialogues of

Plato, the incomplete teachings of Aristotle, or the fragments of Sappho we try to reconstruct the perfect library in our minds, striving for what seems knowable, and contemplating for a moment the barbarity of previous ages. Despite this dream, however, we come to realize that this comprehensiveness is just a mirage. The collection of the Library of Alexandria was surely incomplete, despite boasts to the contrary, and shows us the very limits of the library as a symbol of total knowledge. Another hard truth comes upon us quickly after that: libraries have always been imperfect and distorted reflectors of their cultures.

That striving for full and complete knowledge, however, remains deep in our collective myths, appearing in stories about Prometheus, the Tower of Babel, and Pandora's box. We feel a sense of dread and looming that exists underneath the shining surface of knowledge's promise. Prometheus, bound to have his liver torn out eternally for giving the gift of fire to humanity, is representative of the double-edged sword of information itself. Knowledge comes at a price for those who would wield it. In Pandora's case, we are faced with a beautiful and tempting evil that results in the gift of unintended consequences from seeking out something forbidden or from satisfying our curiosity. For Babel, it is also *babble*. The breadth, depth, and width of this omnivorous omnipresence is the modern internet in all of its confounding glory: all things at all times in perpetual and instant availability. But this comes with the price of a deafening confusion, mental overstimulation, and a decline in shared understanding.

These old stories speak of an even older desire for knowledge and the power that comes with it. From these multiple perspectives, they all have a similar assumption: that the things sought after are true and consequential. But what if, at the heart of these stories, something *were* missing? What if it, too, were illusory? That is a fundamental question that we all keep coming back to: *What is real?* And, conversely, *what is false?* One of the most interesting myths for our time—perhaps one that is the most relevant to life in online virtual worlds—is the Grapes of Zeuxis. In this story, Zeuxis paints a still life of grapes so perfectly that not only are people fooled, but even the birds are compelled to come and peck at them. Zeuxis's Grapes has been lauded as the paragon of human ingenuity and has been seen as one of the ideals of *mimetic* Western art (and perhaps not that far from the current emphasis on ever more realistic CGI in Hollywood blockbusters).

The facsimile of reality becomes more convincing than the real thing, and there is complete willingness on our part at times to buy into this illusion, for we can derive much satisfaction from reveling within it. Art relies upon our suspension of disbelief, the irony and paradox being that through lies and deception we can come to understand and accept fundamental truths better than if merely told the unvarnished truth. Beyond this irony exists a deeper problem, however; *mimesis*, the imitation of reality itself, is a deception that can too easily be taken as real in negative ways. As poet Yves Bonnefoy suggests, Zeuxis's perfect representation of his grapes is "a lure that works all too well; it's trompe-l'oeil deception invites its own destruction" (Bonnefoy, 1992). The illusion of the grapes is ultimately punctured, the colors fade away, and the ripped-up canvas is left disintegrating on stone tiles while the birds starve. The internet is a great analogue to this issue of image versus reality. Might we all sometimes feel the same as these birds when we salivate over perfectly photographed images of someone's breakfast posted on TikTok?

Even now, surrounded by our most sophisticated technologies, people easily fall for tricks and hoaxes, not unlike the Great Moon Hoax from nearly two hundred years ago. When the Webb telescope started sending back its images, scientists were quick to share some results, though one image passed through social media, which a scientist claimed was a sun but turned out to be the cross section of a *chorizo*. Even being aware that something is unreal can still cause confusion in people. Currently, digital avatars like "Imma" and "Seraphine," whose likenesses are rendered into real-live images and videos, show us how we can be simultaneously drawn to and repulsed by the gaps between the fake, the real, and the uncanny valleys that these create. The dissonance of what seems real and what is so obviously fake creates an interesting *frisson*, or thrill, while also creating distinct sensations of disgust (Ong, 2020). Our own feelings and perceptions are constantly challenged when our sense of authenticity and veracity become compromised.

THE PROMISE OF KNOWLEDGE THROUGH INFORMATION

But what compels us onward to new things, even as they both attract and repulse, intrigue and bore? Information seeking has long been seen as related to fulfilling a psychological need, helping us reach higher states of satisfaction and growth. But information itself is just a stone along the path toward knowledge. Place enough stones in front of you and a clear path begins to materialize, but it is one that can only progress forward in increments—stone by stone, bit by bit, item by item—until you find you have progressed while you weren't looking. So perhaps this is a poor analogy. Researcher Bertram Brookes considers information to be less a "thing" that fills up available buckets (such as databases, books, and brains) and more like a process, "which modifies a user's knowledge structure" (Brookes, 1980). The development of knowledge is implied in the process of searching for information, just as knowledge itself is implied to be built upon something incontrovertible, something filled with certitude, and developed with unchangeable truths. The destination may not always be the goal, in other words, and the result may be to arrive back where we started, but the journey is part of the learning process, bringing us closer to the great promise that lies beyond gathered knowledge: *wisdom*.

Some of these unchangeable truths come to us from our use of critical thinking skills fostered by our own native intelligence. Some of these come, like our shock with the Grapes of Zeuxis, from our preoccupations with fact, fiction, and the falseness and truthiness that arrive in both. The most successful way to help us understand what is real and what is false has been the development and adoption of the scientific method. Yet it remains difficult for some people to separate science from pseudoscience; therefore, distinguishing between these, as Karl Popper, Thomas Kuhn, and other philosophers of science have attempted, becomes essential. We need to distinguish good science from bad science, false conclusions from valid ones, data and information from knowledge and wisdom, and even our own good judgment from our prejudices. While it is usually easy for people to distinguish between facts and opinions, sometimes those lines blur in ways that are unclear even to ourselves. Opinions are often just how we interpret what the facts mean to us and what actions are best taken as a result. But facts don't always tell us what ought to be done, and so we look for guidance from others, which sometimes steers us wrong.

We are also notoriously bad at distinguishing good judgment from poor prejudice. The human mind is capable of incredibly imaginative creations but also prone to pitfalls. Some of these pitfalls are minor: we fool ourselves into thinking, for example, that we look better than we really do; or our voices sound wonderful to our ears—until we hear a recording of our voices, stripped of the warmth and familiarity of our own physical bodies. Then we are shocked at the reality of how our subjectivity has clouded the judgments we have made about ourselves. But some of the pathologies, such as racism or conspiracy theorizing, are very detrimental and damage us when we fail to heed how important factual information really is.

THE BASICS OF INFORMATION BEHAVIOR

The lens through which most of this book examines the phenomenon of fake news falls within a subset of library and information science known as information behavior. The topic itself is incredibly broad. As Beth St. Jean writes, the essential quality of information behavior is "information + a verb" (St. Jean et al., 2021, p. 10). This involves examining the physical and mental acts humans employ to incorporate information into their knowledge bases (Cole,

2013). As such, it involves a large array of conditions but boils down to examining an individual's need for information, their actions taken to seek it out, and how they use it once they find it—*if* they find it. Information needs often stem from within, but not always. Information-seeking behavior is analyzed not only by observing individual behaviors and seeking out their motivations but also by examining the behavioral trends of people within larger groups. Within this extremely wide framework, any number of models and theories exist to help explain the ways in which people utilize (or don't utilize) it. Too detailed and complex to cover in detail here, readers can find much more about the various important theories and models of information behavior in the book *Theories of Information Behavior*, a compendium of the discipline's most important research areas.

That overall area of inquiry provides important insight into the motivations and causes of human behavior related to information, focusing on two main areas: cognitive and sociological. These two strands along with a mixing of the two, prosaically called "the multifaceted approach," look at the internal thoughts and processes of information users, their sociological contexts, and the important *locus* of interaction between the two (Cole, 2013). In this text, theories of information behavior will serve as the framework for the investigation of fake news and misinformation, with special focus on affective needs and metacognition, and with a little less focus on information literacy (IL). IL has often been proposed as an essential approach for neutralizing the effects of fake news and misinformation, but it has come under greater criticism recently as not appearing to be sufficiently effective to counteract the worst aspects of fake news.

Affect, as defined in information behavior literature, "more broadly includes emotion, mood, preference, and evaluation, are increasingly viewed as central to the user-centered perspective" (Julien et al., 2005). In this case, we are interested in seeing how emotion and mood impact the ways in which people interact with information—including false information and fake news. As information scholar Diane Nahl suggests, "successful information behavior depends upon continuous coping procedures to regulate negative and positive affective forces operating on individuals in information intense environments" (Nahl, 2005). Such negative "forces" might include irritation, uncertainty, personal stress, and time pressures, while the positive forces include optimism, self-efficacy, pleasure, and interest. Information behavior, therefore, depends upon observing the mental states of the user, who is central to the information seeking and use process.

Brenda Dervin, one of the most influential of researchers into information behavior, posits that information seekers engage in "sense-making," which helps to bridge user perceived gaps in a person's information need. In this regard, fake news might negatively affect the ways in which information users come to understand the gaps in their knowledge base. Some of the problems, then, stem from the user's own information behaviors, though this is not to ignore the wider context of the internet and the ease of access to false information. Notably, Carol Kuhlthau (1993) finds that feelings are integral for the information search process (ISP) but emphasizes that uncertainty leads people to be less willing to continue searching for information in a system. Perhaps, if this principle of uncertainty occurs continuously as it does online sometimes, people will be less likely to seek out reputable sources and may prefer to rely on ones that just make them feel better—like a social media site—even if they are not reputable or, worse, full of outright falsehoods. Information behavior as a research discipline has a lot to tell us all about how likely or how extreme a person's turning to false information and fake news may be. Further complicating this is the direct manipulation of users occurring within the platforms and tools of "surveillance capitalism," as Shoshanna Zuboff terms it. This is a great threat to personal agency if people's information choices can be nudged in certain directions based on the direct online observation and tracking of their subjective feelings and moods.

HOW METACOGNITION GUIDES LEARNING

Of course, improving these issues hinges upon learning *how* we learn and how we come to realize our own strengths and limitations in the course of seeking out information. The concept of metacognition provides a useful framework from which to study the ways in which people learn new information and incorporate it into their knowledge base. It can also provide us with insight into how fake news and misinformation might come to be adopted by people as factual and then spread by the same information users. Disruptions to the self-awareness used to monitor one's own thinking might be considered a kind of metacognitive pathology that impedes one's ability to engage in various types of metacognitive behaviors. The thesis ultimately driving this book is that the susceptibility to misinformation and fake news *may be a function of* the relative strengths and weaknesses in a person's metacognitive abilities, a *misinformation susceptibility factor* that could be quantified. Misinformation and fake news are factors that disrupt a person's "metacognitive taxonomy," a list of important cognitive functions and behaviors that people may engage in while seeking out and interacting with information.

Metacognitive behaviors impact a person's information seeking in several ways. They might impact one's ability to balance thoughts to come to a better understanding of a concept, or they might interfere with a person's attempt to build their base of factual knowledge. Misinformation might also distract users and prevent them from changing course or adapting their research strategies during a search, especially if it appears as an all-encompassing explanation to a complex phenomenon, like a conspiracy theory. Sometimes an information seeker fails to communicate with others about the information itself, making it harder to verify or fact check something with others. Ultimately, one's metacognitive abilities may be predictive of how easily one falls for the false aspects in fake news.

Identifying these problem areas may improve information users' ability to counteract the negative effects. People often need to learn how to better understand their own curiosity, to come to understand why they might be interested in a topic. Sometimes the conflicts between an imposed information need (that is, a school report) and the personal need to discover something new can go unresolved. People can sometimes be unaware, too, of their own personal strengths and weaknesses in terms of learning and need help to pull back and reflect on what they are doing while searching. Using metacognition as a framework and applying it to the fake news model developed from some of my research into fake news, it is proposed that we might be able to understand better how fake news and misinformation come to spread online and dominate information behavior.

WHAT THIS BOOK COVERS

The first part of this book, "Pathologies of Information and the Limits of the Human Mind: Knowledge's 'Fallen' Promise," covers a few serious breakdowns in information behavior, or information pathologies, as I name them, that interfere with how we come to view information and process it as knowledge. These pathologies describe limitations of the human mind and how reaching knowledge and understanding often becomes thwarted by various obstacles. These problems are inherent to both external contexts—that is, encountering conspiracy theories in a particularly partisan social media circle—as well as to one's own internal abilities to learn and synthesize or blend information to create knowledge.

Chapter 1 takes a broad investigation into the problems of information itself, including some of the negative information behaviors we exhibit and the ways in which humanity often fools itself or lies to others. This includes various mental errors, logical fallacies, and perceptual tricks that affect the way we think and perceive. Chapter 2 interrogates the concept of pathology and whether information's use might be considered pathological. I establish the use of the term "pathology" for information behavior—perhaps a controversial or at least eye-opening stance—and determine why it might be appropriate to use the term for the various information use problems we face. I trace the term from its original use in describing physical disease to its adoption in psychology and then later in sociology research. The links between sociology and information behavior research are deep ones. Finally, the chapter looks at how metacognition plays an important role in helping people learn and find information to turn into knowledge. Chapter 3 examines the impact that digital information technology has upon its users, including issues related to surveillance capitalism, e-colonialism, and so-called digital expansionism. Behavioral and mental changes in users brought about by the overuse of information technology and social media are examined as well. I also look at how these technologies might be impacting people's metacognitive skills.

Fake news, of course, is the central theme of this book. The book's second part, "A Brief History of Fake News," will look in depth at the early history of fake news through its adoption in the mass media era and into the digital internet era. Chapter 4 starts off with an in-depth look at the long history of fake news, its antecedents from Ancient Greece to the early printing press era, and the earliest examples of fake stories proliferating in societies. Chapter 5 will examine how fake news and misinformation spread throughout the twentieth century, including looking at notorious fake news stories from the age of predigital mass media. Finally, chapter 6 looks at current developments in fake news, showing how digital media and social media have changed the game by altering the information-sharing landscape and speeding up the process of indoctrination.

Many of the issues about fake news, including what defines it, who creates it, and who consumes it will be addressed in the third part, "Fake News: A Model for the Modern, Internet-Driven Phenomenon." We begin our description of fake news in chapter 7 using the definition of fake news posited in my research with Ahmed Alwan and Eric Garcia, which we describe as "the phenomenon of information exchange between an actor and acted upon that primarily attempts to invalidate generally-accepted conceptions of truth for the purpose of altering established power structures" (Weiss et al., 2021). The unique aspect of our definition is that the two sides of the relationship, the creators *and* the consumers of fake news, are equally important. Entwined, they affect each other in numerous ways for the purpose of sharing something incorrect to destabilize factual information. We view fake news, then, less as a specific genre and its collection of media formats—though these defining formal aspects are important—and more as a series of *shared intentions*. In this regard, the concept mirrors Brookes's conception of information as an ongoing process and not a "thing" merely delivered through various containers. We aim to find what is wrapped up within these intentions and what motives or influences impact the consumption and the sharing of fake news.

Chapter 7 provides a broad overview of this new comprehensive model for fake news; this includes a review of the main relationship in the model, which is the dynamic between the actor (that is, the creator and dissemina-tor of fake news) and the acted upon (that is, the consumer and subsequent sharer of fake news). Discussion also focuses on the contexts developed between micro, meso, and macro worlds in information behavior parlance, showing the influence of various contexts and variables on the interrelated participants of the fake news phenomenon. Importantly, fake news is exam-ined "from a number of different essential perspectives, including its role as a player in political propaganda and disinformation; its role within rumor and the spread of misinformation; and, finally, its role in parody, satire and a term defined as 'political kayfabe'" (Weiss et al., 2020). The rich context and the varying purposes driving fake news become important as I attempt to illuminate the intentions behind its creation and reasons for its proliferation among some groups. Chapter 8 focuses entirely on the creators of fake news and discusses potential motivations and provides insight into the possible ways one might examine and quantify the phenomenon, developing profiles of potential spreaders of fake news. Some of the motivations for sharing fake news might include spreading propaganda, repeating rumors, promote theories, or create parodies, for the purpose of distorting or enabling facts to damage power structures. Finally, chapter 9 examines the consumers of fake news and the personal conditions that might spread it among users. It also outlines profiles of those who are potentially susceptible to its effects. User conditions and characteristics would include the level of online trust a person has, how comfortable they are disclosing personal information about them-selves, how much they might compare themselves to others online, how much fear of missing out (FOMO) anxiety they might exhibit, their level of fatigue from being on social media, their personal identification, and their level of education. Focusing on these conditions would tell us much about how likely a person would be susceptible to fake news.

The fourth part of this book, "The Impact of Digital Fake News," examines the influence that fake news and misinformation have on the wider world, including areas such as education, online communication, and political discourse. Chapter 10 examines how fake news impacts higher education and academic libraries. It looks at how false information can be used as a profit-making tool, as in the case of Alex Jones's Infowars, showing the burden that this places on educators and institutions of learning even as ped-dlers of lies reap obscene profit. The chapter also reviews the impact of false information and conspiracy on learning outcomes. Chapter 11, meanwhile, shows how the premise of information to "inform" and the expectation of factuality has become subverted through the rise of fake news. The chap-ter examines the issues of rising extremism, the use of alternative facts, and fake news in online chat room environments. The chapter also looks at the increased polarization of views in the political arena and examines the political motivations for the use of fake news and the misuses of facts for spin and manipulation.

The final section of the book, "Fighting Fake News: Joining Small and Large Worlds Together," will look at two methods necessary for fighting fake news. Chapter 12 attempts to elucidate ways in which people might neutralize the negative effects of fake news through focusing on the individual. This will be framed in terms specifically of Chatman's concept of the small world of information users; the chapter will examine the metacognitive problem areas in individual users and address issues of metacognition through not only education but also through quantifying and pinpointing specific susceptibilities to false information in people. Chapter 13 provides a wider context to work with beyond the needs and behaviors of the individual. It examines instead the wider scope of "information worlds," which focuses on the greater societal factors impacting information users. The chapter proposes social policymaking to promote good behaviors at a larger scale and wider regional, national, and international strategies for neutralizing the effects of fake news.

COUNTERFACTS AND THE CONTRARY NATURE OF BARE TRUTHS

Finally, a brief note on why this book was named *Counterfact*. With a good play on words, we get the sense of how information is subverted and has been turned into something false, something counterfeit, factually speaking—something *counterfactual*. Much like the *Buck Rogers* television show opening, we are confronted with the use of something real—even artifactual—but placed within a fictional narrative for the sake of deception. Sometimes the deception is harmless—or desired in the case of artistic expression or in parody and satire—but most other times it is detrimental to the user. Those with enough knowledge of the historical background would easily see through the deception of adding documentary footage to a sci-fi story. But for those who are relatively unfamiliar with documentary film practices or are unable to discern the fiction inherent to the medium itself, the show takes on a life of its own. It becomes factually plausible to the viewer or reader, despite all the evidence to the contrary. In that sense, counterfacts replace observed best practices people have developed over years of use with false narratives and unfounded motives that worsen the lives of their believers and even undermine their abilities to discern fact from fiction.

Often, as we see in conspiracy and pseudoscientific theories, the truth is *far* stranger than the fictions we create, and thus forces a pause in people. Conspiracies reveal more about the limitations of the human imagination than they do about the strange nature of reality. While a round earth surely has been proven beyond doubt—and its circumference accurately estimated over two thousand years ago by Eratosthenes using basic geometry—our senses tell us that we're living in flatland. Although some pseudoscience conspiracies can have a crude and seductive simplicity on the surface (that is, gravity explained as if the earth were a rising flat-floored elevator), they betray the lack of real knowledge beyond our limited human perspective. Our senses, as we know, can easily deceive us. Similarly, the quantum world provides us with many counterintuitive theories that challenge the core of our assumed concrete realities. Entanglement, multiverses, and relativity can be difficult to grasp at times. Similar to the loss of confidence and reduced affect people experience when using information systems, much of this reality defies our commonsense assumptions and can cause anxiety. Narratives and counter-facts can be far more comforting and nonthreatening by telling us the things we wish to hear about how the world is constructed. There's something naively comforting to some people about the image of the flat earth as an elevator, crazy as that may seem; the alternative but more accurate view is that we are a tiny, fragile, miniscule world potentially on the edge of destruction at any moment at sea in a violent universe. That narrative provides very little comfort.

It is hoped that "the real" wins out, that the strategies proposed in this book to both identify the potential peddlers of false information along with the strategies to help reorient "true believers" from their erroneous beliefs can become successful. The opposition is fierce at times, but the fight to illuminate goes on. As Charles Mackay, author of the nineteenth-century book *Extraordinary Popular Delusions and the Madness of Crowds*, writes, "Of all the offspring of Time, Error is the most ancient, and is so old and familiar an acquaintance, that Truth, when discovered, comes upon most of us like an intruder, and meets the intruder's welcome" (Mackay, 1932). We must learn, in other words, to accept the intrusion, no matter how discomfiting.

REFERENCES

Bonnefoy, Y. (1992). The grapes of Zeuxis. *Modern Poetry in Translation,* *1*(1), pp. 28–32.

Bowler, L. (2011). Into the land of adolescent metacognitive knowledge during the information search process: A metacognitive ethnography. In Amanda Spink and Jannica Heinstrom (eds.), *New directions in information behaviour* (pp. 93–125). Springer.

Brookes, B. C. (1980). The foundations of information science. Part I. Philosophical aspects. *Journal of Information Science 2*, pp. 125–33.

Cole, C. (2013). Concepts, propositions, models, and theories in information behavior research. In Jamshid Beheshti and J. A. Large (eds.), *The information behavior of a new generation: Children and teens in the 21st century*. Lanham, MD: The Scarecrow Press, Inc.

Dervin, B. (2003). From the mind's eye of the user: The sense-making qualitative-quantitative methodology. In Brenda Dervin, Lois Foreman-Wernet, and Eric Lauterbach (eds.), *Sense-making methodology reader: Selected writings of Brenda Dervin*. Cresskill, NJ: Hampton Press Inc.

Fisher, K. E., Erdelez, S., and McKechnie, L. (2005). *Theories of information behavior*. Medford, NJ: Information Today.

Julien, H., McKechnie, L., and Hart, S. (2005). Affective issues in library and information science systems work: A content analysis. *Library & Information Science Research, 27*(4), pp. 453–66. https://doi.org/10.1016/j.lisr.2005.08.004.

Kindy, D. (2022). Great Moon Hoax of 1835 convinced the world of extraterrestrial life. *Washington Post*. https://www.washingtonpost.com/history/2022/08/14/great-moon-hoax-chorizo/.

Kuhlthau, C. (1993). A principle of uncertainty for information seeking. *Journal of Documentation, 49*(4), pp. 339–55.

Mackay, C. (1932). *Extraordinary popular delusions and the madness of crowds*. New York: L. C. Page.

Nahl, D. (2005). Affective load theory. In Karen E. Fisher, Sanda Erdelez, and Lynne McKechnie (eds.), *Theories of information behavior*. Medford, NJ: Information Today.

O'Brien, H. (2011). Weaving the threads of experience into Human Information Interaction (HII): Probing user experience (UX) for new directions in information behavior. In Amanda Spink and Jannica Heinstrom (eds.), *New directions in information behaviour* (p. 86). Springer.

Ong, T. (2020). Virtual influencers make real money while Covid locks down human stars. Bloomberg. https://www.bloomberg.com/news/features/2020-10-29/lil-miquela-lol-s-seraphine-virtual-influencers-make-more-real-money-than-ever?utm_source=pocket-newtab.

St. Jean, B., Gorham, U., and Bonsignore, E. (2021). *Understanding human information behavior: When, how, and why people interact with information*. Lanham, MD: Rowman & Littlefield.

Weiss, A., Alwan, A., Garcia, E., and Garcia, J. (2020). Surveying fake news: Assessing university faculty's fragmented definition of fake news and its impact on teaching critical thinking. *International Journal of Educational Integrity, 16*(1). https://doi.org/10.1007/s40979-019-0049-x.

Weiss, A., Alwan, A., Garcia, E., and Kirakosian, A. (2021). Toward a comprehensive model of fake news: A new approach to examine the creation and sharing of false information. *Societies, 11*(3). doi.org/10.3390/soc11030082.

PART I

Pathologies of Information and the Limits of the Human Mind

Knowledge's "Fallen" Promise

Chapter 1

Truth, Lies, and Information Pathologies

THE BROAD ISSUE OF INFORMATION AND THE PROMISE OF INFORMING

It's been said that only librarians like searching for information—because everyone else prefers to *find* it. In some ways, given how librarians tend to focus on search methodologies and tools as a discipline and derive immense job satisfaction from providing these services to their patrons, this rings mostly true. Marcia Bates, a professor of library and information science (LIS), pointed out this difference more than twenty years ago. She wrote at the time that an "average person, whether Ph.D. scholar or high school graduate, never notices the structure that organizes their information, because they are so caught up in absorbing and relating to the content" (Bates, 1999). They are *so* caught up, in fact, that "the organization of the information they are using is usually virtually or entirely invisible" (Bates, 1999). The process of the search, then, is entirely secondary, subsumed by the primary goal of utilizing whatever information has been found to the point that the structure within which it all exists recedes to the background.

This invisibility is partly by design and partly a result of user needs and priorities. Information systems designers are primarily interested in offering seamless services to users. This is especially true in most modern libraries, which provide patrons with access to the millions of books and journal articles found in an array of databases, catalogs, or platforms—but presented through a single unified search and retrieval platform. Users generally do not care to know exactly where the content came from as long as they can get to it and satisfy their need for it (whether out of curiosity, a class assignment, a personal project, and so on). They do not need to know exactly how their sausage got made and delivered to their table if all they want to do is eat it. In the off chance that a user does happen to notice the system, it is usually because there has been a problem. Think: broken links, missing documents, fruitless searches, irrelevant results, zero results, too many results, mounting frustrations, and so on. This is the worst kind of publicity in the minds of librarians, as awareness of the system itself not only disrupts the library's main goal to provide information transparently to the user but also draws unwanted attention to the processes and workflows conducted behind the scenes.

Yet given the immense systems we are now working with and increasingly mediated through—systems that now spill over beyond just subject databases or library search catalogs into all aspects of one's personal life—it has become essential for the average user of information systems to start paying some attention to the role and influence that the organization of this information may have on their behavior. In the past twenty years since Dr. Bates pointed out this limited awareness, we have seen immense social advancements and social upheavals, spurred in part by the establishment of international information networks and subsequent social media technologies. If information science is the study of "the universe of recorded information" (Bates, 1999), we now find that the universe has expanded far beyond our human ability to access and comprehend it all. The current omnipresent extent of information technology's reach into our lives was largely unforeseen at the time, hinted at only in science fiction and dystopian cautionary tales. Yet the real-life impacts these technologies have since had upon such widespread areas as politics, governance, personal privacy, and education cannot be understated. It is absolutely a brave new world.

And what of the people in it? The Arab Spring, as Zeynep Tufekci describes in her 2017 book *Twitter and Teargas: The Power and Fragility of Networked Protest*, demonstrates the sudden unforeseen transition from traditional power structures to something new and revolutionary, hinting at the potentially transformational and even aspirational power of information technologies (Tufekci, 2017). Yet as inspiring as the Arab Spring was at the time—now already ten years past—that promise has since soured, as several of the states involved either retained or reverted back to despotism. While some countries did change their constitutions toward more democratic reforms (for example, Tunisia, Algeria, and Morocco), others like Egypt and Yemen fell into violent repression, and Syria suffered through a civil war. New technologies may indeed be revolutionary, but if abused they may just as easily perpetuate despotic governance or consolidate existing oppositional power that can damage fragile democracies.

Around the same time as the Arab Spring in 2013, government contractor Edward Snowden released a trove of information about the United States National Security Agency (NSA), which was subsequently published in

Wikileaks. The release of this information revealed the extensive lengths that the United States and other governments around the world have taken to spy upon citizens of numerous countries (Greenwald, 2014). In the ten years since, the documented interference of Russia and the use of Cambridge Analytica to impact voters in the 2016 US presidential election have truly dampened the democratic and utopian ideals of early 1990s internet. What began as a way to bring content and agency to all in a decentralized power-sharing communications structure, as Tim Berners-Lee originally conceived it, has devolved into a complex knot of competing corporate interests and large-scale government players aiming to control not only the systems providing the infrastructure but also the people using them and the data they generate about themselves.

With these contemporary problems in mind, we reach the reality of total connectivity through the development of the Internet of Things, cloud/mist/fog computing, and quasi-utopian "smart" cities capable of tracking behavior and anticipating needs. Researchers, as a result, will need to find improved methods of understanding the human role in massive information and data-collection systems (Parastatidis, 2009, p. 165). Similar to the totality of the reach of our information systems for not only recording information and collecting data, disseminating information—whether true or false—through these systems is also unprecedented in scale and speed. Researchers studying the data from social media platform Twitter/X have found that false information actually spreads on its platform more quickly than fact, diffusing "significantly farther, faster, deeper, and more broadly" for all types of information (Vosoughi et al., 2018). Notably, it was false information of a political nature—especially when it contained novel information that surprised users—that that reached more people more widely than any other false information (Vosoughi et al., 2018).

Clearly, the stakes are high. Containing the spread and influence of false information becomes much more difficult to achieve when it appears to spread more quickly and more pervasively than truthful information. The early democratizing promise of new digital tools has also created unforeseen havoc on societies, destabilizing as much as energizing us. We need to better examine the people inhabiting and acting within this new world while also examining the external forces both within societies and in the digital tools they habitually use. Theories of information behavior have been one of the main avenues that LIS researchers have used to glean insight into the impact that information systems have on users. But given how excessively powerful the major players dominating the internet have become, how does one uncover—let alone speak—the truth to such power?

INFORMATION IS A PARADIGMATIC PROBLEM

Tracing the history of information itself, we find interesting patterns of development in the concept and how it is applied in both systems and communication technologies. First, we can start with Claude Shannon's modern, electronic systems–based conceptualization of information. What was revolutionary about Shannon's theory was his realization that information in the digital electronic form could be quantified and therefore measured. This leads to the harnessing of that information through communications systems. And as Bates describes it, "once the concept of the system was developed and elaborated, systems could be recognized as underlying countless disparate social, technical, and physical phenomena. Operations research and systems analysis during and after World War II developed these ideas further into a variety of applied realms" (Bates, 1999, p. 1047). This expanded further, where researchers like Parker (1974) and Wiener (1961) start to see these structures and patterns of organization as information itself. Wiener's conception of cybernetics provided an overarching concept of control—from the ancient Greek *kybernētikě* for governance—over these systems. But even more important was the role of the user within these systems. Wiener shows us "that many systems are driven not primarily or only by mechanical forces, but rather are determined by the feedback of information to a governing element of the system" (Wiener 1961). The feedback loop, the dynamically changing set of conditions that are changed in an iterative-like process, allowed information systems to flourish.

Yet despite these developments and clear advances in systems technologies and the awareness of how to both quantify as well as control them, a lack of clarity in the field of LIS persists. Throughout its history, the concept of information has tended to be ill defined and ambiguous. Despite its seemingly clear-cut and pragmatic usage in everyday parlance, *information* (along with the related concept *data*) remains slippery, changeable based upon the context, the discipline in which it appears, or the theoretical frameworks within which it is used. Even in a foundational definition of the scope of information science as a discipline, which Bates (1999) describes as "the world of recorded information produced by human agency," questions nevertheless persist about the nature of information. How, for example, is information *defined*? Is it merely the recorded bits of things, events, or ideas? But how, then, is this concept different than "data," which Rosenberg aptly asserts "has no relation to truth whatsoever," existing as a rhetorical concept without an essence of its own (Rosenberg, 2013, pp. 36–37).

In other words, what *makes* something become information beyond its *being recorded*? Is it part of a hierarchy as some conceptualize it? Or is it a discrete *thing*? Is it an abstraction or is it concrete? Bates rightly highlights that the purpose of information science is to focus not merely on recorded information but also on users' relationship *to* it. Yet going back to Dr. Bates's previous statement, what exactly becomes of *human agency* in a world dominated by electronic devices that mediate our experiences and control our information-seeking behaviors, nudged perhaps by artificial intelligence or algorithms that surreptitiously record us?

Describing and understanding the relationship between users and the ill-defined concept of information may be one of the most difficult aspects of the LIS discipline to reconcile. Indeed, as Yu (2015) writes, "the lack of a solid methodology in defining information has . . . contributed to the divergences of its denotation [within LIS]" (p. 796). The conceptualization of information includes physical and abstract representations, types of data, the products of data processing, the types of messages or communications, and more, with subjective-objective interpretations and tangible-intangible formats further complicating the matter (Yu, 2015, pp. 798–99). The lack of a shared definition for information may ultimately be LIS's largest problem and the one issue most in need of rectification in the discipline overall. Yu's attempt to provide a clear list of twelve "conceptualization clusters" outlines the difficulty LIS has in uniformly defining information.

For the purposes of this book, however, Buckland (1991) provides a sufficiently complex definition of information from three perspectives: "as process," "as knowledge," and "as thing," which Yu (2015) separately denotes as the operational, epistemological, and ontological characteristics of information (p. 808). Buckland further divides information into both intangible and tangible elements. "Information-as-knowledge" is that which helps to reduce uncertainty about any kind of subject (Buckland, 1991, p. 351). It includes whatever we have come to learn and are able to recall and apply to our daily lives in terms of both use and well-being. While "information-as-process" is both the action of "becoming informed"—itself a difficult concept to pin down—as well as the technological and mechanical processing and handling of data (assumed to be digital) by information technologies. It refers to both how we become informed by something and also the systems or processes that provide this information. Finally, "information-as-thing" is composed of the documents and media (for example, the various containers or formats that hold them) used by people for various purposes (Buckland, 1991). This applies to the tangible formats, documents, vessels, and containers that convey various information to us.

Additionally, Yu outlines the operational, epistemological, and ontological characteristics of information that provide us with more classifications of information itself; operational seems to overlap with tangible processes and systems (that is, information as process/ing); epistemological overlaps with knowledge, especially as it applies to meaning and how we confirm facts and truth and reduce uncertainty; ontological deals with the information as thing, the documents and containers, and how they convey meaning to users.

In a notable addition to our understanding of information, Marchionini proposes another way of conceptualizing information as "temporal states in cyberspace" (2008, p. 166), which would include a person's development of the self within cyberspace. This *proflection*, as he terms it, is a person's "conscious and unconscious projections and the reflections that other people and machines create to those projections" (Marchionini, 2008). Stated more simply, proflection is the tracked and recorded sum of a person's actions, interactions, and calculations (automated or otherwise) that go toward developing, curating, and sharing one's online identity. Although this is surely a novel approach, it is unclear if this is a different type of information. Digital identities are rooted within the creation of digital objects and texts, the online actions taken by any given user, and the technological systems that help to process them. Notably, though, proflection might help us understand how users of online systems become radicalized politically, especially through the development of what Cass Sunstein (2001) terms "the daily me."

GAPS IN THE THEORIES OF INFORMATION BEHAVIOR

Despite the long tradition of information behavior research and the numerous theories proposed to help explain and frame how people search and use information, there is still much that is missing in the overall picture. The gaps in these theories point out where our "terra incognita" lies and point out the limits in our ability to fully understand the ways in which people work with and utilize information in the fullest range of their lives, from site-, school-, or work-specific tasks to everyday living and general time spent on computers—not only using them for individual tasks but also online in social media. The following will attempt to delineate a little more of this idea of the "terra incognita" that exists within our discipline and that will be examined in greater detail in chapter 2.

INFORMATION BEHAVIOR RESEARCH AND THE PROBLEM OF RESULTS

The flaws in the previous information behavior research approaches stem from several erroneous assumptions. First, the assumption that user behavior is linear and rational does not hold up under the scrutiny of actual human behavior. Foster's theory of nonlinear information seeking, one theory that provides an alternate view of human search behavior, suggests that we find information in a circular, flowing manner that does not advance in a step-by-step fashion (Foster, 2004). Second, the choices that users make are often assumed to represent a purpose, motive, or reason—usually to fulfill a goal or need of some kind. But this ignores the environmental factors that may actually encourage or foster *irrational* behaviors. Indeed, the concepts of *nonknowledge* (Kempner et al., 2011) and *agnotology* (Proctor, 1995) identify such gaps and obstacles in human knowledge making, helping us realize that there are questions we can neither conceive of nor begin to solve. Agnotology in particular provides a framework for trying to understand how culturally induced ignorance, doubt, and falseness can flourish. Finally, it is debatable whether researchers can draw universal conclusions about human information behaviors based solely on the perfect conditions in a research lab (that is, cf. Sandstrom's [1994] use of "optimal foraging" theory), especially when such controlled conditions are not reflective of users' real-life experiences.

J. David Johnson (2009) in his incisive examination of human information behavior research theories comes to a similar conclusion, writing that "approaches to HIB [human information behavior] have often been rooted in the most rational of contexts, libraries, where individuals come with a defined problem, or information technology systems, that have their own inherent logic." The field of information behavior clearly appears to favor the *purposive acquisition* of information, he argues, as seen in the significantly more populated top-right quadrant in figure 1.1. This focus on purposive acquisition obviously misses much of the messy reality of human nature and behavior, which exists within a much larger set of contexts and environments. This "terra incognita" of human irrationality, avoidance, and nonpurposeful accidental information behavior remains relatively underexamined, as seen in the other much sparser quadrants, especially the bottom-left quadrant focusing on the *accidental avoidance* of information.

To improve upon some of these gaps, Allen et al. (2011) later propose a model based on activity theory, which helps researchers to examine both individual actions and wider societal contexts in a more complex way. They write that the theory "offers a mid-point between the individualist and societist perspective" (p. 785), the two main but divergent approaches in the studying information behavior, and allows researchers to look at individuals within certain social contexts. Its ability to account for both an individual and their social contexts allows the theory "to address a major weakness in current information behavior research" (p. 785). While it is commendable to look at information behavior with a much wider lens, activity theory, like many of the theories shown in figure 1.1, nevertheless continues to ignore

Theories of Human Information Behavior (HIB)

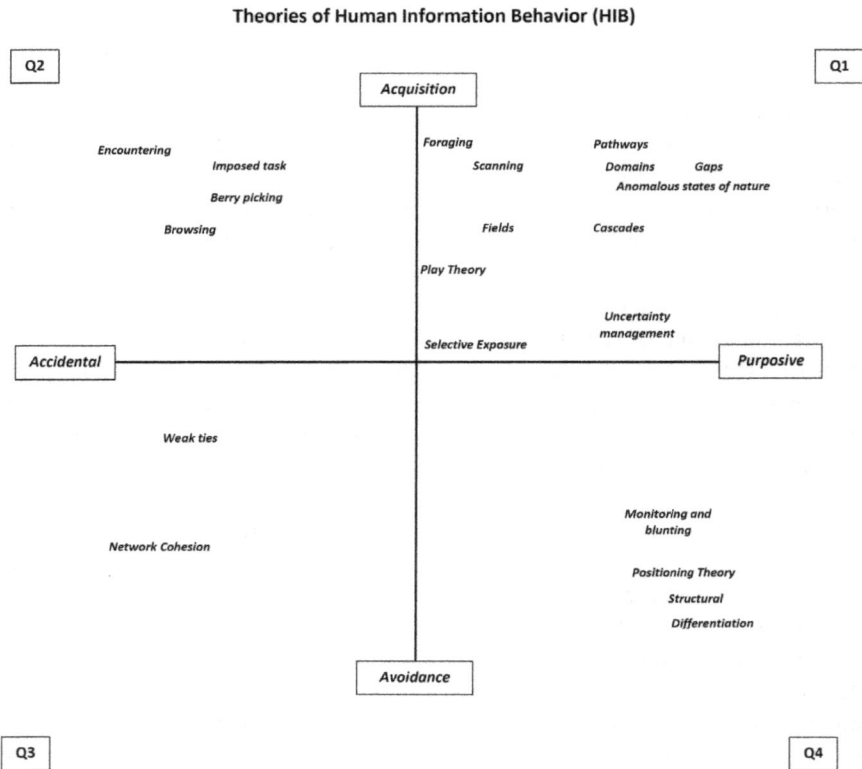

Figure 1.1. Mapping of theories of information behavior along scales of accidental–purposive searching and acquisition–avoidance motives. *Source*: Johnson, 2009.

some fundamental aspects of human psychology. Indeed, as the authors admit, the theory "takes *motivated activity* [emphasis mine] as the central unit of analysis, helping us to illuminate on the cause of information-seeking and information behavior" (p. 782). This approach nevertheless avoids addressing the irrational, bored, apathetic, disengaged, or even aggressive and self-destructive behaviors that people may experience or exhibit while online. Many people, for example, may harbor no clear motive for seeking information and their information needs are neither always clear nor rational and reasonable. People can still be manipulated or nudged into personal actions by overly *oppressive* human-made systems, further compromising the concept of motivation.

Marchionini (2008) asserts that "humans are moving toward a potentially more symmetrical meaning of human-information interaction, where both humans and information objects evolve as a result of and through interaction." While human-information interaction surely must evolve over time, the symmetry that Marchionini expects does not seem to exist. In the years since this was written, information behavior research does not seem to have seriously or properly considered the problem of our place within a surveillance capitalist society that depends upon subverting (or, in the popular Silicon Valley parlance, "disrupting") the long-standing social conditions that influence our information behaviors (Zuboff, 2015). The symmetry, in other words, is destroyed by the exploitative nature of our current information society. Such disruptions and imbalances include reducing our personal privacy (and the sense of freedom and agency that comes with it), marginalizing truthful information (and the sense of certitude that comes with it), monetizing such basic human behaviors as establishing and sustaining friendships, or idly gossiping in confidence among a circle of friends. These disrupted contexts in which so much information behavior is conducted need to be reexamined more clearly and with more skepticism. The current approaches are likely insufficient to tackle the scale and scope problems associated with data and information, especially as they grow beyond human ability to regulate and control them. If the world is indeed in the midst of an era of global surveillance capitalism, as Zuboff argues, then as information professionals, researchers, *and* educators we need to examine how the destruction of privacy for the sake of creating and perpetuating extremely asymmetrical power structures impacts information behavior.

Several information behavior theories over the years have attempted to provide context for users and describe them in terms of environments, grounds, and ecologies. Nardi and O'Day (1999), for example, proposed the concept of "information ecologies" to help explain wider contexts for information seekers. Williamson's (1998) ecological theory of human information behavior focuses on incidental information acquisition, in which people do not always purposefully acquire information. Savolainen's (1995) ELIS theory attempts to incorporate "everyday living," combining both social and psychological factors in information behavior. Erdelez's (1997) theory of information encountering focuses on the opportunistic acquisition of information (OAI) and the accidental nature of information seeking. Pettigrew (1998) and Fisher, Durance, and Hinton (2004) further develop the theory of information grounds, which attempts to widen the areas in which people might seek and encounter information. Sonnenwald's (2005) theory of "information horizons" attempts to include "the role of social networks and contexts in information behavior as a process" and encourages users to develop their own maps to help visualize their horizon. Each of these theories extends the study of information behavior beyond the systems and tools people use to seek it to examine the users and their environments.

However, despite the progress and the promise of these wider approaches that incorporate more holistic and inclusive metaphors for environment and expanded contexts, Tang et al. (2019) conclude that "it remains questionable whether the transition to an ecological perspective of human information interaction in information research has taken place" (p. 578). These so-called ecological and ecosystem approaches are insufficient as they have generally been unable to transcend the weak ties to reality that the metaphorical information ecosystem attempts to establish. The benevolent-sounding "ecology of information" or the more recent "bibliodiversity" (Shearer et al., 2020) make the process of information seeking and information behavior appear naturalistic and therefore an inevitable and inescapable part of our lives. Yet there is nothing inevitable or natural about how information systems are developed, devoted as they are to *control*. Even assuming that human-made digital systems are somehow akin to natural environments nevertheless ignores the reality of human existence. Humans do not exist in a perfect walled-off garden as rational and willful actors; we are, instead, participants (both willing and unwilling) in an unnatural, human-designed, and manipulated set of *unevenly applied* cybernetic-social conditions. Worse, this assumption of naturalness stemming from our centuries-old place in the Renaissance belief in humanity's place at the top of the order of things—that is, as "the paragon of animals"—ignores the irrationality and behavioral pathologies of human behavior that develop among those subjected to oppressive systems and cultures.

Ultimately, by assuming a naturalistic vision of our information systems, we also allow the normalization of surveillance and spying on users of information systems. All online user behavior becomes subject to the abuses of surveillance capitalism. Indeed, the neoliberal conceptualization of personal privacy and identity as tradeable commodities within the framework of surveillance capitalism will come to adversely impact human behavior both online and offline, possibly putting people who are already at risk of marginalization and oppression under further duress. The increased sharing and resharing of fake news, misinformation, and disinformation must also be addressed by new theories and approaches to information behavior.

FOOL ME ONCE, SHAME ON YOU; FOOL ME TWICE . . .

The problems in information behavior research are not limited merely to issues of failure to retrieve sought-after information or identifying obstacles when searching. There also exist issues with the limitations of the human mind and its psychology that have direct impact on the ways in which people use or deal with information, learning, and self-education. We are all very familiar with at least some of the day-to-day limitations of our own perceptions and our own inabilities to truly perceive others, the world, and the causes of many of the things we observe in our lives. Obviously, there are too many of these fallacies and misperceptions to review in extensive detail here. This section will therefore examine just a few of the more well known ones that have more relevance to the study of information behavior.

The avoidance half in figure 1.1 suggests that there is a strong influence within people to omit painful or difficult searches for information, further problematizing the methods we take to research information behavior. As Case et al. (2005) write, "Many models of the information-seeking process . . . do not even consider that information seeking may *not* take place in cases in which people recognize their ignorance about a topic." Case refers specifically to Ellis's behavioral model of information seeking (1989), Kuhlthau's constructive process of information seeking (1993), and Wilson's complementary "nesting" models of information seeking (1999). The lack of consideration for this obstacle for finding information could be considered a significant flaw in certain information behavior models (Case et al., 2005). Some of this avoidance by information seekers is purposeful—such as avoiding a taboo or restricted subject or one that carries criminal liability for seeking it out (perhaps abortion in some states in the near future). But much of this avoidance may be incidental and accidental, subject to our own whims and influenced by our inability to understand ourselves. Those accidental avoidances can also be perpetuated by our own mental lapses, mental breaks, the use of logical fallacies to help buttress our own egos, and by the perceptual tricks our mind plays on us.

COGNITIVE DISSONANCE

In many ways, cognitive dissonance can be seen as a root cause for many problems in human information behavior. The self-perceptions we carry of ourselves can cloud our judgments and affect how we search for things in a less than rational manner. Called "a classic example of "irrationality" (Suzuki, 2011), we lie to ourselves to avoid painful feelings. As Case et al. write, it has "long been noted that people may *avoid* information, if paying attention to it will cause mental discomfort or dissonance" (2005). The impact of cognitive dissonance on information seekers is an important one. In some situations, it can be a determination between life and death, especially when it is related to information about cancer, disease in general, or overall health. The stakes are quite high in identifying the factors that contribute to people not wanting to find out information; it's also important to find out what information clusters and topics people avoid as well as the environmental conditions that people live in that might contribute to this avoidance. Cognitive dissonance clearly contributes to the areas that people avoid when searching for certain types of sensitive information.

MENTAL LAPSES, LOGICAL FALLACIES, AND THE TRICKS OF PERCEPTION

As if that mental barrier to thinking about subjects and topics weren't enough, we are all prone to engage unwittingly in various negative information behaviors, including being influenced by mental errors, employing logical fallacies in our reasoning, and even having our senses tricked in spite of our best efforts. These problems include a significant number of cognitive barriers that we may not be aware we are being influenced by while we seek out information.

Mental lapses: Survivorship bias, for example, shows us that we can be fooled by the presence and existence of something if we fail to consider the wider context. The best known example is from World War II history, when British RAF planes returning from bombing runs in Germany were thought to be the most vulnerable in the areas they were observed to be hit most often: around the wingtips, rear tail assemblies, and the center of the plane. But that was merely a subset of all the planes sent out; the ones that had failed to return had been fatally hit in the more vital areas of the plane: the engines, cockpit, and fuel tanks. They didn't see those because they never returned. What survived to return was merely hit in less important areas and so to reinforce those areas—as was initially proposed—would have been a tragic error, merely protecting less important parts of the plane while leaving the vital parts exposed. This shows just how easily we can sometimes fool ourselves if we are not more careful in our reasoning. In everyday life, just because I've had a long career, avoiding downsizing or never changing jobs, doesn't mean that I'm necessarily the most skilled employee. It may be that I was just lucky to have survived job cuts for that long—or that I was completely, utterly without ambition and chose to stay in one place. Hiring committees, therefore, might not want to hire new employees based on the ones that have been there the longest.

The Dunning-Kruger effect and its near opposite, "imposter syndrome," similarly demonstrates for us how self-knowledge can sometimes go awry; in the former, a person tends to overestimate their abilities and takes their rank as evidence of their abilities—even if none exists. This is an important concept of information seeking as it could be argued that the overestimation of one's knowledge about a subject could influence a person's susceptibility to misinformation. Froehlich (2019) finds that the Dunning-Kruger effect is an accelerant and enhancer of the effect of fake news because "people are uncritical about their own abilities and uncritical of their lack of critical thinking." They lack, he writes, "the intelligence to recognize it" (Froehlich, 2019). Imposter syndrome, meanwhile, preys upon those who think they are underqualified to do their work, despite being knowledgeable and talented for a work position. Additionally, our own personal knowledge of something also impacts how we react and interact with others. In the curse of knowledge, we sometimes assume that everyone knows a piece of information that we have learned and assume that someone has the same background as us. The largest problem for academia is that an expert will sometimes not change their level of discourse and engage in overuse of jargon without explanation or will adopt language that is overly and compulsively "hedging," resulting in unclear and indecisive communications. It is no wonder that the sagest advice given by the oracle at Delphi, the ancient worlds' source of wisdom, was "know yourself"—probably the hardest thing one can possibly do.

Finally, in the case of information behavior, confirmation bias tends to be the most difficult as well as impactful influence upon those who search for information—especially when it comes to the topics of misinformation and fake news. Confirmation bias is "the tendency to preferentially view information that is consistent with one's opinions or hypotheses, [which] has a significant impact on decision making" (Nickerson, 1998). In other words, people will seek out, believe, and reinforce the information they already believe to be true. This is problematic when dealing with the spread of false information and can be very difficult to amend. Suzuki and Yamamoto (2021) assert that "confirmation bias can be a significant problem in web search behavior because confirmation bias that occurs when users search the web for information about food, clothing, housing, and politics can significantly impact society." Most alarming, people tend not to "change their prior beliefs very much . . . even if they spend a lot of effort searching for information" (Suzuki and Yamamoto, 2021). This fact exposes some of the problems inherent to models of information search, which mainly rely upon examining the purposive acquisition of information. When the purpose is to reinforce beliefs that are patently false, the ability to counteract the negative effects of misinformation becomes compromised.

Logical fallacies: Yet we also fall prey to problems of thinking itself, failing to conduct our reasoning and thinking in proper ways. Failure to identify logical fallacies is probably one the major reasons why fake news and misinformation are able to proliferate. As Yakub et al. (2020) suggest, many of the techniques in fake news and misinformation obscure the false logic in fake news stories by exploiting "reliability cues" so that even if the reasoning is completely erroneous, they nevertheless "pass as reliable and trustworthy." These fallacies, notably, comprise a number of tricks that people may not be aware of, including the use of nonsequiturs, which are often conclusions that aren't necessarily the logical result of the facts. People occasionally will generate false comparisons and draw erroneous conclusions from them just because one thing seems similar to another. We sometimes will also fall for things like false dilemmas, where it appears there are only two choices for outcomes but there are instead numerous potential results. This is especially the case in politics where only two sides are presented on an issue in order to get people to vote for one party. People can engage in hasty generalizations, using evidence that may be unrepresentative of the whole picture. This happens often in conspiracy theories and pseudoscience, like flat earth theories, that omit or fail to account for the significant body of evidence proving the contrary. People engage in circular reasoning as well, stating a hypothesis as being true but then failing to provide the further justifications to support that hypothesis; ultimately, they only provide a rehash of the original statement itself. People also believe in testimonials too much even when the expertise of such a person may not be relevant to the subject at hand. As we will see in later chapters, informal networks online (especially chat rooms and discussion forums) can have an outsized influence on whether or not someone believes a piece of information.

Perceptual errors: Finally, in addition to both mental errors and the logical fallacies, the human mind also engages in various perceptual errors. In particular, the human mind engages in the cognitive distortion of "selective perception," which is a condition that occurs whenever we focus our attention on something, but what we see is based on our *expectations*, causing us to not consider the rest of the information presented. Commonly seen among sports fans complaining about fouls and poor referees (immortalized by the famous Hastorf and Cantril [1954] study of the Princeton-Dartmouth game), selective perception gives rise to the fact that people, especially partisans, will see the same event differently. Their view of it is in actuality dependent upon expectations they hold prior to the event.

Perceptual errors, however, can be extremely damaging in the case of stereotyping and in self-serving bias (SSB), where people can become marginalized based on such skewed perceptions; SSB has been shown to change people's "fairness principles" (Deffains et al., 2016). When people begin to blame the victims for their own problems while crowing about their own successes, for example, self-serving bias is often a culprit. In one study, SSB predicts "a tight relationship between wealth and the perception of the causes of poverty," meaning that those who are wealthy are more apt to believe they deserve their wealth as a result of their virtuous actions (that is, hard work, persistence, energy) and also more apt to believe the poor lack these good qualities (Deffains et al., 2016). They are also less willing to accept that their success might have been a result of luck or random events. Conversely, the poor may be less likely to blame their own actions for their situations and shift the blame of their fortunes entirely upon their external circumstances and environments.

This stark divide in perception mirrors our own political divides on the issues of taxation and wealth distribution. However, the reality of each person's station in life may be more complex and contradictory than either of these two starkly different perspectives provide. Indeed, the reality is that so many of us succeed through a combination of skills, hard work, and luck, while at the same time we also will suffer setbacks through external events as well as our own poor decisions. Taking this further, in the case of fake news and misinformation, people may fall for stories that help to buttress these self-serving biases even if evidence to the contrary proves them to be inaccurate. Fighting the influence of fake news can be incredibly difficult if built-in personal biases like these must be first penetrated, like personal bubbles, and subsequently burst. Sometimes the task is impossible.

TOWARD A THEORY OF "INFORMATION PATHOLOGIES"

Given the vast array of problems in human perception, reasoning, and understanding, it should come as no surprise that an assumption of rationality or linear progression in seeking out and finding information can be misleading. In fact, it should come as no surprise that people fall into mistaken beliefs, considering the varied and impressive array of pitfalls people encounter in their everyday lives. Far more surprising and notable are those who engage directly and rigorously with fact and truth and avoid such pitfalls. Indeed, assuming rationality in information behavior should be approached delicately as most of our information seeking is likely influenced by our emotional states or affect (Nahl, 2005).

Certainly, new approaches in information science and information behavior research are moving beyond just examining rational and reasoned purposeful acquisition of information. While this is an essential cornerstone to understanding information behavior, it is emphasized more often because it is the most readily observable and arguably most linear in its approach. The more recent adoption of Allen's action theory, for example, provides us with a wider context that takes both individuals and their societies into account. However, it is still somewhat dependent upon rational actors who are constantly aware of their place within the world; it assumes that purposeful actions are the starting point for the research. But researchers are now also beginning to focus on showing information technologies' inherent *unnaturalness* and their so-called uncanny valleys of artificiality. The assumptions that people generally exhibit rational behavior online is a dangerous one as it sweeps some habitual behavioral pathologies, such as failing to adequately identify and counter misinformation online, under the rug.

We need to corral, instead, the various theories of negative behavior that appear across the information behavior landscape, including information overload, procrastination, apathy, satisficing, power imbalance, surveillance chill, fake news, and more, in order to better understand the impact that technology is having on us. We need to look into the unfettered influence of information technology on users of all ages, and how cognitive development may be altered through constant use of social media not only in children but also in adults (Carr, 2012). By focusing on such problems and inherent behavioral pathologies, we can bridge the gaps in current theoretical models of information behavior. These issues have risen in prominence over the past twenty-five years as digital technologies have become the dominant forms of communication and distributing culture, encompassing nearly all aspects of our culture.

The following chapter, in particular, will focus on the concepts of pathology in more detail to get at a workable definition of information pathologies—especially in terms of how these pathologies relate to the three types of information—as process, thing, and act. We will examine the concept of pathology in far more detail and will suggest a new, updated way of visualizing the information behavior landscape's "terra incognita."

REFERENCES

Allen, D., Karanasios, S., and Slavova, M. (2011). Working with activity theory: Context, technology, and information behavior. *Journal of the Association for Information Science and Technology, 62*(4), pp. 776–88.

Bates, M. J. (1999). The invisible substrate of information science. *Journal of the American Society for Information Science, 50*(12), pp. 1043–50.

Buckland, M. (1991). Information as thing. *Journal of the American Society for Information Science, 42*(5), pp. 351–60.

Carr, Nicholas G. (2010). *The shallows: What the internet is doing to our brains.* New York: W. W. Norton.

Case, D. O., Andrews, J. E., Johnson, J. D., and Allard, S. L. (2005). Avoiding versus seeking: The relationship of information seeking to avoidance, blunting, coping, dissonance, and related concepts. *Journal of the Medical Library Association, 93*(3), pp. 353–62.

Deffains, B., Romain E., and Thöni, C. (2016). Political self-serving bias and redistribution. *Journal of Public Economics, 134*, pp. 67–74. https://doi.org/10.1016/j.jpubeco.2016.01.002.

Ellis, D. (1989). A behavioural approach to information retrieval design. *Journal of Documentation, 45*(3), pp. 171–212.

Erdelez, S. (1997). Information encountering: A conceptual framework for accidental information discovery. In P. Vakkari, R. Savolainen, and B. Dervin (eds.),
*Information seeking in context: Proceedings of international conference on
research in information needs, seeking and use in different contexts* (pp. 412–21).
Taylor Graham.

Fisher, K. E., Durrance, J. C., and Hinton, M. B. (2004). Information grounds and
the use of need-based services by immigrants in Queens, NY: A context-based,
outcome evaluation approach. *Journal of the American Society for Information
Science and Technology, 55*, pp. 754–66.

Foster, A. E. (2004). A nonlinear model of information seeking behavior. *Journal of
the American Society for Information Science and Technology, 55*, pp. 228–37.

Froehlich, T. J. (2019). The role of pseudo-cognitive authorities and self-deception in
the dissemination of fake news. *Open Information Science, 3*(1), pp. 115–36. https:
//doi.org/10.1515/opis-2019–0009.

Greenwald, G. (2014). *No place to hide: Edward Snowden, the NSA, and the U.S.
surveillance state*. New York: Metropolitan Books/Henry Holt.

Hastorf, A. H., and Cantril, H. (1954). They saw a game; a case study. *The Journal
of Abnormal and Social Psychology, 49*(1), pp. 129–34. https://doi.org/10.1037/
h0057880.

Johnson, J. D. (2009). An impressionistic mapping of information behavior with special attention to contexts, rationality, and ignorance. *Information Processing and
Management, 45*, pp. 593–604.

Kempner, J., Merz, J., and Bosk, C. (2011). Forbidden knowledge: Public controversy
and the production of nonknowledge. *Sociological Forum, 26*(3), pp. 475–500.

Kuhlthau, C. C. (1993) A principle of uncertainty for information seeking. *Journal of
Documentation, 49*(4), pp. 339–55.

Marchionini, G. (2008). Human–information interaction research and development.
Library and Information Science Research, 30(3), pp. 165–74.

Nahl, D. (2005). Affective load theory. In Karen E. Fisher, Sanda Erdelez, and
Lynne McKechnie (eds.), *Theories of information behavior* (pp. 39–43). Medford,
NJ: Information Today.

Nardi, B., and O'Day, V. (1999). *Information ecologies: Using technology with heart.*
MIT Press.

Nickerson, R. S. (1998). Confirmation bias: A ubiquitous phenomenon in many guises.
Review of General Psychology, 2, pp. 175–220. doi: 10.1037/1089-2680.2.2.175.

Parastatidis, S. (2009). A platform for all that we know: Creating a knowledge-driven
research infrastructure. In T. Hey, S. Tansley, and K. Tolle (eds.), *The fourth paradigm: Data-intensive scientific discovery* (pp. 165–72). Microsoft Research.

Parker, E. B. (1974). Information and society. In C. A. Cuadra and M. J. Bates (eds.),
*Library and information service needs of the nation: Proceedings of a conference
on the needs of occupational, ethnic, and other groups in the United States* (pp.
9–50). Washington, DC: USGPO.

Pettigrew, K. E. (1999). Waiting for chiropody: Contextual results from an ethno-
graphic study of the information behavior among attendees at community clinics.
Information Processing and Management, 35, pp. 801–17.

Proctor, R. 1995. *Cancer wars: How politics shapes what we know & don't know about cancer*. Basic Books.

Rosenberg, D. (2013). Data before the fact. In L. Gitelman (ed.). *Raw data is an oxymoron* (pp. 15–40). MIT Pres.

Sandstrom, P. E. (1994). An optimal foraging approach to information seeking and use. *The Library Quarterly, 64*, pp. 414–49.

Savolainen, R. (1995). Everyday life information seeking: Approaching information seeking in the context of "way of life." *Library and information Science Research, 17*, pp. 259–94.

Shearer, K., Chan, L., Kuchma, I., and Mounier, P. (2020). Fostering bibliodiversity in scholarly communications: A call for action. *Zenodo*. http://doi.org/10.5281/zenodo.3752923.

Sonnenwald, D. H. (2005). Information horizons. In K. Fisher, S. Erdelez, and L. McKechnie (eds.), *Theories of information behavior* (pp. 191–97). Information Today.

Sunstein, C. (2001). *Republic.com*. Princeton, NJ: Princeton University Press.

Suzuki, M., and Yamamoto, Y. (2021). Characterizing the influence of confirmation bias on web search behavior. *Frontiers in Psychology, 12*. https://doi.org/10.3389/fpsyg.2021.771948.

Suzuki, T. (2011). Complementarity of behavioral biases. *Theory and Decision, 72*(3), pp. 413–30. https://doi.org/10.1007/s11238-011-9268-1.

Tang, R., Mehra, B., Du, J. T., and Zhao, Y. (2019). Paradigm shift in information research. *Proceedings of ASIS&T 2019 Annual Meeting*, pp. 582–85.

Tufekci, Z. (2017). *Twitter and tear gas: The power and fragility of networked protest*. Yale University Press.

Vosoughi, S., Roy, D., and Aral, S. (2018). The spread of true and false news online. *Science (American Association for the Advancement of Science), 359*(6380), pp. 1146–51. https://doi.org/10.1126/science.aap9559.

Wiener, N. (1961). *Cybernetics.* Second edition. Cambridge, MA: The MIT Press.

Williamson, K. (1998). Discovered by chance: The role of incidental information acquisition in an ecological model of information use. *Library and information science research, 20*(1), pp. 23–40.

Wilson, T. D. (1999). Models in information behaviour research. *Journal of Documentation, 55*(3), pp. 249–70.

Yakub, G., Knight, S., Kitto, K., and Fray, P. (2020). The absence of a media literacy toolbox: Working towards an evaluation tool. *Communication Research and Practice, 6*(3), pp. 259–76. https://doi.org/10.1080/22041451.2020.1802844.

Yu, L. (2015). Back to the fundamentals again. *Journal of Documentation, 71*(4), pp. 795–816. doi: http://dx.doi.org.libproxy.csun.edu/10.1108/JD-12-2014-0171.

Zuboff, S. (2015). Big other: Surveillance capitalism and the prospects of an information civilization. *Journal of Information Technology, 30*(1), pp. 75–89.

Chapter 2

Can Information's Use
Be "Pathological"?

The impetus behind developing a concept of information pathologies is ultimately to develop a counterpoint to engineering-based approaches to information behavior research. The models and theories often assume that human needs for and uses of information can be most efficiently accommodated by the development and testing of systems and devices or through the observation of the behaviors of their users in controlled conditions (Bates, 2005, p. 13). While the approach has been dominant in information behavior research and has certainly yielded important results that indicate clear patterns in user behavior, we nevertheless cannot ignore the fact that there are deep-seated inconsistencies in human behavior, stemming from numerous causes—including the socially pathological—that may not be possible to fully address in a human-made system or in information seeking models that function as "an idealized set of steps" (Bowler and Nesset, 2013). A major aim of this approach is to pinpoint flaws and ignored problems so that design can improve. To paraphrase Erich Fromm, it is hoped that human behavior in all its unpredictability and irrationality can be the force that drives changes in information system design and not the design that compels people to change their behaviors.

The use of the word "pathology" is somewhat unexplored in past research. Because it is not well established in information science, it is therefore important to take a look at the justification for using this term. We will look more closely at the development of the term through history and trace how it might impact library and information science and, ultimately, how it might help us understand human information behavior.

ON THE CONCEPT OF PATHOLOGY AND
INFORMATION PATHOLOGIES

Pathology and Social Pathologies

The concept of "pathology" originates from the health sciences and generally describes how various physical and environmental conditions affect the health and well-being of people. The concept includes ways to promote and secure health, the measures taken to prevent physical diseases, and the methods used to help detect sources of various health problems, including the conceptualization of disease itself, disease vectors that spread it, and the personal hygiene necessary to prevent or alleviate it. Notably, the concept has not remained confined to physical health sciences. In particular, pathology was next adopted by psychology, where it is now applied in the examination of the causes of psychological diseases and ailments. Gradually, though, the concept of pathology expanded beyond its original examination of individual health and well-being into a wider, more social-oriented theory of what ails groups of people. Widespread psychological ailments noticed in much larger groups ultimately spurred the question of whether society itself was ill in some way. R. C. Smith in his book *Society and Social Pathology: A Framework for Progress* (2017) argues that not only can individuals be pathological, but their societies can be as well (p. 20). Drawing from the theories of Theodor Adorno and Herbert Marcuse, Smith asserts that social pathology is a *universal* condition, occurring "across cultures and epochs," regardless of political and societal conditions (p. 125).

Yet the issue is not merely that negative human behaviors occurring on massive scales necessarily means that societies are inherently pathological. Some of the issue is that there is a dichotomy between individuals and the societies they exist within. To bridge this gap between individual and social perspectives, sociologists have begun to look, notably, at "systems theory," which has ironically been central to information and computer science studies for decades. Smith argues, "scientific approaches in systems theory and system thinking offer important conceptual tools when it comes to understanding the pathological and systemic character of contemporary crises and their interrelation" (2017, p. 16). Other researchers, such as Nafeez Mosaddeq Ahmed, elucidate "systemic interconnections between a number of global crises from water scarcity and food insecurity to climate change; potential energy crisis; food insecurity; economic instability; forced migration; international terrorism; mass surveillance and increasing militarization" (Smith, 2017). Additionally, "negative or unhealthy social systems . . . are reproduced largely on the basis of pathological patterns of human action and behavior" (p. 20).

We can draw inferences as well as conclusions about individuals' pathological behaviors based upon the patterns observed within the large-scale systems they inhabit. Indeed, Smith argues that social pathologies are *systemically* connected. Interrelated crises therefore have an impact upon people's "patterns of mental and physical disturbance" (2017, p. 21). Taking this a step further, we can apply this concept of negative social systems to how *information* systems are created and adapted by societies, and how they are subsequently used by individuals within those societies. Indeed, "Individuals can suffer social ailment inasmuch as social phenomena can be the product of social ailment" (Smith, 2017). The internet, social media, information use, and behavior can be viewed as related to and interrelated with the wider social pathologies even as they are developed by members existing *within* them. As the main tools used by people within societies, information systems may indeed create, exacerbate, and perpetuate social pathologies, not dissimilar to the ways in which Safiya Noble (2018) has shown that search image algorithms can exacerbate and perpetuate racist imagery.

Information Pathologies

If we can assume as valid that "social pathology in the medical sense can also entail the study of the relation between disease and social environmental conditions" (Smith, 2017, p. 43), then we might also be able to apply this to information behavior studies as well. Along these lines, information pathology might be viewed as the study of the relationship between social pathologies—especially negative and antisocial behaviors—and the conditions surrounding information and information technology systems that create, exacerbate, and sustain them. Notably, some researchers have begun to describe fake news in terms of disease pathology itself. Piccialli et al. (2021) identify fake news as an "infectious pathogen" in the information ecosystem with social media platforms forming as a metaphorical host spreading the fake news infection. Olan et al. (2022) later subsequently carry this concept further with an exploration of a fake news conceptual model based upon the use of the "disease triangle." In this respect, utilizing the concept of pathology within information science is not unjustified. However, metaphors like disease and pathology are perhaps several steps away from models, even, in terms of their accuracy in reflecting reality. Indeed, some of the links to human information behavior are not delineated clearly enough in this concept of pathology. The next section will examine the interplay with this theoretical approach and that of social environments.

Information Behavior Theories and Models

Marchionini (2008) provides us with a clear direction for information behavior research. "A major challenge for information scientists," he writes, "is to develop techniques and tools to study human-information interaction from a social perspective" (p. 173). Humans exist in a hybrid world, he argues, inhabiting a mixture of both physical and digital environments. The transition between these two environments as well as the effect it has on people need to be examined more clearly—especially in light of the problems (that is, hate, lies, bullying) that spill out from online groups into the real world. The problem still remains, though, of how to examine not only individuals but also their wider contexts, especially as those contexts are fluid and the boundaries that used to separate physical worlds from digital or cyber worlds become more permeable or layered upon each other. Thivant (2005), for example, depicts a typical representation of information behavior in figure 2.1, which breaks information behavior into "streams of experience" and "incidental information." This shows the interaction of the user with information in a rather straightforward linear manner, though occasionally looping back to previous conditions and repeating as needed. Starting at the top left with "information needs," which are fueled by our "streams of experience," user behavior branches into information seeking or information use. The process then moves beyond use and into management and production—lofty goals, it should be noted, for the typical information user. Noted in the margin above the diagram, are some acknowledgments of trouble, including uncertainties and stressors, cognitive gaps, suppression, and avoidance. These are

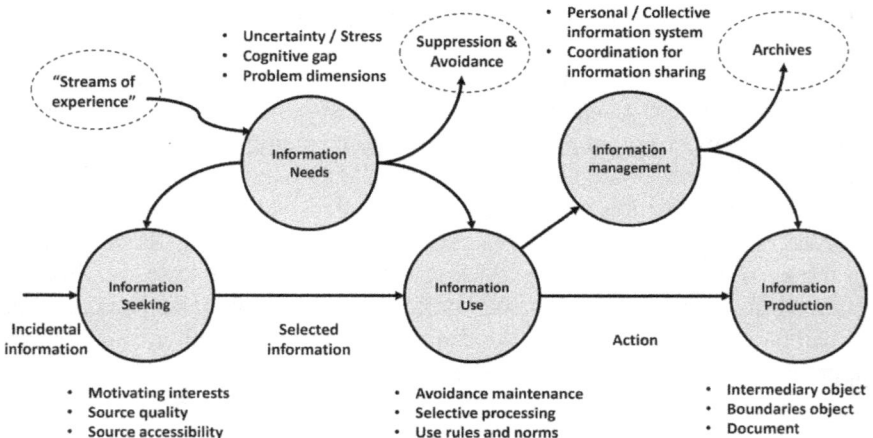

Figure 2.1.   Information behavior activities diagram. *Source*: Thivant, 2005.

identifiable problems in human behavior, but this is a simple model that is not quite able to reveal the full scope of problems impacting information users.

The model seems to break down in the absence of a clear understanding of how information is vetted in the first place. First, the concept of information itself seems unclear. "Incidental information" seems to imply a wide range of information existing out there in the world, yet it glosses over the inherent problem of verifiability and truthfulness *in the information itself.* For example, it is possible that fake news, which seemingly fools users into some semblance of belief in its source's veracity, could become part of the user's pool of incidental information. If this is later selected and then produced as more information in the form of an object or document, it can easily "poison the well." The model essentially assumes that the information being used "incidentally" is *verifiable*—and that is a very problematic assumption, indeed. The model also assumes that users will come to know the differences between common knowledge, facts, and their own beliefs. Significantly, the model also might not be able to handle bad actors, or the people whose information needs (that is, motives) and information uses (that is, actions) are tantamount to the bad faith spreading of *disinformation.*

The emphasis on a primarily linear process of information use, such as Kuhlthau's information search process (Kuhlthau, 1993)—that series of "idealized steps" according to Bowler and Nesset—belies the reality that life is messier and far more complex than models such as these are able to depict. Furthermore, our information societies are sometimes compromised by the external interference of various factions. It is difficult, then, to take users' unspoiled reason and self-willed sense of purpose as a given. People sometimes harbor no motivation for why they seek out something. People sometimes do not understand why they are looking for something much less have the motivation to complete their tasks. Some forget what they are looking for as they fall into the eternally distracting rabbit holes of online browsing. Some get overwhelmed with too many choices or too much information.

More problematic is the possibility of system control and developer bias that are often ignored when focusing on the actions of an individual user. Users do not always see how they are being manipulated by automated opinions, AI-generated bots, other users, or limited choice constructions nudging them in a certain direction. Responses forced out of users and the impact of system tracking and surveillance clearly compromise the information-seeking model, which still insists that information system architecture is a transparent and benevolent construction. Yet our information systems are the product of this particular society designed at this specific moment in time to meet the ends of its original creators first, and probably the needs of some of its users second. It glosses over the fact that the internet and all information systems are *human-made* systems with decided slants toward the creators and handlers of information, increasingly seen as a proprietary commodity.

Looking at another model can help us to see the pervasive problem of being unable to account for all variables in information behavior. Allen et al.'s (2011) adoption of activity theory (Engeström, 2000) is an attempt to rectify some of the problems missing from narrower information behavior contexts. The authors explain that activity theory helps them to both "analyze information behavior as a collective and [as an] individual process" (p. 781). To bridge wider social conditions with an individual user, they use Engeström's activity system diagram that includes "other elements such as community, the division of labor, and rules/norms" (2000). Yet if we look at figure 2.2, describing "collective activity—formation of assignment and individual activity seeking information," we are shown two identical diagrams, where one is assumed to be the larger context, incorporating more variables and a larger scope, and the other is the individual's narrower context. They describe this repetition as both "an overview of the activity and its context" (in the case of the former) and "an in-depth analysis or explanation of the information behavior" (in the case of the latter).

The problem with this approach, however, is that the larger context is conceptualized as identical to the smaller, and vice versa. It is as if they are imagining each part of this system as a completely identical element, much like a fractal or Mandelbrot set, mathematically capable of being sized up or down, from collective group to individual component in perfect scale *ad infinitum*. This seems untenable as a theory as it is merely a metaphoric

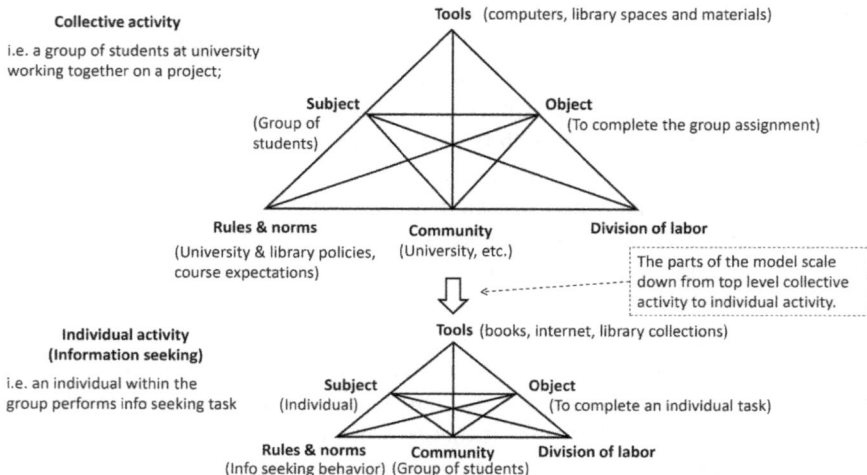

Figure 2.2. Collective and individual activity systems. *Source*: Allen et al., 2011, p. 782.

conceptualization of a small set of the many variables that impact human behavior and human behavior occurring in relation to information. We have seen all too often how problems of scale alter computer systems and user behavior; what an individual does when using a system by themselves surely does not perfectly mirror the behavior of a hundred let alone a hundred *million* users. Humans are one thing when seen as individuals—unique and atypical as single data points—but they become quite different when moving and acting as a herd.

An assumption of collective-individual uniformity becomes problematic when looking at the purpose or motive of an activity. The model, like many other models in LIS and human information behavior research, assumes a clear objective and purpose for all members of the community, as well as an assumption of identical understanding and interpretation of rules and norms established within a group. Yet all of our activities cannot be assumed to be identical. Scope, scale, size, and inter- and *intra*group dynamics each need to be considered. Adding more people to a group necessarily complicates how people behave. Divisions of labor, for example, are not always fair, and specialization is not always welcome. Sometimes people are forced to do work they dislike despite their inherent qualities and qualifications—that is, relegated to note taking or fetching coffee and tea, like many women in Japan, for example. Some of this is due to long-standing "traditions" or deep-seated societal prejudices, while some of this is due to seniority and other ways in which certain workers are privileged over others. Interpretations of shared texts—such as a syllabus in a university class or a mission statement for a corporation—can also vary widely, resulting in wildly differing actions.

It is clear, too, that Allen et al.'s action theory may be insufficient to help navigate some of the more difficult and widespread information problems that exist. In particular, action theory may have trouble with increased levels of anonymity and the subsequent loss of accountability or social penalties in online systems. Trolling, in particular, muddies the waters of objective discourse. The negative and antisocial behaviors found online cannot be addressed solely by applying action theory. Perhaps if the theory reexamines its assumptions of motive, rules, and norms, and the fluid natures of online communities themselves, the theory might be improved. Otherwise, it may not be a viable way forward. It will be up to information scholars as well as practitioners to examine the impact that information has on people and point out where pathologies exist—not only as users of the systems but also as users impacted *by* the systems. Ultimately, we need to find more sophisticated methods for examining the behavior of users, individually, in small groups, and in large crowds.

Plotting Information Behavior Theories and Recognizing "Terra Incognita"

One approach to improve this situation would be to pinpoint what each theory of information behavior attempts to examine and then highlight what it is *unable* to address. In the previous chapter, we examined the ways in which information behavior research has tended to focus much more on the *purposeful acquisition* of information, with a significant amount of research theories looking into understanding why people actively seek out information and the conscious steps they take to find it. There appears to be much less LIS information behavior research conducted in the accidental and avoidant quadrants where people either were influenced by such issues as taboos or cognitive dissonance, which dampened or curtailed information seeking. Some of this is related to the lack of significant models and paradigms that exist in LIS for these areas.

Indeed, examining human information behavior in the areas that lack specific intent on the part of an information user can be extremely difficult. Ann Kerwin's (1993) six states of ignorance can help us to reframe this in more detail:

1. *all the things people know they do not know* (**known unknowns**);
2. *all the things they do not know they do not know* (**unknown unknowns**);
3. *all the things they think they know but do not* (**errors, false truths**);
4. *all the things they do not know they know* (**tacit knowing**);
5. *all the things they are not supposed to know but may find helpful* (**taboos**);
6. *all the things too painful to know, so suppressed* (**denial**).

This list is a useful foundation for further research into the fickle and irrational natures of people, a way to get beyond information behavior research's "rational approaches to irrational problems," as Johnson describes it, that miss "the 'blooming confusion' of the real world" (Johnson, 2009, p. 596). Importantly, the types of ignorance people exhibit are not exclusive to any particular group; they are universals that we all face. We are all aware of some of the things that we do not know, those "known unknowns," which are often the easiest things for us to imagine and to articulate to others. Yet there are also things that we are not aware of and that we also do not know. We are also prone to error and false information (labeled as "false facts" earlier), and the things we think we know but don't. These errors and false facts apply greatly to our many misunderstandings about the world and represent a large underexplored area rife for research. These fall in the "accidental avoidance" quadrant, which can be seen in Johnson's mapping of Kerwin's states in figure 2.3. Tacit knowing is also on the somewhat accidental acquisition side, which is something that we know but may be unaware that we know it. Finally, taboos and denial, while similar in that they are both evidence of purposeful avoidance of information or facts, provide us with insight into the things we cannot know but want to and the things too painful to know and therefore repress or suppress.

As mentioned previously, LIS and human information behavior researchers have focused primarily on the "known unknowns" (top-right quadrant), the purposeful acquisition of information. The remaining three quadrants, however, which include "unknown unknowns" (top-left quadrant), "false truths" and "errors" (bottom-left quadrant), and "taboos" and "denial" (bottom-right quadrant), are generally less well addressed. These quadrants speak to the subconscious, the underexamined self, and the deep-rooted conscious and

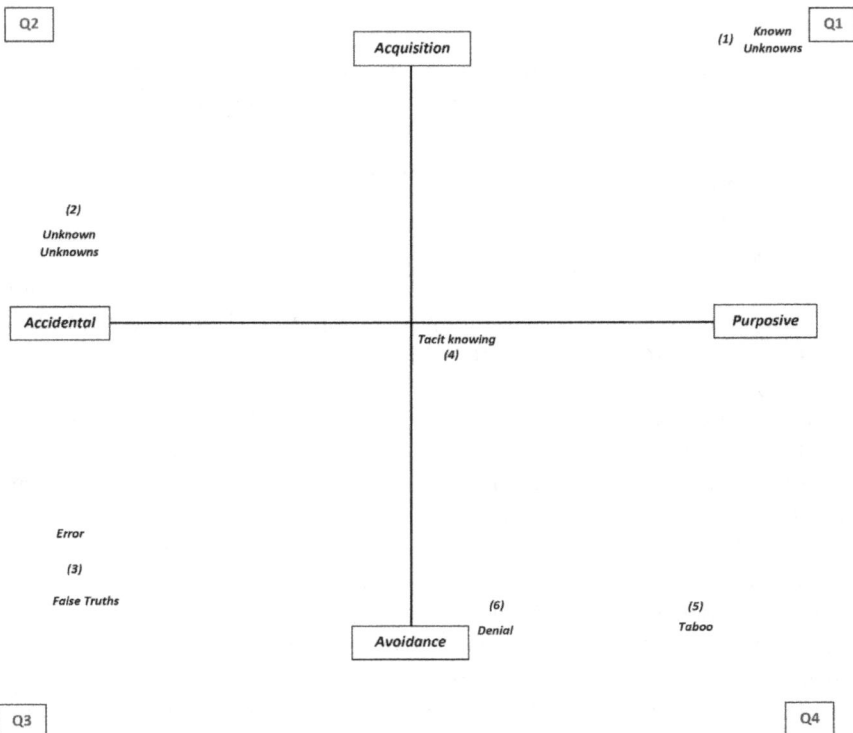

Kerwin's six states of ignorance

Figure 2.3. Kerwin's types of ignorance in human information behavior as mapped by Johnson. *Source*: Johnson, 2009.

unconscious desires to avoid awkward, painful, forbidden, or cognitively dissonant concepts, ideas, and facts.

The one drawback with Johnson's original model, however, is that it does not accommodate the overarching and manipulative contexts of digital information systems and platforms, especially their nudging and behavioral conditioning abilities, their built-in protocols of adaptive control (for example, targeted advertising and cookies), and their complicity in data tracking and online surveillance. These must surely have an impact on human information behavior as well. Indeed, many of the information pathologies that arise from the conditions inherent to information systems, including the root causes of misinformation and fake news, are not necessarily situated or clearly identified in this frame. In other words, our "terra incognita" in information behavior research may sometimes lay *within* the borders of Johnson's model but may also extend *beyond* them as well, where system factors would play an outsized role in shaping user behavior. So how, then, do we account for these unexplored areas in human information behavior theory? We will examine this in more detail in the following section.

"TERRA INCOGNITA": FUTURE PROBLEMS AND UNANSWERED QUESTIONS

A Mapping of Information Pathologies

As psychoanalyst Erich Fromm suggests, it is impossible to make someone "sane" by forcing them to adjust to their society. The society, instead, must be adjusted to the individual. Similarly, we cannot make people adjust to information systems and then assume they will adapt to or learn to accept many of the systemic problems and pathologies they incubate, harbor, or amplify. We must, rather, look at ways to investigate and adjust systems to meet the needs of *all* people who use them. Toward this end, using Johnson's mappings as a template, we can plot an aggregation of information behavior theories according to their examination of accidental or purposive information seeking behavior and motives of information avoidance or acquisition.

Figure 2.4 categorizes human information behavior theories and models by their contexts. Information systems and libraries clearly dominate the top-right corner, with their focus on purposeful acquisition of information, while more amorphous groups, such as small worlds and fragmented social worlds, would comprise the bottom quadrants of accidental and purposeful avoidance of information. The map plots research theories associated with information behaviors (in black text), which help to explain ways in which people find and acquire information (that is, pathways, foraging, scanning,

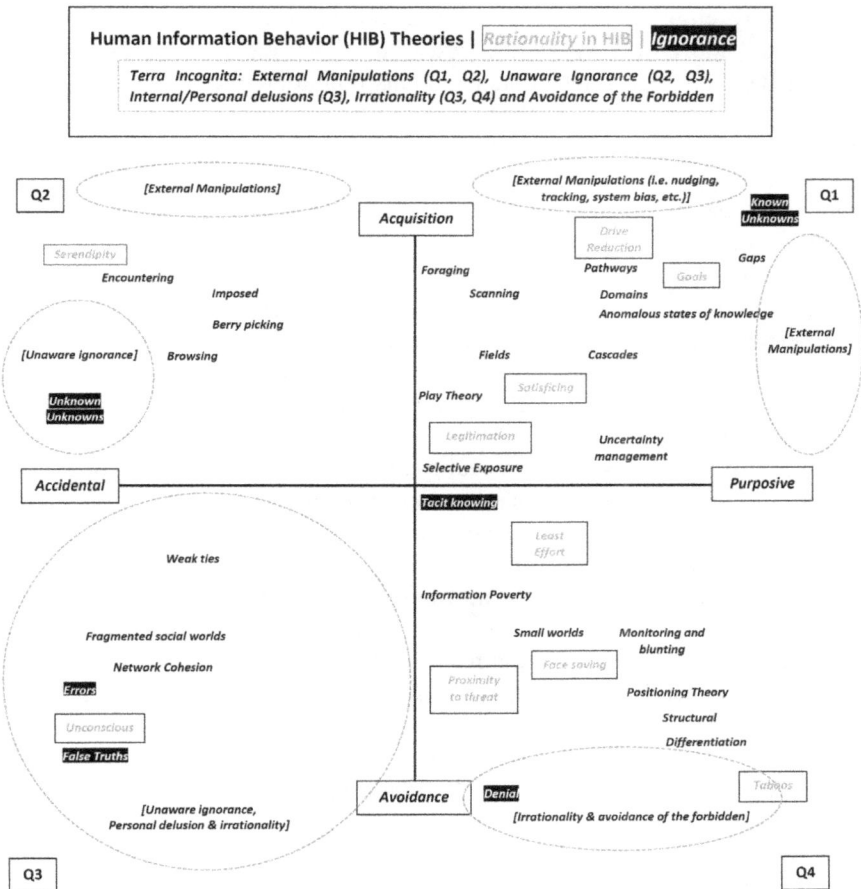

Figure 2.4. Map of human information behavior theories, their information contexts, conceptions of rationality, Kerwin's six states of ignorance, and "terra incognita" of human information behavior along the accidental-purposive and acquisition-avoidance axes.

encountering, berry picking, monitoring, and blunting, etc.). Finally, the assumptions of rationality inherent to information behavior models is plotted (in gray text surrounded by a black box), showing the ways in which people react to or are motivated by methods of information seeking (that is, via serendipity, satisficing, creating goals, unconsciously, or with the least possible effort). Kerwin's six states of ignorance have also been added in white text with a black background as a further reference point, helping the reader to get a sense of how the various types of ignorance play a role in the seeking out of information.

The gray circles with black text indicate information behavior's "terra incognita," those sections in the research where we seem to be missing approaches and theories to understanding nonrational and underdescribed information behaviors and where information pathologies may be appearing. External manipulations would include such things as nudging (a method used to direct people to choose something choice designers prefer), tracking, built-in system biases, and the use of surveillance to monitor behavior.

Other areas of our "terra incognita" include those conditions where we are unaware of our own ignorance on a subject; some of this condition may be covered in the Dunning-Kruger effect, for example, which observes that incompetent people are often largely unaware of their incompetence in an area. According to the theory, people can habitually overestimate their knowledge or abilities and are therefore prone to greater error. This also relates to the way in which people are not entirely rational or objective in their thinking and may avoid looking at the reality of their situation. Finally, purposeful avoidance nevertheless remains relatively understudied in information behavior, often from the influence of personal denial and taboo subjects. Taboos and other types of forbidden knowledge, in particular, can have a pernicious effect on people, especially if the information needed is for health purposes— say for abortion access or sex education—yet remains entangled inextricably to a society's social or even legal restrictions.

Importantly, while looking at these categories in the aggregate, we observe that the majority of the research and contexts studied in information behavior fall within the top-right quadrant, which emphasizes the study of the *purposive acquisition* of information. Yet the contexts for human information behavior remain evenly distributed throughout the human experience with information. Problems such as information poverty—which falls within accidental avoidance of information quadrant—and fragmented worlds (falling in purposeful avoidance) seem overall less studied in LIS research and perhaps much harder to approach experimentally.

Indeed, the emphasis on striving to anticipate a person's "known unknowns" (found in the top-right, purposeful acquisition quadrant) may arguably be *the defining approach* to research into human information behavior and is largely the main focus of much library-centric research in general. The lower-left quadrant, in contrast, which contains the accidental-avoidant sides of human information behavior, remains relatively understudied. One reason for this is that it is often particularly difficult to incorporate unknown quantities and unpredictable attitudes into the *pragmatic* and *programmatic* missions of libraries themselves and overall information research itself. Librarians in particular may find research into these amorphous areas anathema to their stated missions *as* librarians because one of the very basic assumptions of librarians is that they are there to serve and fulfill their patrons' information needs. At the very least librarians may find these areas impractical to pursue as necessary areas of research because they often fail to meet the immediate and practical needs of their library's users.

As Kuhn has suggested, such thorny and unresolvable problems in scientific disciplines are often abandoned out of practical, economic, and career-oriented concerns, resulting in a "normal" phase of science and inquiry that attempts to better articulate the most dominant theoretical paradigms (Kuhn, 1970, p. 24). It may even be difficult to conceive of how to approach these areas, especially as it is easier to measure an *occurrence* rather than an *absence* of something (Kempner et al., 2011, p. 481). However, this is not to say that identifying information pathologies would have little impact on "known unknowns" or purposive information seeking. In fact, scholars may need to consider how even purposeful information seeking may be influenced by factors such as nudging, choice architecture, tracking and surveillance programs, or the biases built into information technologies, systems, and platforms that provide the avenues for such purposeful acquisition.

What impact do flaws in an information system have on individuals and their wider society?

The concept of information pathology raises a number of questions about how to understand information behavior in a society. What systemic issues can be identified through an information pathology lens? Because systems are built by people, for example, do flaws inherent to humans wind up as *systemic* flaws? Noble's important book *Algorithms of Oppression* (2018) argues that this may be the case. Discriminatory results appearing in a Google image search stem from the human developers of the algorithm, which is in turn reflected in the images retrieved for the user. How quickly and rapidly might information pathologies spread through typical information behaviors? Or, in the case of "counterfacts," what are the motivations for sharing or creating something like fake news or misinformation? Some of these motivations are unclear, and as a result solutions to fight them are equally imprecise.

Definitions of fake news, as well, are often muddled. Weiss et al. (2020), for example, examine how teaching faculty at a master's-granting state university in California define and understand fake news. Most solutions to the problem of fake news in LIS literature address how librarians teach the concept to students and conclude that if librarians could just *reach* them, students would learn to neutralize its effect on them. Yet this approach by itself may be insufficient. The authors call for a unified definition of the concept that attempts to corral the individual's role within a system, its adversaries, and the system itself. They define fake news as a "phenomenon of information exchange between an actor and acted upon that primarily attempts to invalidate generally-accepted conceptions of truth for the purpose of altering established power structures" (p. 12). This definition could be seen as part of a new approach to information studies, based on assumptions that there are unanticipated breakdowns in wider social systems. The antidote to fake news has often been seen through a narrower lens of information literacy, which assumes, much like information behavior, that actors in information systems are at bottom rational choice makers, vested in their own self-improvement, and that they can become resistant to manipulation so long as they become aware—via instruction—of information literacy strategies (Oltmann, 2018; Cooke, 2018). But this remains problematic.

This new definition, however, accounts for the wider societal problems facing online information and general social behaviors. Weiss et al. write, "what binds both sides of the fake news phenomenon—'the actors' and 'the acted-upon' as we have defined them—is the suspension of disbelief coupled with the spread of false information. The two threads are indelibly intertwined, needing both sides to complete and perpetuate the cycle" (2020, p. 11). In other words, they identify that the wider causes of fake news must be examined from both a personal perspective—that of the actors and the acted upon—as well as among the wider social dimensions that foster these systemic information problems. Calling for information literacy as a main solution to the problem of fake news is too limited in the face of lopsided systemic power imbalances, especially if one side holds all the cards in spreading misinformation with little or even no penalties for doing so. In one telling example, not one of the members of the Kremlin-backed troll farm Internet Research Agency, which is documented to have interfered in the 2016 US presidential election, has been remanded into US custody for misinformation transgressions (Mueller, 2019).

Additionally, fake news needs to be seen as part of the wider social phenomenon from which it stems. We need to see the factors that allow for its rise and ability to spread so easily. It seems that using information literacy may be just a bandage covering a much deeper and more widespread problem. Information behavior's reliance on the rational actor while emphasizing information literacy as the main salve to the problem might not resolve inherent social pathologies, as the main theories provide room only for benevolent, purposeful, and "good faith" actions. It is no wonder that information researchers and library educators may struggle to devise responses to the fake news phenomenon aside from the commonsense advice of information literacy or treating library patrons as if they were vessels to be filled with the right facts.

From a social pathology perspective, the effects of denialism and fake news must further be seen as a combination of numerous multidimensional factors. They cannot be seen merely as the problems of poorly created or implemented information literacy programs in libraries that (1) are part and parcel of the social fabric to begin with and (2) ignore the wider society by focusing primarily on sources of information (that is, gatekeeping). Smith sees the problem of climate denial, for example, as a consequence of numerous social pathologies. He warns that we must seek "to understand human behavior not according to a one-dimensional model or framework, but how, from a dialectical or dynamic interactive perspective, it is affected by genetic inheritance, psychological and emotional development, as well as by general experience (social or otherwise)" (Smith, 2017, p. 132). With this in mind, we can see that LIS's overemphasis on the addressing the "known unknowns" in information behavior (that is, if students only knew where to find the right sources, they'd never believe false things) may be woefully underequipped to address willful as well as unconscious denialism.

"Beyond" Cognition: Toward Meaningful Realities and a Metacognitive Approach

It is clear that what has been missing from much information behavior research is a look at wider social pathologies and their impact on user actions. While focusing on the linear process and the rational actor in information behavior models, researchers may have missed some of the more complex interplay between users and the powers wielded by or even through such institutions themselves. Information research must endeavor to include a wider look at the concepts related to social pathologies. Such information pathologies would serve to both identify as well as examine the systemic problems of information in all its incarnations and forms, especially as it relates to the inherent abuse of power in an information society, the diminishment of personal agency and privacy, and systemic oppression caused by surveillance capitalism's asymmetrical power structures. If we ignore the growing power imbalance between IT/social media companies and their users, we may never reach an accurate understanding of negative online information behaviors. Libraries may lose their foothold within the information economy. Library policies of free access to information may be slowly depleted of their influence. As Luciano Floridi writes, "the design of a meaningful reality is . . . a social and ethical obligation that we have towards each other" (2013, p. 332). Identifying the problems with information and information behavior will help us to fulfill the goal of contributing to developing a meaningful reality.

Thinking of Thought Itself

But how do we begin to create a more meaningful reality? One of the ways in which we might do this is through the development and improvement of our metacognition skills. As touched upon briefly in the introduction, meta-cognition is seen as "a form of self-aware thinking that can help one monitor one's own thinking" (Bowler, 2011, p. 94), or more simply: "thinking about thinking" (Rhodes, 2019). The concept provides a useful framework to study the ways in which people learn and incorporate information into their bases of knowledge. Disruptions to these skills may contribute to some of the information pathology problems we notice in information user behavior. Metacognition itself comprises three components: "[1] knowledge of one's self; [2] knowledge of the nature of a cognitive task in relation to one's own cognitive abilities, and [3] knowledge of how and when to . . . use cognitive strategies to complete a cognitive task" (Bowler, 2011, p. 96). The important thing to remember is that the person is assumed to be thinking and pondering their own knowledge and understanding of something while also generally confirming or refuting their mastery of it. It is also seen as a task-oriented approach, with an acknowledgment that someone may not necessarily have a good understanding of that task.

Metacognition is theorized as operating on two levels, the object level, which consists of a person's actions and thoughts "as they take place in the world," and the meta level, which seems to stand outside the object level to observe and monitor a conscious goal or task (Rhodes, 2019). Awareness of the activity in play, in other words, is separate from the activity itself. This awareness may be scalable and may reach higher states of even greater self-awareness. Nelson and Narens (1990), important researchers in the field of metacognition, argue that an initial meta level may have yet another meta level that monitors that meta level, and so on.

The tasks we endeavor undertake within the framework of metacognition can therefore fall under a large array of activities. Bowler posits that we can examine an information user's metacognitive abilities by looking at the following behaviors that users demonstrate during their searches: balancing, building a base, changing course, communicating, connecting, knowing that you do not know, knowing strengths and weaknesses, parallel thinking, pulling back and reflecting, scaffolding, understanding curiosity, understanding memory, and understanding time and effort (Bowler, 2011).

The first several provide insight into how people grow into their roles as information seekers. In *balancing*, the user is confronted with the task of choosing between various options, requiring a significant amount of evaluation to decide which option among many would be best. Some of the problems identified by Bowler include information overload—the negative feeling associated with too much information that creates a temporary disen-gagement from a search—as well as choice paralysis, especially if the choices that need to be balanced appear to be equally credible. The benefit of being strong in this area, however, gives the information user the ability to better choose the best and most credible sources while at the same time warding off problems related to too much information.

For *building a base*, it is suggested that students develop a search through small incremental blocks, almost like a road or a building's foundation, in order to successfully reach their information goal. Dervin (1999) and Kuhlthau (1991) provide the theoretical base for this in their information research. Much of the work related to this is done through browsing for information, finding synonyms or keywords, brainstorming or mapping terms together in order to see a wider perspective and a bigger overall picture. What is useful about Dervin's approach is that she sees sense-making "not set forth as if [it] were merely a purposive, linear, problem solving activity." It is, instead, "merely a subset of human possibilities" (Dervin, 1999, p. 46).

Similarly, *changing course* is another metacognitive technique that requires information seekers to first assess whether their original search approach has been successful and to next decide how to modify or alter the direction to improve search results. The important similarity between these first three is the realization that a multipronged approach with an adjustable net, so to speak, may yield better results. The user has to be aware, though, of the wider picture while simultaneously remembering the ultimate goal. The role of "information seeker" becomes essential to these first approaches.

But the next couple metacognitive skills, *communicating* and *connecting*, seem to take things beyond just adopting the role of information seeker by helping one to realize that intelligence is in the connections between self and others. This broader realization puts the seeker in the wider context of information as a medium between users and seekers. Talking and discussing plans or verifying information with others works as a useful strategy to help solve problems. Similarly, connecting is a "linking" process, in many ways "the act of defining the relationships between nodes in a mental map" (Bowler, 2011, p. 109).

Another cluster of skills involves developing clearer self-knowledge, including awareness of some rather negative things: one's ignorance as well as one's weaknesses relative to one's strengths. Knowing that you do not know something is partly about identifying the gaps in one's knowledge but also a painful acknowledgment of one's own limitations. This is a step toward Socratic wisdom (knowing that you know nothing). Belkin's anomalous states of knowledge and Dervin's sense-making base their theories on these gaps in knowledge, focusing on a person's awareness of "not knowing." Still, it is a rather optimistic take on personal ignorance, as the person is aware of such gaps and has a tempered, rational response to this. But the fact remains that many of us remain ill informed about what we do not know because it is an uncomfortable, even irrational, feeling. Similarly, a person's self-awareness of their strengths may outweigh their awareness of their weaknesses. We often know—or think we know—what we are good at, but coming to acknowledge and accept our own ignorance or poor skills can be a difficult thing, especially as it might be tied up with negative emotions such as shame or embarrassment. Transcending these is often a difficult obstacle to overcome.

In the end, the thinking skills associated with metacognition involve the understanding of several important personality traits: one's curiosity, one's memory, and one's expenditure of time and effort. Each of these is reliant upon the information seeker's ability to regulate their interests and emotions while also remaining aware of the wider perspectives and obligations that may be forcing them toward a conclusion to their tasks. As is often the case with students, for example, they find an aspect of an assigned school task that turns out to be far more interesting than the original project and get interested in this at the expense of finishing it. The ability to balance the needs of the task with the desire to learn more and spend more time on something not central to their work is seen as an essential metacognitive task. It is about prioritizing one side of a natural tension between two forces—curiosity and obligation—that are sometimes in opposition to each other. Yet managing one's time and understanding the need for persistence is also a key concept for ensuring that results of information seeking are satisfactory.

Metacognition, Information Pathologies, and the "Terra Incognita" of Information Behavior: The "Susceptibility Factor"

Ultimately, as an important theory, Rhodes finds that "applications of meta-cognition are present in virtually all areas of research within psychology," which would include education, health, clinical psychology, law, and more (Rhodes, 2019). Metacognition as applied to library and information science does seem to have a natural alliance as focus on retrieval of information and incorporating it into personal needs overlaps with education and psychology disciplines. This explains why metacognition provides a useful and important support for studies into information literacy, as Bowler and Nesset show. Yet there are some difficulties in understanding just how effective metacognition can be. Frith explains: "First, there seem to be two forms of self-monitoring. There is an explicit form, which is slow and deliberate, while there is also an implicit form, which is rapid, automatic and can occur without awareness. The question remains open as to whether this implicit form of self-monitoring should even be called metacognition. . . . Second, the explicit form of self-monitoring, as we shall see, is highly susceptible to error" (Frith, 2012). This problem with error, as we have seen, is central of much of our information behavior inquiry. It is possible that the problems with error itself helps to spread false information.

Ultimately, the issues facing one's ability to understand how one understands something is tied up with the ways in which the "terra incognita," those understudied and sometimes irrational influences that prevent people from finding out information—those pesky information pathologies, or "chaos" as Brenda Dervin (1999) might call it—interact with our rational intentions to understand and learn, as well as our affective needs and wants. The story of how fake news and misinformation sometimes interfere with our ability to find knowledge is the story of this interaction between these various influences. Indeed, if metacognition is self-awareness used to monitor one's own thinking—the thinking about thought itself—then information pathologies are those things that can disrupt this awareness, resulting in a kind of "metacognitive pathology."

Misinformation and fake news, it could be argued, find ways to disrupt the typical methods people take to monitor their thinking. Therefore, the major hypothesis of this book is to suggest that one's *susceptibility* to misinformation may in fact be as much a function of a relative strength and weakness in a person's overall metacognitive abilities. This leads us to consider whether there is perhaps a metacognitive susceptibility factor. The impact of one's susceptibility to these information pathologies limits one's effectiveness as a user of information and an identifier of false information, misinformation, disinformation, and general fake news.

REFERENCES

Allen, D., Karanasios, S., and Slavova, M. (2011). Working with activity theory: Context, technology, and information behavior. *Journal of the Association for Information Science and Technology, 62*(4), pp. 776–88.

Allmer, T. (2012). *Towards a critical theory of surveillance in informational capitalism*. Peter Lang.

Bates, M. J. (2005). An introduction to metatheories, theories, and models. In K. Fisher, S. Erdelez, and L. McKechnie (eds.), *Theories of information behavior* (pp. 1–24). Information Today.

Bowler, L. (2011). A metacognitive ethnography. In A. Spink and J. Heinström (eds.), *New directions in information behavior* (pp. 93–125). Emerald.

Bowler, L., and Nesset, V. (2013). Information literacy. In J. Beheshti and A. Large (eds.), *The information behavior of a new generation: Children and teens in the 21st century* (pp. 45–63). The Scarecrow Press, Inc.

Cooke, N. A. (2018). Critical literacy as an approach to combating cultural misinformation/disinformation on the internet. In D. E. Agosto (ed.), *Information literacy and libraries in the age of fake news* (pp. 36–51). ABC-CLIO, LLC.

Dervin, B. (1999). Chaos, order, and sense-making: A proposed theory for information design. In R. Jacobson (ed.), *Information design* (pp. 35–57). Cambridge, MA: MIT Press.

Engeström, Y. (2000). Activity theory as a framework for analyzing and redesigning work. *Ergonomics, 43*(7), pp. 960–74. https://doi.org/10.1080/001401300409143.

Floridi, L. (2013). *The ethics of information.* Oxford University Press.

Frith, C. D. (2012) The role of metacognition in human social interactions. *Philosophical Transactions of the Royal Society of London,* B, Biological Sciences, *367*(1599), pp. 2213–23. https://www.ncbi.nlm.nih.gov/pmc/articles/PMC3385688/.

Jeanes, E. (2019). Hawthorne effect. In *A dictionary of organizational behaviour.* Oxford University Press.

Johnson, J. D. (2009). An impressionistic mapping of information behavior with special attention to contexts, rationality, and ignorance. *Information Processing and Management, 45*, pp. 593–604.

Kempner, J., Merz, J., and Bosk, C. (2011). Forbidden knowledge: Public controversy and the production of nonknowledge. *Sociological Forum, 26*(3), pp. 475–500.

Kerwin, A. (1993). None too solid: Medical ignorance. *Knowledge: Creation, Diffusion, Utilization, 15*(2), pp. 166–85.

Kuhlthau, C. C. (1993). *Seeking meaning: A process approach to library and information services.* Ablex.

Kuhn, T. S. (1970). *The structure of scientific revolutions.* Second edition. University of Chicago Press.

Lamdan, S. (2019). Librarianship at the crossroads of ICE surveillance. *In the library with the lead pipe.* http://www.inthelibrarywiththeleadpipe.org/2019/ice-surveillance/.

Marchionini, G. (2008). Human–information interaction research and development. *Library and Information Science Research, 30*(3), pp. 165–74.

Mueller, R. S. (2019). *Report on the investigation into Russian interference in the 2016 presidential election: Submitted pursuant to 28 C.F.R. §600.8(c).* US government official edition.). US Department of Justice.

Nelson, T. O., and Narens, L. (1990). Metamemory: A theoretical framework and new findings. In G. H. Bower (ed.), *The psychology of learning and motivation,* 26 (pp. 125–73). New York: Academic Press.

Noble, S. U. (2018). *Algorithms of oppression: How search engines reinforce racism.* New York University Press.

Olan, F., Jayawickrama, U., Arakpogun, E. O., Suklan, J., and Liu, S. 2022. Fake news on social media: The impact on society. *Information systems frontiers: A journal of research and innovation,* pp. 1–16. https://doi.org/10.1007/s10796-022-10242-z.

Oltmann, S. M. (2018). Misinformation and intellectual freedom in libraries. In D. E. Agosto (ed.), *Information literacy and libraries in the age of fake news* (pp. 66–76). ABC-CLIO, LLC.

Penney, J. W. (2016). Chilling effects: Online surveillance and Wikipedia use. *Berkeley Technology Law Journal, 31*(1), pp. 117–82.

Piccialli, F., di Cola, V. S., Giampaolo, F., & Cuomo, S. (2021). "The role of artificial intelligence in fighting the COVID-19 pandemic." *Information Systems Frontiers,* 23(6), 1467–1497. https://doi.org/10.1007/s10796-021-10131-x.

Rhodes, M. G. (2019). Metacognition. *Teaching of Psychology, 46*(2), pp. 168–75. https://doi-org.libproxy.csun.edu/10.1177/0098628319834381.

Smith, R. (2017). *Society and social pathology: A framework for progress.* First edition. Palgrave Macmillan.

Thivant, E. (2005). Information seeking and use behaviour of economists and business analysts. *Information Research: An International Electronic Journal, 10*(4). http://InformationR.net/ir/10-4/paper234.html.

Weiss, A., Alwan, A., Garcia, E., and Garcia, J. (2020). Surveying fake news: Assessing university faculty's fragmented definition of fake news and its impact on teaching critical thinking, *International Journal for Educational Integrity, 16*(1). https://doi.org/10.1007/s40979-019-0049-x.

Zuboff, S. (2015). Big other: Surveillance capitalism and the prospects of an information civilization. *Journal of Information Technology, 30*(1), pp. 75–89.

Chapter 3

Ceding Truth to Power

Information Behavior and Life in a Digital Cage

NAVIGATING INCREASINGLY POLICED WATERS

In the previous chapter, a lot of ground was covered regarding information pathologies and metacognition. One of the clearest ways in which we can deal with negative information behaviors is through engaging in "thinking about thinking." Some of these cognitive strategies have been widely adopted for information literacy initiatives, which attempt to improve student learning outcomes. Librarians and libraries have been quick to address the problems of fake news and misinformation through the implementation of tools and educational programs centered on information literacy, especially the Association of College and Research Libraries (ACRL) *Framework for Information Literacy for Higher Education*. The strategies and tools suggested in the information literacy framework have been suggested by many librarian practitioners as a method to help mitigate these problems (Auberry, 2018; Cooke, 2018; Jones-Jang et al., 2021). These guidelines have been successful—to a point. In the process of focusing on information literacy strategies, however, the wider political and sociological changes wrought by the near-universal adoption of internet technologies and the misinformation and fake news that they help to spread wind up being less prioritized. As a result, much is missed regarding the wider causes of misinformation's creation and spread and the strategies needed to mitigate them. It's hard, in other words, to see the forest for the trees. The question remains how users can navigate the problems of Big Data, monetized personal information, and surveillance while finding the information they need.

One of the major shortcomings of library and information science has been in the area of examining the library's place within a capitalist society, especially as it pertains to information tracking and data brokering (Lamdan, 2019). It is difficult sometimes to see librarians' obligations and roles objectively given how closely libraries are entwined with the engines of economic growth within our societies, contributing significantly to the information economy (for example, book publishing, database purchasing, film streaming services, etc.) as well as the information ecosystem (for example, sharing, vetting, repurposing, and inventing new knowledge). The benefits of this situation are seen to outweigh the drawbacks, and librarians surely do not wish to see themselves as complicit in a system that exploits its own users. Tellingly, however, many of the most well-known vendors that libraries support financially have undergone significant shifts in their business focus. Data brokering in particular has taken over a significant number of vendors that previously were primarily book, digital content, or database publishers. ProQuest—now part of the publicly traded analytics company Clarivate—began as a service providing graduate student master's theses and dissertations in microfilm format. It later evolved into online database publishing and now is but one arm of a multinational corporation that focuses on information services and products in the form of collected user data. Clarivate's website reveals that their "real world data product includes more than 300 million longitudinal covered lives, 2 million healthcare providers and 98% of payers in the United States, with visibility into 100 million electronic health records" (Clarivate, 2022). That last figure represents nearly one in three people in the United States, many of whom are the users of and stakeholders in our libraries, including students, faculty, staff, administrators, and community members at large. Clarivate's shift in business focus is ultimately reflective of the history of many media platforms and the economic power they have wielded since the 1900s. The "medium is the message," Marshall McLuhan says, designed to perpetuate itself through the content it broadcasts and collects.

Another takeaway from this shift is that libraries are no longer primarily siloed entities creating a walled-off "separate peace," so to speak, with spaces cloistered from the external world, stocked with books and other print or analog media as buttresses against it. Instead they have become part of a much wider interconnected mechanism, their silos dismantled and dispersed, inextricably bound to the creators and aggregators of the content they hold, linked voluntarily and involuntarily through this decentralization of their spaces and power to the philosophies the companies espouse and the social and political policies they influence. These companies are representative of a new capitalism that has, as Smith suggests, "introduced new social, economic and political forces, as well as certain distinct structural and cultural motivations . . . [that] naturalize needless suffering and irrationality" (Smith, 2017). This suffering and irrationality stem from the specific economic pressures placed upon people, in particular those vulnerable to hardship and the negative effects of inequality.

While many librarians are vehement in their beliefs that libraries *are* the great equalizers in a democratic society—and the recent history of libraries does bear this out, mostly, though occasionally at *certain* times for *certain* people—libraries still exist within a wider societal context at the mercy of and as contributors to those forces. Recent politically conservative attempts to ban or even burn library books in the States of Texas and Virginia, for example, have been met with organized resistance from librarians, whose missions are often intertwined with making sure that information remains open to all and without stigma. That people still turn to libraries in these times and appreciate their stance against censorship means they still appear to represent a common public good and the heart of the egalitarian spirit. But how long can this last, especially when surveillance-linked capitalism begins to influence a society's basic functions, its thoughts about itself, and the role of information, ideas, and knowledge within it?

Roger Shattuck writes in *Forbidden Knowledge: From Prometheus to Pornography*, "open knowledge appears to stand for modernity itself" (Shattuck, 1996), which seems to have near-universal appeal in the liberal West and other first world well-functioning democracies. But he finds that even within these societies people still strongly believe that some knowledge should *not* be shared. Some things must be kept walled off, including one's personal privacy. These concerns, however, are often disregarded and seen as antithetical to forward-thinking technocrats. In fact, to suggest knowledge or technology should be restricted in any way often courts accusations of censorship or Luddism (Shattuck, 1996). There are still issues with the widespread release of information that is *truly* dangerous in an existential sense, for example, including the manufacturing of nuclear weapons, the unleashing of dangerous weaponized viruses, or the release of compromising information that can endanger people. Such threats logically and pragmatically need to be kept under tight legal controls.

There are also ideas and concepts, perhaps less existentially dangerous than nuclear weapons, that are nevertheless considered taboo in many cultures. Certain ideas that are taboo come to be avoided by people within those cultures. As discussed in chapters 1 and 2, taboos are fairly underresearched in the LIS field, further marginalizing the application of findings in the field. Certainly, to spread this information within a culture that finds something taboo or forbidden could cause consternation or dismay among members operating within it. What is important, however, is that not all open knowledge is seen as an unequivocal public good. Not all knowledge is seen as beneficial in all cases, and the sharing of this knowledge may be seen as reckless or dangerous. This includes personal information, one's sense of privacy, and the autonomy to decide for oneself what happens with that information.

UNEQUAL POWER AND THE INDIVIDUAL

Despite the underlying influence of taboos, forbidden knowledge, and personal privacy, there has nevertheless been a conflation of open knowledge with personal information in the way that the current internet era operates. The immense aggregation of personal data on a widespread scale, considered part of the five Vs of Big Data—velocity, volume, value, variety, and veracity—exacerbates this problem (Weiss, 2018). Information technology now has the capacity to record so much about a person's behavior that it can pinpoint identities and erode one's privacy at much faster speeds and far more extensively and accurately than in the past. It is at this point that one must address the power imbalance that arises from this creation and sharing of data at hyper scales. This overreach of an unfettered and unregulated openness, prying into our personal lives, may be *the* defining feature of the current interconnected online world.

These hidden forces often dictate what ideas ultimately end up as dangerous and influence what may be seen as "forbidden." Sensing its destabilizing effect, some may rush to condemn false information, but how does the idea of "forbidden" actually work within a digital world where almost anything goes within it? Conceiving of something as "dangerous" and "verboten" may unintentionally contribute to its appeal. Espousing dangerous or destabilizing ideas may be some of the thrill people find when encountering fake news, something that we will look at in more detail later in part III of this book.

BEYOND TABOO AND DENIAL, CAN IDEAS BE DANGEROUS?

While every society is constantly reconsidering and reevaluating what constitutes taboos and forbidden information, the concept of a dangerous idea has its roots in the desire to preserve the stability and sustainability of a culture, for "protecting certain beliefs (or illusions), deemed vital for the individual or for society" (Bénabou and Tirole, 2011). To threaten violence is to also impose the concept of the forbidden on someone else who doesn't share that concern, usually someone seen as dangerous and therefore a threat to the society. To criticize capitalism in American society, for example, is to risk reactionary comments and even political violence. Given the real threats to local libraries and librarians in places like Texas, Oklahoma, and Virginia, this is not merely an abstract threat. The fear of capitalism's breakdown drives the threats and the denialism of anything that contradicts its reputation. The constant denial of climate change and capitalism's outsized role in the energy consumption driving carbon emissions is another example of how ideas bend to political power. It is *verboten*, in other words, to find fault with this system. Yet criticism keeps systems healthy by identifying the flaws that weaken and destroy them. To deny this criticism allows a system to become inflexible and brittle. This is where Americans are now.

SURVEILLANCE (*AND*) CAPITALISM

Most people generally accept their current situation online as the way things are, thinking it is only natural that Facebook, Twitter/X, Netflix, and Google, with their enormously popular services, have overtaken the web, controlling its information flows and impacting our physical and personal bandwidth. Acquiescence to the concept of Big Data and its so-called grand bargain for users has led us to this point, making it seem like it was inevitable. But it wasn't and it need not remain this way. Corporate interests currently dominating the web may overshadow the internet's early egalitarian and utopian vision of a free-flowing system of information and communication, but that independent spirit still exists and still attracts users to the internet. Tim Berners Lee, in his thirtieth anniversary letter to the World Wide Web in 2019, exhorts us to "make the web available for everyone" and "hold companies and governments accountable for the commitments they make" (Berners-Lee, 2019). That spirit of individualism, while very much alive, does hang in a precarious balance. The question remains how we might modify or improve the internet so that we might curtail the system of surveillance and exploitation of the data collected and brokered from that system or the incentives that drive it.

As capitalism adopts surveillance as a main method of growing capital, *laissez-faire* policies have allowed IT companies to amass a huge power imbalance that results from the exploitation of personal privacy through mining and selling personal data at immense profit (Zuboff, 2015). Libraries are in danger of being consumed by this shift, not only from vendors but also from within. For their part, libraries have not been entirely immune to the temptations of patron tracking. In academic libraries especially, there is a strong push to track students in order to find out what makes them succeed or fail, with the aim for many to find clear correlations between student use of a library and overall GPA or graduation rates. While intentions may be good, student tracking initiatives could result in further erosion of student privacy. The impact this lost sense of privacy may have on student mental health and well-being is not yet determined. According to Katherine Mangan in her report "The Surveilled Student," students are increasingly monitored on campuses across the United States, especially with regard to anticheating software used in remote learning classes (Mangan, 2021). 54 percent of institutions currently use this type of monitoring software and 23 percent have expressed their intention to adopt it, conceivably reaching nearly 80 percent of all institutions in higher education. Other types of monitoring include active video surveillance of students (23 percent of colleges and universities), passive video surveillance (39 percent), and monitoring the software on students' computers (23 percent) (Mangan, 2021).

Further complicating the issue of assessment in libraries is that the nature of surveillance and its impact on the surveilled remains unresolved. Surveillance as an object of study generally falls into two dominant theories: panoptic and nonpanoptic. Michel Foucault, the founder of the panoptic theory of surveillance, argues that surveillance is always negative as it is "connected to coercion, repression, discipline, power, [and] domination" (Allmer, 2012, p. 41). Foucault sees such power to surveil as centralized (that is, in the hands of a government agency or secret police), where a society is controlled and repressed. In other words, there can ultimately be no such thing as "good" surveillance. This interpretation seems especially apropos in light of the uneven amassing of power and capital characteristic of surveillance capitalism and the lack of consent regarding privacy that have occurred.

Nonpanoptic surveillance theories, on the other hand, tend to see surveillance as equally usable for all people, often beneficial (like tracking your child or tracking student progress), and therefore only negative if they are used in negative ways. This pragmatic rather than absolutist approach suggests that surveillance is more a neutral behavior, equally enabling or constraining depending upon the situation and the variables involved (Allmer, 2012, p. 40). This approach may work best for many student initiatives that rely on student data and tracking to better understand areas where students both succeed and underperform academically.

However, the problem of rationalizing student tracking as overall benevolent (that is, academic success initiatives, improved or accelerated graduation rates, and so on) is that nonpanoptic surveillance tends to "overlook the power asymmetries of contemporary society and . . . convey the image that private actors are equally powerful as corporations and state institutions" (Allmer, 2012, p. 42). Such egalitarian concepts of diffused, personal surveillance—which may exist at the individual level—often miss the reality that a greater, more centralized power ultimately comes to coerce and control both the individual surveillant and the surveilled. No matter how much an individual can potentially keep track of someone else—that is, their next-door neighbors—this surveillance act will necessarily be minor in comparison, not only in scale and scope but also in terms of legal impact. It takes the centralized power of the state itself to enforce punitive actions against the other person.

Furthermore, the direct negative effects of surveillance on information seeking behaviors are well documented. Penney's (2016) research on the effect of the Snowden files disclosures reveals that people are less willing to search for controversial topics when they become aware of widespread surveillance activities. The well-documented Hawthorne effect demonstrates that people behave differently when they know they are being watched (Jeanes, 2019). Similar effects may impact students. Should they come to believe that libraries are effectively functioning as an arm of the surveillance state, students may reject libraries as free and safe spaces for personal inquiry, one of their most enduring and positive features. Surveillance capitalism perpetuates the mass-scale, interconnected panopticon, while hiding behind the illusion of a flattened, egalitarian digital world. However, the unseen but very real power imbalances of surveillance capitalism are not only destroying privacy, they are also interfering with libraries' goals of institutional neutrality and, ultimately, marginalizing librarians' long-held positions as mediators and experts of quality information resources. The failure to address these ongoing social issues in information behavior research would be tragic.

SURVEILLANCE (*IN*) LIBRARIES

Because libraries generally function outside the cutthroat world of the billion- and trillion-dollar IT titans and are relatively cloistered institutions compared to the rough-and-tumble world of politics and business, it is easy to downplay their part in all this and to assume that librarians have little to do with the wider machinations and "real-world" problems of the greater society. It's easy to assume that libraries have a minimal impact in the world of surveillance capitalism, beyond the library profession's general advocacy for patron privacy. Libraries have certainly done much to bolster this reputation, including the general stance against protecting patron privacy as outlined in the American Library Association's (ALA) policies. Public positions against government surveillance, such as fighting against the PATRIOT act post-9/11, have also burnished library reputations and largely protected Americans against invasive laws. But focusing solely on these past actions severely downplays the role that libraries play in the contemporary information economy and the clear relationship that libraries have had with companies that currently deal in surveillance and data tracking.

In the early 2000s, during the height of the book digitization efforts of Google, libraries were partners in the mass digitization of nearly twenty to thirty million print books (Weiss, 2014). Mass digitization projects that started in the mid-1990s and early 2000s, such as UMI's theses and dissertations (now ProQuest), gave libraries a clear path to contributing works of great cultural value to the online environment. These digitization projects have undoubtedly provided libraries with beneficial services, especially with the HathiTrust or the fiercely independent and sometimes bleeding-edge Internet Archive, which have both far surpassed anything Google accomplished, despite its deep pockets to throw money at any problem. Yet some of these projects, Google Books in particular, and traditionally supported vendors that have recently pivoted to other services may also entwine the library in a mesh of trade-offs hidden in the various corporate collaborations and agreements that many libraries have entered into.

Many of the large publishing companies like RELX (aka Elsevier) and Clarivate no longer focus purely on journal publishing and database content aggregation. They are, instead, pivoting to the tracking, collection, and analysis of user data, which is where the largest potential for profits appears to exist, given the unequal power balances and general lack of overarching regulations. They have pivoted so much that publisher Elsevier, according to Ulrich Herb, can be said to no longer be primarily in the business of distributing and selling scientific publications but is instead in the business of "information analytics" (Herb, 2019). Of course, cost cutting and adapting to meet market demand are at the heart of capitalism itself. Adapt or die, is the rule of thumb. Eastman-Kodak, despite inventing the digital camera in the mid-1970s, remains a notable case study in failing to shift from analog technologies to digital platforms. Successful companies, in other words, find ways to adjust to market demands.

Other companies once known primarily for other goods and services have joined the trend to collect user data to sell to data brokers. These organizations exist across the full range of business sectors, including media and publishing (that is, Disney, Viacom, etc.), telecoms (AT&T, mobile carriers, etc.), IT platforms (Google, Facebook, Amazon, etc.), finance (lending, credit, collection agencies, etc.), and retail (brands, travel, etc.) (Wolfie, 2017). Notably, the public sector in the form of utilities and law enforcement is also gathering and selling data about customers and constituents. Some companies collect specific types of data, ranging from customer management data (that is, Acxiom and MailChimp), advertising technologies (Adobe, Neustar, ad networks), business IT (FICO scores, Palantir), risk data (Equifax, LexisNexis), and marketing data (Acxiom, etc.) (Wolfie, 2017). Many of these companies overlap the types of data they collect, making it extremely difficult to determine specifically what is collected and for what purpose.

The problem of such widespread surveillance becomes worse when confronted with the realization that some data brokers have worked with law enforcement and other agencies, including the FBI, Pentagon, and US

Department of Homeland Security. Acxiom, for example, had hired former military personnel on its board of directors to work as lobbyists for the Department of Defense and Homeland Security in order to "set up the technological systems for total surveillance of the U.S. and global population" (Foster and McChesney, 2014). Acxiom later worked with the airline JetBlue to use public and private traveler records in a purported defense against terrorist attacks. RELX, for its part, was reported to have provided data to ICE (Lamdan, 2019). In 2005, Choicepoint, formerly a data aggregator and later a part of LexisNexis Risk Solutions (another RELX subsidiary), "sold significant amounts of personal information on 145,000 consumers to a group of identity thieves in California, resulting in at least 700 known cases of fraud and identity theft" (ACLU, 2022). Ultimately, the shifts that long-standing library vendors have undergone have unfortunately compromised privacy for libraries, their staffs, and their users.

SURVEILLANCE IS DEADENING FOR LIBRARY USERS—AND FOR LIBRARIES

History demonstrates what happens when libraries lose the trust of their communities, especially when they are seen as the tools of a repressive regime. Sometimes libraries are convenient targets for political aggression, but other times they become part of the social control apparatus and central to the monitoring of information and how it is disseminated (Knuth, 2003). A library also need not be attacked from barbarians from abroad to be ruined. Sometimes that happens from within. Soviet libraries, for example, were heavily censored and had their collections revised or weeded based on the prevailing politics of the day. This ongoing and decades-long reaction to perceived external and internal threats by Soviet leadership severely compromised the trust of users (Rogers, 1973). Some who grew up during the era saw that merely borrowing books was risky: "You could get punished if you were caught reading. That was precious time stolen from productive work; child labor was routine in that quasi-paradise" (Bradatan, 2023).

Clearly, with the yearly attempts to censor books in libraries across the United States these issues persist. Libraries in a free society need to push back against the threat to control information by continuing to assert their core ethical values. One would like to think in a post–*Roe v. Wade* United States, for example, that library patrons would still be able to learn about reproductive health without being tracked or having their searches blocked or redirected. Seeking out such information should be unfettered, but this is by no means guaranteed. One cannot take for granted the ability to seek information without the fear of reprisal. The stark reminder of how easily a sense of freedom can be broken plays out in people's information-seeking behavior, including when using libraries. Many women may now perceive negative consequences when seeking out information about abortion in some regions of the United States, which may negatively impact their well-being. Elfreda Chatman's theory of information poverty (1987) is especially illuminating here. She suggests that the decision to risk exposure about a personal problem is often *not* taken due to a perception that negative consequences outweigh the benefits. In other words, people—women especially—often have to weigh the personal risks of seeking out certain information. If the risk seems too high for them, many will cease looking for that information, which ultimately can become "a maladaptive closed loop," where a necessary action (that is, going to a doctor) is not taken and one's condition gets worse (St. Jean et al., 2021).

But this is a far wider problem than a regional interstate issue. If patrons feel their searches are being monitored and that law enforcement could potentially spy on their inquiries—even within the library—the dampening effect on patron information seeking behavior will likely increase. As mentioned previously, Penney's research shows that just being cognizant of the *possibility* of being observed while seeking certain subjects alters user information behavior. Subjects in his research were found to be far less willing to look up topics they thought were controversial when made aware of the NSA's PRISM surveillance program. Other studies find similar dampening effects on user information behavior. Marthews and Tucker find that "cross-nationally, users were less likely to search using terms that they believed might get them in trouble with the US government" (Marthews and Tucker, 2014). They ultimately warn of government surveillance's potential "chilling effects" on the overall search behavior of internet users. Ignoring or downplaying the issue of surveillance will not only impact students' trust of libraries in general but may also narrow research topics that might be seen as too controversial in an overly politicized and polarized society. Considering that the stakes are much higher for certain segments of the population, it is imperative to review how much and how far reaching the surveillance of library patrons may be by certain information technology companies.

E-COLONIALISM AND "DIGITAL EXPANSIONISM"

Related to online surveillance—and the motives that drive it—are the concepts of e-colonialism and digital expansionism. We have reached a state where data "pervade everything, with subjectivities and life chances exposed to and possibly altered by new forms of 'algorithmic governance'" (Fraser,

2019). In this conception, colonialism is not a complete analogue to the systemic exploitation of Indigenous peoples by Western powers that occurred across the globe over several centuries. It is instead how people are "dispossessed and alienated" from the information about and made by themselves (Fraser, 2019). Still, patterns of exploitation in new forms nevertheless persist, involving old subjects as well as creating new ones. It should perhaps come as no surprise that the term for using the data collected on us is to "mine" the data, an extractive process that, in the real world at least, may be one of the most dangerous and exploitative jobs one might ever do that also causes significant damage and upheaval to physical environments.

The driver of e-colonialism itself is the profit made from the data collected on potentially billions of users who are in positions of weakness and more easily exploited for their "resources." While their activities are screened and monitored for the sake of an establishment's safety and international stability, users' predilections, desires, wants, needs, and fears are also mined for their advertising dollars. As Coleman remarks in a discussion about the exploitation of people on the African continent, "largescale tech companies extract, analyze, and own user data for profit and market influence with nominal benefit to the data source. Under the guise of altruism, large scale tech companies can use their power and resources to access untapped data on the continent. Scant data protection laws and infrastructure ownership by western tech companies open the door for exploitation of data as a resource for-profit and a myriad of uses including predictive analytics" (Coleman, 2019). In similar ways to the diamond, the extraction of the human resource—"blood data," as it were—comes at a significant human cost. What is important to note is that this exploitation is not regularly countered given the weakness of the laws, the deep pockets of the companies in control, and the "enabling legal construct" surrounding the collection of data that serves to perpetuate it (Cohen, 2015).

Yet the push for "openness" is sometimes unwarranted. While librarians often advocate for the open sharing of information, we have to be careful of the downside to this practice. Not every group will benefit from being openly identifiable. Marginalized groups in particular—groups normally associated with exploitation and subjugation both currently or historically, including Indigenous and LGBTQ people—are vulnerable to the unequal power balances advocating for open information. These unequal power balances include not only the loss of one's autonomy, privacy, and solitude but also the unwitting extraction and monetization of "a particular set of information-based extractive endeavors," which Cohen describes as the "biopolitical public domain." This results in and "shapes practices of appropriation and use of personal information" (Cohen, 2015). In other words, the openness of this extracted data about ourselves is not always on our own terms, encroaching upon our ability to control what others see or hear about us as well as our ability to withdraw from the public sphere. Information exposed in this newly created quasi-corporate public domain allows for the unintended appropriation of cultural materials and personal information as well as the erosion of one's sense of personal privacy. The conflation of human and social identity with the data about the person is rife for exploitation if mishandled in the systems designed to extract that data. The algorithms indeed oppress us.

Sacred texts, which are often meant to be shared solely among the initiates of a group or culture, fall along these lines of misappropriation. Those within a culture must be allowed to uphold their right to share ideas and writings among themselves without the prying eyes of a generalized but increasingly politicized and power-imbalanced openness. To inquire into these ideas is to pry into something that the creators and living embodiments of these cultures may prefer to keep among themselves. Or at least they would prefer to have the autonomy to determine whether to share them or not. Many sacred texts are considered to be part of the public domain, given their age as documents, yet the ownership and stewardship of those texts needs to be considered as much from a cultural perspective as from a legal one. The right to determine how far and wide the information found in sacred texts should be disseminated ought to be left up to the members of those cultures. Some in these cultures will find the unfettered digitization of their works to be distasteful or an encroachment of their cultural values. As Manžuch writes: "conflicting and contradictory interests, power relations, and political and legal contexts have a huge influence on the decisions taken by archives, libraries, and museums" (Manžuch, 2017). The decision to digitize has not always been transparent—as in the case with the Google Books Project and its notorious nondisclosure agreements forced upon various universities (Weiss, 2014)—and the motives employed to justify it are not always appropriate.

The lack of autonomy to determine the parameters of sharing certain information in these situations is telling. Despite the overall importance and benefits of openness, privacy often becomes a casualty to open knowledge. The movement to "decolonize" research, which centers "concerns and world views of non-Western individuals, and respectfully knowing and understanding theory and research from previously 'Other(ed), perspectives" (Thambinathan and Kinsella, 2021), attempts to address this loss of agency in the subjects of digitization projects. Some libraries have attempted to alleviate the problems of digital encroachment, or "decentering" the digital library, by working closely with the Indigenous cultures in question to provide them with necessary preservation services, while also striving to not encroach upon their cultures through unwanted digitization and online dissemination of their sacred texts. Such strategies fall within a growing trend of creating decolonized Indigenous archives and engaging in "digital repatriation," which "create electronic surrogates of items that are then theoretically available to the source communities that created them" (Senier, 2014). Such surrogates are then kept restricted on behalf of that community, helping to build relationships of trust between the libraries and the dominant societies they often represent and the Indigenous cultures that may have been exploited by them in the past.

HOW SOCIAL MEDIA AND IT MAY
DISRUPT OUR WAYS OF THINKING

Aside from the problematic nexus of privacy and surveillance, our social media and the IT companies that develop and manage these platforms have further impact upon our lives than we may generally consider. "Disruption" has long been the term used in Silicon Valley to describe a revolutionary overturning of long-established markets, accomplishing the greatest amount of change with the newest ideas. But it has also become synonymous with radical social and behavioral changes in not only industries but also in any number of areas not traditionally related directly to businesses, including education, health care, government oversight efforts, and so on. While Elizabeth Holmes may currently be the most notorious example of this desire to "disrupt" at all costs, there are numerous examples throughout the past twenty-five years that range the gamut from full-on scam (as with Theranos) to revolutionary but fading (Facebook, Uber, Twitter/X), to untouchable (Google and Amazon)—for now. These may change in a few years, or even tomorrow. But are there problems with behavioral and mental changes brought about by the overuse of information technologies and social media. Do the platforms we use "disrupt" how we think or modify our behaviors? Do they interfere with or instigate the ways in which we interact with others in online communities? A significant amount of research suggests this is the case.

Le Roux and Parry (2021), in one notable experiment, find that "students often become trapped in a cycle of repeated self-regulation failure which results in the procrastination of academic tasks," meaning that rather than pay attention to their classroom lectures or engage actively in their studies, they would instead prefer to interact with and consume content on social media. The students' inability to self-regulate speaks partly to the ability of social media platforms to gain and control a user's personal attention. The loss to learning is significant. Carr in his book *The Shallows* suggest that while the internet "grants us instant access to a library of information," it also has the potential to reduce our "ability to know, in depth, a subject for ourselves, [and] to construct within our own minds the rich and idiosyncratic set of connections that give rise to a singular intelligence" (Carr, 2010, p. 143). What has occurred is a loss of memory and contextual understanding, much like what Plato suggests will happen in his dialogue *Phaedrus*: "they will appear to be omniscient and will generally know nothing; they will be tiresome company, having the show of wisdom without the reality" (Plato, 2008). When our knowledge is placed outside of our minds into objects or repositories—or those "external written characters," as Plato calls them—we lose both the ability to recall the information and to deeply interact with it as knowledge. This has occurred at a massive scale and at surprisingly fast recall speeds with the proliferation of the internet. We can fool even ourselves into thinking we are wise and knowledgeable when all we need to do is conduct a quick search on our favorite search engine.

Considering our metacognition skills, too, we find that the ways in we used to interrogate a text or review a source of information have been altered, sometimes in negative ways. The overuse of social networking sites can contribute to "a variety of mental health problems, including loneliness and addiction, among young adults" and "other behavioral and substance addictions, namely, withdrawal, conflict, tolerance, relapse, salience, and mood modification" (Balıkçı et al., 2020). Information technology can disrupt the traditional ways in which people acquire thinking skills, complicating the ways in which we deal with and downplay numerous problematic information sources, including fake news, conspiracy theories, and misinformation. As Balıkçı et al. further suggest, such interference into a person's metacognition beliefs may "lead to the implementation of maladaptive coping strategies" (2020). Such coping strategies may involve failing to check rumors and otherwise interfere with normal reasoning but may also involve riskier transgressions, including descending into alcohol and drug abuse, gambling, and internet addiction.

Jaron Lanier, former engineer for Google and well-known public intellectual and tech gadfly, has suggested that people, celebrities in particular, may be suffering from what he calls "Twitter Poisoning." Despite the rather lurid and sensational name, he may have a point. The suggestion is that the algorithm, guided partly by engineering and partly by the psychological methods of operant conditioning (made famous by the Skinner Box), controls the user through a series of steps that can encourage maladaptive and addictive behaviors. He argues that the similar behaviors of such disparate personalities as Elon Musk, former President Trump, and Kanye West indicate something sinister is at work. That their disparate personalities—and one can hardly find more dissimilar-seeming people—appear to merge into identical bullying and antisocial behaviors suggests that the common denominator is "social media disease" (Lanier, 2022), which humans are not equipped to handle for all the undue attention social media gives. Celebrity in this regard becomes yet another way in which a person loses their sense of self and privacy, not dissimilar to the feelings people get when they realize their actions are being watched. While Lanier's idea is fascinating, the suggestion that these celebrities are suffering from a metaphoric poisoning, similar in symptoms to the addictions unique to Twitter/X and social media, is somewhat difficult to conceptualize fully and may be somewhat simplistic overall.

However, this is a danger for anyone who proposes a model to explain something: the metaphors for our understanding of the world—both digital and physical—can break down at times due to the abstractions at the heart of their conception. For example, throughout part I of this book, there have been many allusions made to the gaps in information behavior research, in particular the general focus on the purposive acquisition of information in the LIS discipline. The other aspects of information behavior—the nonpurposive, the avoidant, and the serendipitous—tend to be less well understood and examined. Indeed, Cole and Leide suggested in 2006 that LIS was "just beginning" to explore human information behavior more thoroughly (Cole and Leide, 2006).

But, unsurprisingly, there are also problems with the models in human information behavior that incorporate mixed or weak metaphors within them. We refer to these conditions online in any number of ways, including through illness (natural or chemical), pathologies (social and physical), pollutions, cyberspaces and cyberterritories (or as Fraser calls it, *digital geographies of flow and territory*), environments, zones of contact, grounds, information poverty zones, emergent and chaos theory behavior (cf. Diresta, 2022), and so on. Even now, in attempting to be objective and clear about understanding of human behavior in an online situation, it is difficult to avoid the narrative making and storytelling inherent to these models in order to impart clearer meaning to the reader. Researchers struggle to find new metaphors, models, and theories for the situation we now find ourselves in. But if we have trouble finding ways to describe our situation, how can we ever begin to push back against the tide of ongoing endemic problems in information systems? How do we find "antidotes" to the poisoning, as Lanier describes it? How do we find ways to control or limit the murmuration and "emergent toxic behaviors" as Diresta visualizes them? How do we protect, as this author describes it, against information pathologies and push back against those who would have us all cede truth to power?

So, in order to proceed, we must make do somewhat with the incompleteness of our models and the weakness of our metaphors while being cognizant of the fact that various factors, positive and negative, nevertheless continue to impact the ways in which we interact with and use information. When examining information behavior models, we can strive for improving the awareness of our overall online environment and ensuring they accurately describe the users within these systems. Yet many of the causes of user behavior remain unclear and inconclusive; some of the models we use miss the true manifold complexity in which people live out their lives, rarely remaining still and constant—more often, in fact, becoming unpredictable and inconsistent—and unequivocally impacted by the stimuli of the outside world and the motives of their internal one. We return, again and again, to the dichotomy of objectivity and subjectivity, and the ways in which the two inform and entwine with each other. We return to the areas of our "terra incognita," those places that defy, at times, a complete understanding of what we do and why we do it when interacting with information. Perhaps the models fail us at times, but we work with them anyway, derive our meaning and impose our narratives to get at a better understanding of ourselves.

With this complexity and lingering sense of incompleteness in the context of information behaviors, the next few chapters will look at the past history of fake news and misinformation to review the historical record for similar analogues from the past. While this book has so far examined the current practices and issues related to information behavior in digital information systems, there remains the need to look back at the longer history of fake news and misinformation. The models currently in use can be informed better by looking at what people have done in the past under different conditions. If one can find similar behaviors in the past, it may explain some universals that transcend time and place. And so the next part of this book will begin to look at the longer history of fake news and misinformation in the hope that the context can provide some illumination on the universality of some of the information problems everyone is facing and just how much current technology may or may not amplify them.

REFERENCES

ACLU. (2022). FAQ on ChoicePoint: The ChoicePoint ID theft case: What it means. *American Civil Liberties Union (ACLU)*. https://www.aclu.org/other/faq -choicepoint.

Allmer, T. (2012). *Towards a critical theory of surveillance in informational capitalism*. Peter Lang.

Auberry, K. (2018). Increasing students' ability to identify fake news through information literacy education and content management systems. *The Reference Librarian, 59*(4), pp. 179–87. https://doi.org/10.1080/02763877.2018.1489935.

Balıkçı, K., Aydın, O., Sönmez, İ., Kalo, B., and Ünal-Aydın, P. (2020). The relationship between dysfunctional metacognitive beliefs and problematic social networking sites use. *Scandinavian Journal of Psychology, 61*, pp. 593–98.

Bénabou, R., and Tirole, J. (2011). Identity, morals, and taboos: Beliefs as assets. *The Quarterly Journal of Economics, 126*(2), pp. 805–55. https://doi.org/10.1093/qje/ qjr002.

Berners-Lee, T. (2019). Tim Berners-Lee's annual letter on the World Wide Web's 30th anniversary. *Quartz.* https://qz.com/1568798/tim-berners-lees-annual-letter -on-the-world-webs-30th-anniversary.

Bradatan, C. (2023). I know what savage fear really lies at the heart of the American Dream. *New York Times.* https://www.nytimes.com/2023/01/02/opinion/failure -romania-america.html.

Carr, Nicholas G. (2010). *The shallows: What the internet is doing to our brains.* New York: W. W. Norton.

Chatman, E. A. (1987). Opinion leadership, poverty, and information sharing. *RQ, 26*(3), pp. 341–53.

Clarivate. Real World Data. (2022). Clarivate. https://clarivate.com/products/real -world-data/.

Cohen, J. E. (2015). The biopolitical public domain: The legal construction of the surveillance economy. *Philosophy & Technology, 31*, pp. 213–33. http://dx.doi.org /10.2139/ssrn.2666570.

Cole, C., and Leide, J. E. (2006). A cognitive framework for human information behavior: The place of metaphor in human information organizing behavior. In Amanda Spink and Charles Cole (eds.), *New directions in human information behavior* (pp. 171–202). Dordrecht, Netherlands: Springer.

Coleman, D. (2019). Digital colonialism: The 21st century scramble for Africa through the extraction and control of user data and the limitations of data protec- tion laws. *Michigan Journal of Race and Law.* https://repository.law.umich.edu/ mjrl/vol24/iss2/6.

Cooke, N. A. (2018). *Fake news and alternative facts: Information literacy in a post-truth era.* ALA Editions.

Diresta, R. (2022). How online mobs act like flocks of birds. *Noema.* https://www .noemamag.com/how-online-mobs-act-like-flocks-of-birds/.

Foster, J. B., and McChesney, R. W. (2014). Surveillance capitalism: Monopoly finance capital, the military-industrial complex, and the digital age. *Monthly Review.* https://monthlyreview.org/2014/07/01/surveillance-capitalism/.

Fraser, A. (2019). Curating digital geographies in an era of data colonialism, *Geoforum, 104*, pp. 193–200. https://doi.org/10.1016/j.geoforum.2019.04.027.

Herb, U. (2019). Steering science through output indicators & data capitalism. *Proceedings of the 23rd Congress of the European Society of Veterinary and Comparative Nutrition*, Turin, Italy. https://digitalcommons.unl.edu/scholcom /125/.

Jeanes, E. (2019). Hawthorne effect. In *A dictionary of organizational behaviour.* Oxford University Press.

Jones-Jang, S. M., Mortensen, T., and Liu, J. (2021). Does media literacy help identification of fake news? Information literacy helps, but other literacies don't. *The American Behavioral Scientist, 65*(2), pp. 371–88. https://doi.org/10.1177 /0002764219869406.

Knuth, R. (2003). *Libricide: The regime-sponsored destruction of books and libraries in the twentieth century.* Westport, CT: Praeger.

Lamdan, S. (2019). Librarianship at the crossroads of ICE surveillance. *In the library with the lead pipe.* http://www.inthelibrarywiththeleadpipe.org/2019/ice-surveillance/.

Lanier, J. (2022). Trump, Musk and Kanye are Twitter poisoned. *New York Times.* https://www.nytimes.com/2022/11/11/opinion/trump-musk-kanye-twitter.html.

le Roux, D. B., and Parry, D. A. (2021). Off-task media use in academic settings: Cycles of self-regulation failure. *Journal of American College Health, 69*(2), pp. 134–41. DOI: 10.1080/07448481.2019.1656636.

Mangan, K. (2021). The surveilled student. *The Chronicle of Higher Education.* https://www.chronicle.com/article/the-surveilled-student?utm_source=Iterable&utm_medium=email&utm_campaign=campaign_3492351_nl_Academe-Today_date_20220107&cid=at&source=ams&sourceid=.

Manžuch, Z. (2017). Ethical issues in digitization of cultural heritage. *Journal of Contemporary Archival Studies, 4*(4). http://elischolar.library.yale.edu/jcas/vol4/iss2/4.

Marthews, A., and Tucker, C. E. (2014). Government surveillance and internet search behavior. *SSRN Electronic Journal.* 10.2139/ssrn.2412564.

Penney, J. W. (2016). Chilling effects: Online surveillance and Wikipedia use. *Berkeley Technology Law Journal, 31*(1), pp. 117–82.

Plato. (2008). *Phaedrus.* Benjamin Jowett (Trans.). Project Gutenberg. https://www.gutenberg.org/files/1636/1636-h/1636-h.htm.

Proctorio. (2022). Securing the integrity of online assessments. Proctorio. https://proctorio.com/.

Rogers, R. A. (1973). Censorship and libraries in the Soviet Union. *Journal of Library History, Philosophy, and Comparative Librarianship, 8*(1), pp. 22–29.

Senier, S. (2014). Digitizing Indigenous history: Trends and challenges. *Journal of Victorian Culture, 19*(3), pp. 396–402. https://doi.org/10.1080/13555502.2014.947188.

Shattuck, R. (1996). *Forbidden knowledge: From Prometheus to pornography.* New York: St. Martin's Press.

Smith, R. (2017). *Society and social pathology: A framework for progress.* First edition. Palgrave Macmillan.

St. Jean, B., Gorham, U., and Bonsignore, E. (2021). *Understanding human information behavior: When, how, and why people interact with information.* Lanham, MD: Rowman & Littlefield.

Thambinathan, V., and Kinsella, E. A. (2021). Decolonizing methodologies in qualitative research: Creating spaces for transformative praxis. *International Journal of Qualitative Methods, 20.* https://doi.org/10.1177/16094069211014766.

Waxman, O. B. (2021). Librarians grapple with conservative efforts to ban books. *Time.* https://time.com/6117685/book-bans-school-libraries/.

Weiss, A. (2014). *Using massive digital libraries.* Chicago: ALA TechSource.

Weiss, A. (2018). *Big Data shocks.* Lanham, MD: Rowman & Littlefield.

Wolfie, C. (2017). Corporate Surveillance in everyday life: How companies collect, combine, analyze, trade, and use personal data on billions. Cracked Labs. https://crackedlabs.org/en/corporate-surveillance/infographics.

Zuboff, S. (2015). Big other: Surveillance capitalism and the prospects of an information civilization. *Journal of Information Technology, 30*(1), pp. 75–89.

PART II

A Brief History of Fake News

Chapter 4

The Early Origins of Fake News

MYTH, LEGEND, AND HISTORY

The first part of this book focused primarily on the theoretical constructs and frameworks surrounding the development of human information behavior, including how metacognition plays an important role in the development of user information skills and how problems related to information use in the digital era might be construed from the perspective of pathologies. While fake news and misinformation were touched upon in this first part, it was not a central concern. Rather, more focus was given to the ways in which people are seen to use information, for better and for worse, and how the gaps in our models miss some of the motivations for and causes of these behaviors. Werner Heisenberg's well-known quote is apt here: "What we observe is not nature itself, but nature exposed to our method of questioning" (Gleiser, 2018). Our understanding of reality is based more upon *how* we look into it, what questions we are able to conceive and formulate, and only then come to find evidence for. If our models are accurate, we find something new and are able to perceive the world generally as it is. But if our models are incomplete, we view the world in an incomplete manner, leaving room for errors in our perceptions of the world. While science thrives on finding and correcting that error, much of the activities in the rest of our lives don't always meet this high standard. We are left, perhaps, unaware of our own ignorance. In fact, our misconceptions take root in this gap between what we think we see in nature and the limited nature of the questions we choose (or have chosen for us) to ask about it. As described by Thomas Kuhn, we sometimes see only the questions and methods applicable for a specific paradigm, missing the potential questions and approaches that may lurk hidden elsewhere, waiting to be uncovered. Like being armed with the proverbial hammer, everything starts to look like a nail in need of a good pounding.

The next part of this book, however, will examine the historical contexts of fake news and misinformation, spanning the distant past in the earliest eras of writing from the Classical Greek age through to printing press and the development of science hoaxes in the early nineteenth century. Like information overload—the condition where people feel overwhelmed by too much to learn or look through to find information and gain knowledge—the telling of lies through written and oral communication has a long and illustrious history found across cultures and societies. There are also historical embellishments that occur over time through the development of myth, legend, and national and ethnic origin stories. As Bosworth (1971) writes, "Propaganda and history are often inseparable," and he is not far off the mark, for it is the telling of narratives—both the true ones and embellished ones—that helps us find meaning. This section will examine just a small slice of that varied and convoluted history, tracing a confusing blend of fact and fiction, truth and lie, that often makes it difficult to know what happened definitively in the past.

One word of caution: this is not an exhaustive look. There are just too many examples that one could delve into at length across numerous cultures, histories, and traditions. While other chapters will focus on more recent times, including the mass media age of the late nineteenth and twentieth centuries and the current digital social media age, this chapter focuses on a few of the earliest examples of fake news. The wide range of topics includes false histories, false events, hoaxes, and other types of misleading information passed off as legitimate discourse. Special consideration will be made for the technology that allowed for false information to spread more easily: the printing press.

A TRUE HISTORY OF LIES

Some consider outright lies to be the direct antecedents to our current forms of fake news. As McQueen (2018) suggests, "fake news is a lie," which likely "originated with the dawn of human speech." Though this book will not attempt to go *that* far back in time to speculate on whether lies were integral to the development of human language itself and all of its signs, symbols, and interpretations—"everything," as author and semiotician Umberto Eco (1976) asserts, "which can be used in order to lie"—it will focus briefly on the idea of lying and briefly trace how concerns about it have run through our literature and culture. Indeed, for Eco, the reality is that both lies *and* the truth are bound together and used to equal effect in our languages; for if something "cannot be used to tell a lie, conversely it cannot be used to tell the truth" (1976). In fact, he concludes, it is impossible to say anything *without its potential to be formulated as a lie*. In that regard, we are simultaneously freed yet constrained by our conceptions and expectations of the truth as they intermingle with our fixations and predilections for the false. In other words, lying is a feature not a bug of our communications, something that is in constant play in any utterance we make.

Of course, on the surface of things, telling lies is perceived as one of our society's major ills, regulated legally in terms of libel and slander but also in the general sense that those "frank lies," as Jacques Derrida has called them, that people tell with "deliberate intention to deceive" (La Caze, 2017), serve to breach one's sense of trust and hamper cooperation, without which a society cannot function. This utilitarian approach to the definition of lying is meant to discourage those more damaging aspects of deception, including fraud and theft, that fray at societal cohesiveness. Yet in spite of the great reliance on trust and cooperation and the mechanisms in place to enforce those things to make societies work, lies remain ubiquitous. There are numerous examples of the types of lies that people take for granted and even consider to be an acceptable trade-off for something else. Societies generally have developed nuanced approaches to lies and often allow them within the strict guidelines of their cultures; *honne* and *tatemae* in Japan, for example, function to allow the lies that spare the embarrassment of others in order to keep their society running smoothly and without open conflict. It is done in service to *wa*, or harmony. The United States, a society that unlike Japan embraces open disagreement, nevertheless tolerates the "white lie" that harms few, if any, in its telling. The white lie remains widespread and generally accepted as a necessary, if not desired, part of daily life, despite the hardline and unnuanced definitions about lying that we may sometimes impart to our own children!

Discussions about the impact and necessity of lies in a society are central concerns as far back as Plato's *Republic*—and it might be speculated with a fair degree of certainty that they likely go back even further in time than that. Plato in particular mentions—and not disapprovingly either—how humans have a tendency to lie for their specific advantage, such as "in dealing with enemies" to deceive and thwart them, or to console friends who "in a fit of madness or illusion are going to do some harm," which would be "useful . . . [as] a sort of medicine or preventative" (aka "the little white lie") (Plato, n.d., 382d). Plato also mentions the uses of mythology and how "we make falsehood as much like truth as we can, and so turn it to account," meaning that people can create moral and ethical lessons for their lives based upon stories that are factually false but nevertheless illuminating (Plato, n.d.). Yet that falseness is truly beside the point. Indeed, the uses of these types of functional lies appear long-standing and well known throughout history, showing up in false decrees, as false histories, within hagiographies, and inhabiting myths and legends.

However, other lies are seen more negatively than the intentional or "frank" deception of others. Plato reserves his harshest judgment for what he calls the "true lie," in which a person has become "deceived or uninformed about the highest realities in the highest part of themselves" (n.d., 382b). This lie is the most hateful for Plato as it concerns a person's ability to perceive reality itself and, ultimately, impacts their very souls. The self-deceived in Plato's perspective are incapable of seeing the world clearly and without distortion. As an aside, it should be noted that much of the handwringing about this type of self-deception mirrors the ways in which people currently despair over those duped by cults, in thrall to con artists, or deceived by conspiracy theories and false information.

ANCIENT ANTECEDENTS

In ancient eras, art, narrative, and propaganda tended to blend with the regimes that sponsored the arts (Woodford, 2003; Bosworth, 1971). Should we consider the false statements of despots and kings written into their decrees or on the walls of their temples and public art to be part of the misinformation and characterize it as the "fake news" of their era? In some ways, perhaps, this is an easy line to draw, though it vastly oversimplifies things. Alexander the Great was deified, for example, as a "child of Zeus" (Jowett and O'Donnell, 1992, p. 53) in order to rival or replace the mythical Heracles in the minds of his subjects and had his image minted onto coins, drawn onto pottery, and sculpted into marble. These symbols of propaganda "serve[d] as a constant reminder of the various subjugated populations just where the center of power resided" (Jowett and O'Donnell, 1992). And that is often the issue with false narratives: they are designed to perpetuate those in power, with myths concocted to buttress their claims on subjugation and the ruling class.

Certainly, embellished historical accounts can turn into a blend of the myth, facts, and false narratives. Ancient accounts often blended epic, lyric, and dramatic poetry with long-existing oral traditions, further complicating the relationship between truth and fiction (Baragwanath and de Bakker, 2012). Indeed, as Classical Greek scholar Antonis Tsakmakis finds, the exemplars of ancient Greek history would navigate "between creative imagination and accurate, critical reasoning, between the real and the ideal, between the local and the ecumenical, between experience or verisimilitude and the truth of poetic or mythical imagery, between the power of rulers and the power of the word" (Tsakmakis, 2015). Central to this is not just that dichotomy between something truthful (that is, verisimilitude) and something false (that is, poetic license)—as we in the modern world tend to obsess over—but a continual negotiation between the two sides depending upon the contexts and purposes of the writing itself. As Plato points out in *The Republic*, the embellished parts of such histories mix with real events to make a specific moral point. Notably, well-known narratives assumed to be true are also debunked to show the importance of reason and the drawing of reasonable and logical conclusions.

Where, however, do we draw the line in a world that blends fact, fiction, and narrative? Does it even matter? The ancient Greeks' line was certainly a bit more blurred than ours today and may indeed point to our very own current situation as well as our futures given the widespread blending of false digital forms, deep fakes, photoshopping, and other digital manipulations that appear to blend fact and fiction in similar ways.

Importantly, the history that has come down to us from the Ancient Greeks—specifically from Herodotus (484–425 BCE), Thucydides (460–400 BCE), and Xenophon (430–355 BCE)—has been notable for not only its accuracy in some parts but its extreme inaccuracy in others. While a number of factors contribute to this, including the issues related to gathering evidence available to them, some cultural aspects impact these histories. Herodotus, for example, has been known to employ both myth and truth paradoxically relying on both (Baragwanath and de Bakker, 2012, p. 10); further, the historian has been seen to emphasize "artful deception and quick-thinking acts that promote self-preservation" in his work (Lateiner, 1990, p. 231), describing how such events might be plausible. But at the same time, Herodotus also attempts to call out the outright damaging fakes and con artists: "He exposes palpable frauds, mercenary, political, spiritual, and cultic, while leaving the decision on other disputable instances open" (Lateiner, 1990, p. 245).

This paradox of *mythos-logos*—of myth versus truth—confounds many of the scholars who study him. For example, Darius, the ancient Persian ruler who invaded Greece, is shown by Herodotus to have fallen victim to a hoax in which an inscription written on Queen Nicotrix's tomb entices him to plunder it (Georgiou, 2002, p. 81), but Darius finds it empty but for another inscription reprimanding him for his greed: "If you were not insatiable for money and covetous, you would not have opened the coffins of the dead" (Georgiou, 2002, p. 80). Generally, Darius is portrayed as a ruler motivated by greed, and this episode seems to be par for the course. Yet this story of deception in the form of written communication appears to be a fabrication. Upon further review, Herodotus, it is argued, seems less interested in documenting Darius's greed. Instead, Herodotus may be playing up Nicotrix's deception to show his readers how a "woman manages to overpower and trick him from her grave" (Georgiou, 2002). While it portrays the Persian ruler in a bad light, hitting typical themes of greed and avarice, it lands in a very different way. It is, instead, very much a pointed lesson for us all and a message to not believe everything that we read—*even the very thing we are reading right now*—for deceptions may be hidden there lying in wait. "All Cretans are liars," we are told, and we might believe it until they confess, "by the way, *I'm* a Cretan." The paradox defies solution by its very nature, and the paradoxes raised in Herodotus's work describe the very nature of history itself: a fabricated tale that *somehow* imparts the truth.

Thucydides, though a contemporary of Herodotus and far more methodical in his approach in describing the Peloponnesian War he lived through, similarly seems "to promise more authentic material than he really does provide" (Tsakmakis, 2015), often failing to give readers evidence of his sources used for describing the war itself. While some of his intent seems to be for imparting reportage on the war to his readers and to posterity, the possibility of embellishment and false narratives persists, sometimes to obfuscate or misdirect, but other times to illuminate something of importance—as in video reenactments today—that the creator wants to share and emphasize with a specific audience. Perfect verisimilitude may not be as important as the ethical considerations brought up by the event itself. The paradox remains a confounding aspect of the ancient history.

The purposes of early history appear, at times, to provide a number of different results: some for the reportage on the likelihood fantastical events or beasts, some on the recounting of actual events, and some on the debunking of false narratives. The twin problems of falseness and inaccuracy appear to be baked into narratives that also attempt to impart a lesson. The goals of the historical accounts may not have been the same as we are accustomed to. Rather than being purely "scientific and cognitive" (Nicolai, 2015), the ancient *historia* are concerned more with "creating paradigms" that provide political, societal, or ethical standards for people to follow in day-to-day life. That they happen to be fact based and verifiable in some sections may be a fortunate but not always intended side effect of the work.

Indeed, we find that later pretype eras were also not immune to the problems of rumors, false narratives, and unconfirmed histories. A *thousand* years after Thucydides, a time when the fading Roman empire has split into two precarious regions, fictional narratives persist in historical writings. As Darnton describes it, Procopius, a historian living in sixth century CE. Byzantium, compiled "dubious information, known as *Anecdota*, which he kept secret until his death, in order to smear the reputation of the Emperor Justinian after lionizing the emperor in his official histories" (Darnton, 2017). That slippery movement from true to false is perhaps at heart one of our main problems overall. The falseness appears to be an essential part of the literary historical conventions in practice at the time and in pre–printing press eras, when authorized and definitive texts were impossible to find, given the need for scribes to copy pieces by hand. Before we judge, however, the sloppiness and even ignorance of the scribes (their grammar mistakes are glaring sometimes), consider all the variant readings of the New Testament in Greek to get a good sense of how difficult it is to keep even the most sacred and valued of canonized texts in Western culture from sliding into misprints and errors.

Sometimes attitudes toward error may be more a matter of expediency than the modern desire for accuracy. Umberto Eco has written about the various forgeries that were "perpetrated in the course of the Middle Ages" but argues that the motivation for these forgeries, false documents, and doctored content stems not from the desire to create "distrust and disorder," as it might be characterized today, but to "confirm their faith in something (an author, an institution, a current of thought, a theological truth) and to uphold an order" (Eco, 2014, p. 249). Again, this is not too far afield from the conventions seen in classical Greek *historia* and the potentially positive impact of the blurring of the fine line between what is true and false, real and fake. It is very similar to the paradoxical Ship of Theseus, which over time had all of its original parts replaced with new ones. The way to sidestep the paradox of whether it is the real ship or not is to point out that its "authenticity" is beside the point. The ship's existence allows people to point back in time to a chain of custody and remembrance that serves as the object's provenance at a time when forensic sciences were nonexistent.

It is perhaps important, then, to point out that the modern problem with the "fake" in fake news may be a product of contemporary values shaped by technologies that allow for instant fact-checking and near-omniscient vigilance. These values may be largely *unshared* by those in previous eras, who held few illusions of ever being able to verify any object or to conduct quick and accurate fact-checking of sources. Ultimately, from what Eco concludes, we "do not know how the people of the Middle Ages, with their ingenuous concept of authenticity, would have judged this brash and cynical concept we have of noningenuous falsification" (Eco, 2014). Ultimately, the more we delve into the past and see the myriad ways in which fabrications and falsifications blend with historic narratives and the desire to impart moral and ethical lessons within them, the more alienated we can become from our current insistence that facts *must* be immutable. As we look back in time to periods that are less flush with information, we are confronted with societies that placed less stock in verifiable truths and more value on *ethical outcomes*. In the current world, people strive toward something authentic, whether it be an object, an experience, an identity, or a persona, and usually derive righteous judgment from that authenticity and the authority it seems to convey. But this was not always the case—for better and for worse.

EARLY FAKE NEWS, MISINFORMATION,
AND THE TRAGEDY OF BLOOD LIBEL

Indeed, one of the more lurid and tragic events in late medieval European history was the murder of the child Simon of Trent in 1475—later sainted and worshipped as a martyr—which shows the dangerous side of unchecked rumors and lies. The stories surrounding the event ultimately serve as a vessel carrying forth false narratives and ugly stereotypes about Jewish people that persist through nearly five hundred years of history until the twentieth century, though similar accusations about blood sacrifice had been common for centuries prior to Simon's death throughout the medieval period (Hsia, 1992). The events surrounding the story involve the murder of the child, Simon, who had gone missing days prior to the Easter holiday, and the subsequent torture and persecution of the Jewish suspects in whose home the body of the boy had been found. The suspects denied involvement—and it is likely the body was planted there—but eventually confessed to the crime after being compelled through various methods of torture. The suspicion and stereotypes already held by the Christian townspeople soon devolved into paranoia about Jewish ritual murders of Christians (Hsia, 1992). Although this narrative was debunked numerous times over the centuries by skeptical researchers and historians, rumors about it persisted through the twentieth century, aided in part by an invention of immense magnitude: the printing press.

THE IMPACT OF GUTENBERG

The invention of the moveable type printing press was a seismic event for the medieval world and was "one of the most revolutionary inventions in history," as many historians have suggested (Dittmar, 2011). It has certainly had an outsized influence on the development of our modern civilization from the moment of its adoption, influencing the foundations of our societies from copyright and its concept of "possessive authorship" (Loewenstein, 2002) and libel laws (McCorison, 2010) to the challenging of old religions (for example, Luther's printed pamphlet "95 Theses" [Heming, 1998]) and development of new governments (for example, American democracy and First Amendment [Humphrey, 1992]), with the spread of truth through scientific inquiries (for example, scientific journals [Walsh, 2006]), or even "at the heart of the Renaissance theatre revival" (Peters, 2003). It has had outsized impact on "the ways ideas were disseminated, promoted the accumulation of human capital, and played a key role in the evolution of business practices"

(Dittmar, 2011) as well as improving commerce and the development of cities as engines that spurred economic growth.

However, the advances "had many unforeseen consequences, including the wider circulation of fake news in the Western world" (McQueen, 2018, p. 17). As printing expanded in "concentric circles" (Barbier, 2006) outward from a single press in Mainz in 1450 to nearly 120 cities throughout Western Europe by 1500—a span of merely fifty years—fake news began to flow as well "from spectacular stories of sea monsters and witches to claims that sinners were responsible for natural disasters" (Soll, 2016). Similarly, the martyrdom of Simon "lived on for a long time" due to the impact of the press. By the seventeenth century numerous poems, hagiographies, paintings, and representations were being distributed that "celebrated the death" of the child (Hsia, 1992, p. 132). The cult of the boy's martyrdom may have become dispersed far more widely through these new types of mass-printed materials, carried further not only by the ease of their cheap printing methods but also by the spreading out of the technology itself across Europe.

Notably, while the original manuscripts and documentation about the trial of Simon were written by scribes and never mass produced using the nascent printing press, later rumors and accusations of "blood libel" that had come to a head in this trial were spread through the development of the printing press. Martin Luther's own publication *On Jews and Their Lies* in 1546 helped to cement the spread of antisemitic prejudice throughout Europe (US Holocaust Memorial Museum, 2022). Sadly, superstitions and accusations about Jewish "ritual use of Christian blood" (Hsia, 1992, p. 133) persisted through the twentieth century, especially in issues of *Der Stürmer*, published during the Nazi regime in Germany in the 1930s (McQueen, 2018).

Just as important to consider as the proliferation of false narratives through easily printed materials is the fact that the press also helped to solidify power structures already in place while simultaneously destabilizing others in decline. As Doyle writes, "the printing press heightens the importance and power of controlling and manipulating information" (Doyle, 2019), but this is applied unevenly across different countries and histories. On one hand, though Gutenberg felt that the Catholic church would be strengthened by his invention, it ironically helped to foster several anti-Catholic revolutions, among which Martin Luther's *Disputatio pro declaratione virtutis indulgentiarum (The 95 Theses)* were printed using the very technology to weaken the very institution it was intended to bolster.

By the time of the age of the Enlightenment in the 1600s, printing presses had become "the hallmark propaganda tool across religious and state institutions" (Doyle, 2019). No better example of consolidating power can be found during the Spanish colonial occupations of South America. In this case, the press serves to solidify the ruling Spanish government's hold on their colonies to both spread power as well as establish their language as the dominant means of communication. Indeed, the number of books printed in Native American languages declined from 31 percent of titles published in 1539 to just 3 percent by 1600; the shift reflects their increasing "imperial dominance over the colonized and 'Christianized' natives" (Doyle, 2019) and dramatizes the contributing role that printing press technology played in the destruction of Indigenous cultures. Importantly, changing long-held narratives and beliefs also involves changing stories and twisting shared truths to serve power. But forcing the exchange of one set of beliefs for another destabilizes what people see as factual. Skepticism, especially the radical kind that discredits everything, would be able to take better hold in this untended and wild ground where prior cultural understandings of events and occurrences are supplanted by new ones sanctioned by the government in power. As we see in conspiracy theories, radical skepticism comes to fuel these wild beliefs and reveals the believer's deepest suspicions about power and their mistrust about how it is wielded.

COLONIAL AMERICAN NEWSPAPERS

As the press in Europe became an established technology, it amplified benefits as well as drawbacks. While the press could be seen as an engine of growth in economic terms and attendant social improvements such increased as literacy rates and public health (Dittmar, 2011), it could also serve as an agent of destabilization. Europe contended with this destabilization not only within their home countries but also in their colonies. Though Spain's grasp on the Indigenous cultures of Central and South America was strengthened through their systematic destruction of native culture, the opposite appears to have happened in the British colonies in America. Revolution was in the air and the press was central to the foment that ultimately resulted in war and protracted conflict. The repression of ideas and the freedom to resist tyranny through free expression becomes a point of contention between the British Crown and the colonists (Humphrey, 1992). American newspapers ultimately play an essential role in the democratic evolution of the United States, but at the expense of British rule. In fact newspapers were not only conveyors of information, they were also symbols of freedom in their own right. In other words, the medium *was* the message, and the concept of a public press was "a weapon to be used by the people in their constant struggle against those in power" (Humphrey, 1992, p. 97).

Yet colonial America was just as awash in false information, too, contributed in part by newspapers employing fake news, misinformation, and other false narratives during the war to confound the enemy. Indeed, Benjamin

Franklin, one of America's most well-known founding fathers, contributed hoaxes in support of the colonialists' efforts to defeat the British. Franklin, apprenticed as a printer from an early age, had come to use the press throughout his life at various stages—as a newspaperman in Massachusetts and Pennsylvania and as statesman—at moments in time when he felt it was crucial to sway public opinion "on issues that mattered to him" (Mulford, 2008, p. 492).

While stationed in France to raise money and awareness on behalf of his new country, Franklin established a press in Passy, France, which produced in 1782 the hoax newspaper titled *Supplement to the Boston Independent Chronicle* (Mulford, 2008). Franklin created a broadside for a fictitious newspaper with two different articles on each side with fake advertisements to give it a more authentic look. The article on the front side of the paper recounts wartime atrocities of the British and their Indian allies, while the reverse-side article concerns the wartime imprisonment of colonial Americans.

But both are themselves "literary hoaxes" (Mulford, 2008). The general purpose of the hoaxes was to garner support for the United States and to plant false stories among British society in order to discredit their war effort and manipulate public sentiment. Franklin in particular hoped for an international "outcry against Britain's alliance with Native Americans" (p. 196). It is not clear how successful the hoax was at the time, but it appears that the British were hardly fooled, with Horace Walpole characterizing it as much a parody as a deception (Dowd, 2015, p. 193). Yet the paper was published widely and seems to reappear through history, and "spreads as truth in our own time" (p. 193). Of course, Franklin was no stranger to printing false news stories and his longtime habit of doing so "nipped at his reputation" even during his own lifetime (p. 195). As a result, this wartime hoax cannot be seen as an outlier in Franklin's output. It is, instead, a prime example of the power of printing itself, the temptations that come with it, and how false ideas persist, even through the centuries.

Similarly, when passed down from earlier generations legends can become ingrained in a culture, until they seem both foundational and definitive. In America, a gold fever that never broke after centuries of colonization by European powers would rise and fall in prominence during different periods in its history (Dowd, 2015, p. 167). The result of unfounded rumors and legends about gold and untold riches—many of which were originated in the Spanish colonies, specifically—in this era were "highly persistent" and "fed off one another" until they led to violence and bloodshed (Dowd, 2015, p. 37). The consequences were dire for some, especially for the Native Americans who happened to be living in the regions where the hunt for gold was acute. The false idea that refuses to die in spite of evidence remains a palpable danger, even now, but especially so for the powerless and the disenfranchised.

POSTREVOLUTION AMERICA: SCIENTIFIC
HOAXES AND PENNY PRESSES

After the revolution, which had been highly influenced by the press itself, and the enshrinement of press freedoms in the First Amendment of the Constitution in 1787, the American press takes off, developing and growing in reach as the country matures. But the spread of fake news and false narratives did not end with the maturing of the newly established free press in America; indeed, it may have gotten worse. The destabilizing power of a free press was evidenced in how easily newspapers could "be used for bad purposes, such as defaming someone's character or ruining a person's reputation" (Humphrey, 1992, p. 97). The issues of power and antityrannical sentiment at the heart of the colonial-era presses that came to the forefront prior to and during the American Revolution eventually fought back against the issues of fake news with extreme backlash. This backlash, resulting in the development of better journalistic standards by the twentieth century, will be examined in more detail in the next chapters.

Nevertheless, as the new nation matured and the press grew larger, there were significant growing pains. As McQueen details it, in the early decades of the 1800s most newspapers were too expensive for everyone except the upper classes. Average rates of 6 cents per issue, coming to roughly $10 per year—approximately $350 today—were too much for most laborers and workers to spend their earnings on. Circulation in New York City among a population of 250,000 people was merely 26,500 among eleven daily newspapers (McQueen, 2018, p. 20). Topics were also geared toward the merchants, politicians, and the wealthy. But that focus changed with the introduction of *The Sun*, the first "penny press" newspaper, selling issues at 1 cent each or $3 per year (approximately $106 today) (note: prices taken from Concannon, 2022). While certainly radical in the sense that information could reach the poor and lower classes, spurring desire for literacy in particular, the real shift in the so-called penny presses was in the content itself. Stories in *The Sun*, for example, focused on "the sensational" and were "strongly seasoned with sex, romance, intrigue, violence, [and] death" (Concannon, 2022)—all the kinds of stories *The Sun*'s founder, Benjamin Day, believed that most regular, working-class New Yorkers were more interested in reading about. Once its popularity soared, imitators and competitors emerged, each trying to outdo the other for the prize of the highest circulation. And it seems to have worked: *The Sun*'s circulation alone was in the thousands per day with new papers reaching similar figures within months of launching (p. 21).

But the lurid stories soon morphed into something else: the hoax. The era from 1835 to 1880, as recounted in Lynda Walsh's book *Sins Against Science*, represents a significant time of literary hoaxes and fake news stories related to science, with more than a dozen high-profile stories gaining notoriety. Four writers, two as well known to us today as they were then, contributed several of these popular science-related hoaxes during the era, including Edgar Allan Poe, Mark Twain, Richard Adams Locke, and Dan De Quille (Walsh, 2006). Incidentally, the derivation of the word hoax itself, as Fredal (2014) reveals, may be *hocus*—meaning to play a trick on someone—which is a shortening of the pseudo-Latin incantation *hocus pocus*. At any rate, the hoax has long roots that extend far past the word's seventeenth-century coinage, traceable back to the ancient Greek historians, including Herodotus. Being "at its core thoroughly rhetorical" the hoax manipulates its audience through a deception that is not meant solely to fool them but also to ridicule something else (Fredal, 2014, p. 75). For that reason, the hoax that fools no one is a failure as much as the hoax that is never discovered (p. 78). The point is that the hoax must be deceptive enough to draw attention to itself but not too deceptive that its wider target—perhaps arrogant researchers claiming earth-shattering novelty—cannot be called out for their behavior.

This dynamic is at play in several of the hoaxes of the time, including The Great Moon Hoax of Richard Adams Locke, Mark Twain's petrified man hoax, and Poe's balloon hoax. In each, the revelation of the hoax may have been as important as the trick itself. Mark Twain's fossilized man, in particular, is revealed through the text—when read carefully—to be "sitting up and thumbing his nose at the reader" (Walsh, 2006, p. 1). Poe revealed his trickery by "getting drunk and standing on the steps of *the Sun* trumpeting his forgery to potential subscribers" (p. 33). Locke's hoax, however, was a sensation—hence the later term "sensationalism"—and the biggest driver of newspaper sales through its thoroughly false depiction of alien life on the moon. Though initially reticent, Locke later claimed that his story was meant to satire a famous astronomer who had come up with a "bizarre plan to communicate with moon beings through geometric shapes" (p. 66). Yet for all these flights of fancy, they were each as much a critique of how science had become a spectacle, both for the audience who might believe every word of it and for the purveyors of that information, for example, the sensationalist press and the scientists who were seen as witting or unwitting accomplices in trumpeting their own discoveries.

IMPLICATIONS OF THESE ERAS OF FAKE NEWS AND HOW THEY RELATE TO NOW

So what lessons for today can be drawn from these disparate times and events besides the fact that fake narratives have had a long and sometimes lurid history? What threads unite these various types of lies, tall tales, forgeries, myths, legends, hoaxes, and fake histories together aside from their persistence over time? A number of important issues, it can be argued, come to the forefront despite the randomness of events, the multiple variables involved, the varying motivations creating them, and the great differences in time and cultures.

First, there is a consistent blur within many cultures between informal narratives and official histories, where the myths, legends, and rumors of a region coalesce into a story that people *want* to believe—or force others to believe—in order to receive or impart desirable social benefits. These range from Alexander the Great's apotheosis to the philosophies and motivations driving manifest destiny in the United States to the false promises of the Gold Rush. These are the stories people want to tell each other, the polite fictions they want to believe about themselves, or the false narratives they impose upon others to control them. The false images and narratives persist to this day, just in a different form and with different personages embodying these things. Much like the banner image of a muscle-bound Donald Trump toting a machine gun, Rambo style, it speaks to the desires for something beyond just a perfect rendition of a subject. It speaks to the desire for a fantasy that uplifts or empowers the believer as much as it does for fulfilling one's own private "truth" regardless of how "real" it is or how little evidence exists to support it. The downside is when that empowerment is serviced in violence against others.

Second, another thread that runs through many of these false narratives and fake news is one of power and its preservation. Propaganda, as Bosworth demonstrates in his examination of Alexander the Great's death, remains inextricably tied to histories, especially at times of great upheaval or when dynasties are interested in establishing and consolidating their power. Specifically, many false narratives betray the central concern that power is fragile, and so they strive to eliminate potential overthrows. Preserving power through false narrative and fake news becomes a common thread, leading to widespread state-sanctioned belief. The false narratives about Jews using blood sacrifice similarly betray a fear of and paranoia about the dominant culture's fragility, as do the repression of the native languages in Mexico and other Spanish colonies. Yet, conversely, American colonial presses were able to harness revolutionary spirit as a force for positive change, precipitating a distinct evolution from colony of a world power ruled by a king to a nascent democratic republic—though not without resorting to fake news!

Third, the nineteenth-century literary hoaxes and their critiques of the sciences need not be seen entirely as an outlier in history that has no antecedents, even if the scientific method itself is fairly new. The issue is instead more about the types of discourses seen as trustworthy, what we use to determine trust, and how that trust can be both subverted—much like hackers will subvert systems they break into—for negative results (to fool people) or for positive (to instruct and delight those who are in on the joke). In the case of the nineteenth-century science hoaxes, we are dealing as much with parody and satire as we are with interrogating truth and the powers that determine whether one narrative is seen as more trustworthy than another. The positive takeaway from hoaxes in general is that they force people to reevaluate knowledge that has been taken for granted. They also show how people can be fooled not only by the content itself but also by the format that packages that message. The fact remains that the format in which information is shared can convey as much meaning to the consumer as the message itself. Nicotrix's hoax in Herodotus's *Historia* was all the more convincing because it was written in stone on her tomb.

Finally, even now we must deal with our own mistrust and bias when attempting to consider the reality of historical events or figures and the blurring of their truths. It may seem obvious to everyone now when reviewing the old hoaxes and myths that various events could *never* have taken place or that they were clearly lies all along. People often believe that they would never fall for such ruses. The seducer is always the most obvious to those who are not being seduced, after all. But this may be the wrong approach. These false stories can tell us much more about prevailing concerns of the time than anything else. Unfounded stories and news essentially "give us entry into the concerns of those who took them seriously" (Dowd, 2015, p. 293).

A recent example might be the changing and evolving status of little-known "Emperor Sponsion (Sponsionus)," whose likeness appears on ancient coins initially found in Transylvania, "once a far-flung outpost of the Roman empire" in 1713 (Ghosh, 2022). For a significant time, and especially during the nineteenth century, these coins were considered fakes, assumed to be hoaxes used to fool coin collectors, especially as Sponsionus appears nowhere in the ancient written record. However, researchers have since reexamined the coins and found evidence that they may indeed be as old as they were first purported to be. The coins are too similar to other verified ancient coins in their composition, form, and damage sustained through centuries of use. The new evidence changes the perspective of the present as well as the understanding of the past. Now, rather than writing the figure off as a historical hoax, scholars are weighing potential theories on who the person might actually have been.

The change in perspective, though, is similar in approach to the ancient writers' histories themselves: reexamining the assumptions of falseness and truthfulness with new evidence that comes to light. The concept of a hoax, however, has a long and complicated history, especially in nineteenth-century America—whose motivations are not unlike the development of fake news and misinformation in our current digital era, which Walsh (2006) sees as operating "at the nexus of scientific and literary epistemologies," criticizing the specialized rhetoric of groups they find threatening (Walsh, 2006). The hoax turns out to be similar in intention, in some ways, to some of the kinds of fake news stories that are constantly spread online: a way to get at what we *want* to be true while also finding ways to ridicule or denigrate perceived adversaries and even enemies. As we will see in the next chapter, the technologies of the modern world moving beyond the printing press further impact our ability to parse truth and fiction but with a much larger reach than ever before.

REFERENCES

Baragwanath, E., and de Bakker, M. (2012). Introduction: Myth, truth, and narrative in Herodotus' *Histories*. In Baragwanath and de Bakker (eds.), *Myth, truth, and narrative in Herodotus*. Oxford University Press. https://doi.org/10.1093/acprof:oso/9780199693979.003.0001.

Barbier, F. (2006). L'Europe De Gutenberg: Le Livre et L'Invention de la Modernite Occidentale. Paris: Belin.

Bosworth, A. B. (1971). The Death of Alexander the Great: Rumour and propaganda. *Classical Quarterly, 21*(1), pp. 112–36. https://doi.org/10.1017/S0009838800028846.

Concannon, M. (2022). 1830–1839: Prices and wages by decade. Library Guides at University of Missouri Libraries. https://libraryguides.missouri.edu/pricesandwages/1830-1839.

Darnton, R. (2017). The true history of fake news. *New York Review of Books*, February 13.

Dittmar, J. E. (2011). Information technology and economic change: The impact of the printing press. *The Quarterly Journal of Economics, 126*(3), pp. 1133–72. https://doi.org/10.1093/qje/qjr035.

Dowd, G. E. (2015). *Groundless: Rumors, legends, and hoaxes on the early American frontier*. Johns Hopkins University Press.

Doyle, A. (2019). Tracing "fake news": The printing press, social media, and politics. *The Criterion*. https://crossworks.holycross.edu/criterion/vol2019/iss1/6.

Eco, U. (1976). *A theory of semiotics*. Indiana University Press.

Eco, U. (2014). Fakes and forgeries in the Middle Ages. In *From the tree to the labyrinth: Historical studies on the sign and interpretation*. Harvard University Press.

Fredal, J. (2014). The perennial pleasures of the hoax. *Philosophy & Rhetoric, 47*(1), pp. 73–97. https://doi.org/10.5325/philrhet.47.1.0073.

Georgiou, I. E. (2002). Women in Herodotus' "Histories." Thesis. Swansea University. http://cronfa.swan.ac.uk/Record/cronfa43005.

Ghosh, P. (2022). Gold coin proves "fake" Roman emperor was real. BBC News. https://www.bbc.com/news/science-environment-63636641?utm_source=pocket -newtab.

Gleiser, M. (2018). How much can we know? *Nature, 557*(7704), pp. S20–S21. https: //doi.org/10.1038/d41586-018-05100-5.

Hsia, R. P. (1992). *Trent 1475: Stories of a ritual murder trial.* Yale University Press in cooperation with Yeshiva University Library.

Humphrey, C. S. (1992). *This popular engine: New England newspapers during the American Revolution, 1775–1789.* University of Delaware Press.

Jowett, G., and O'Donnell, V. (1992). *Propaganda and persuasion.* Second edition. Sage Publications.

La Caze, M. (2017). It's easier to lie if you believe it yourself: Derrida, Arendt, and the modern lie. *Law, Culture and the Humanities, 13*(2), pp. 193–210. https://doi -org.libproxy.csun.edu/10.1177/1743872113485032.

Lateiner, D. (1990). Deceptions and delusions in Herodotus. *Classical Antiquity, 9*(2), pp. 230–46. https://doi.org/10.2307/25010930.

Loewenstein, J. (2002). *The author's due: Printing and the prehistory of copyright.* University of Chicago Press. https://doi.org/10.7208/9780226490410.

McCorison, M. A. (2010). Printers and the law: The trials of publishing obscene libel in early America. *The Papers of the Bibliographical Society of America, 104*(2), pp. 181–217. https://doi.org/10.1086/680925.

McQueen, S. (2018). From yellow journalism to tabloids to clickbait. In D. E. Agosto (ed.), *Information literacy and libraries in the age of fake news.* Denver, CO: Libraries Unlimited.

Mulford, C. (2008). Benjamin Franklin's savage eloquence: Hoaxes from the press at Passy, 1782. *Proceedings of the American Philosophical Society, 152*(4), pp. 490–530.

Nelson, Heming, (1998). A history of newspaper: Gutenberg's press started a revolution. *Washington Post.* https://www.washingtonpost.com/archive/1998/02/11/a-history -of-newspaper-gutenbergs-press-started-a-revolution/2e95875c-313e-4b5c- 9807-8bcb031257ad/.

Nicolai, R. (2015). The place of history in the ancient world. In John Marincola (ed.), e*A companion to Greek and Roman historiography* (p. 11). John Wiley & Sons, Inc.

Peters, J. S. (2003). *Theatre of the book 1480–1880: Print, text, and performance in Europe.* Oxford University Press. https://doi.org/10.1093/acprof:oso /9780199262168.001.0001.

Plato. (n.d.). *Republic, Book II*, 382a–382d. B. Jowett (Trans.). Project Gutenberg. https://www.gutenberg.org/files/55201/55201-h/55201-h.htm.

Soll, J. (2016). The long and brutal history of fake news. *Politico Magazine.* https://www.politico.com/magazine/story/2016/12/fake-news-history-long-violent -214535/.

Tsakmakis, A. (2015). Historiography and biography. In *A companion to Greek literature* (pp. 217–34). John Wiley & Sons, Inc. https://doi.org/10.1002/9781118886946 .ch14.

United States Holocaust Memorial Museum. (2022). Blood libel. *Holocaust encyclopedia*. https://encyclopedia.ushmm.org/content/en/article/blood-libel.

Walsh, L. (2006). *Sins against science: The scientific media hoaxes of Poe, Twain, and others*. State University of New York Press.

Woodford, S. (2003). *Images of myths in classical antiquity*. Cambridge University Press.

Chapter 5

Fake News in the Twentieth Century

Propaganda, Misinformation, Conspiracies, and How New Technologies Helped to Spread It

[Circa January 1897]Frederic Remington: "W.R. Hearst. New York Journal, N.Y.: Everything is quiet. There is no trouble here. There will be no war. I wish to return."

W.R. Hearst: "Remington, Havana: Please remain. You furnish the pictures, and I'll furnish the war." (From Creelman, 1901)

PRECURSOR TO THE TWENTIETH CENTURY: THE ERA OF YELLOW JOURNALISM

As unique and interesting as the previous chapter's broad discussion of mythmaking, history, false narratives, rumors, hoaxes, and misinformation has been, the era that seems most similar to our own is the era of yellow journalism, which took off in the mid-1890s and lasted through the early 1900s. In many ways the yellow journalism years appear to reach a similarly widespread feeling of outcry and fever pitch of scandals as it does today, making it feel like a direct precursor to current modern cycles of rumor, fake news, and sensationalized political discourse. Certainly, there are at least a few factors that seem more similar between then and now than the period occurring after yellow journalism and before the internet, dominated, as it was, by radio and television but regulated more tightly by the FCC until the 1980s.

As we saw with the various literary hoaxes carried out through newspapers in the early part of the nineteenth century, it becomes clear that incentives to print false information—especially the immediate profit and fame for publishers and hoaxers alike—were just too great to resist and that "there was very little to lose in printing fake news" (McQueen, 2018, p. 22). Yellow journalism, an intensifying outgrowth of that earlier hoax era, was the result of a growing "circulation war" that started in the 1890s between the two most famous newspapermen in the nineteenth century, William Randolph Hearst and Joseph Pulitzer. The intense rivalry between Hearst's *New York Journal* and Pulitzer's *New York World* helped establish mass media and its distribution for the late nineteenth and early twentieth centuries. Some trace the impact of this rivalry and the excessive practices of yellow journalism itself—though *wrongly* one must emphasize—to the outbreak of the Spanish-American War in 1898.

Though a newspaper circulation war seems rather quaint now, with price reductions of *one cent* instigating these conflicts, given the immense changes in information technology since then, it is similar in terms of the ways in which information came to be shared on a much broader and quicker scale. Much like the five Vs (volume, value, variety, velocity, and veracity) of the Big Data era, the newspaper wars themselves seemed to presage similar problems of the information and surveillance age, with increased reach, a quick turnaround for daily publishing, problems of scale for fact-checking, and the eclipsing of fact-based news stories with false stories, sensationalism, and political manipulation.

But why call it *yellow* journalism? The name seems to connote the fusty discoloring of old paper and newsprint, as if pointing to its slapdash and cheap pulp quality that—of course, we tell ourselves—only the *uneducated* would fall for. In retrospect, the medium betrays its dubious meaning through the brittle decomposing pages of a bygone era. Of course, in a more highly race- and class-conscious era, yellow seems to imply old-fashioned personal cowardice or a virulent Asian race baiting projecting personal prejudices into the use of the color in our idiom. But that overlaying cultural detritus, while it may provide some room for online speculation to fuel assumptions about the name, belies the whole story, which appears to have a more prosaic origin.

The backstory goes as follows: there was no lack of invention in publishing during this time in publishing, and Joseph Pulitzer, in particular, was a great innovator for the newspaper business. He was using, for example, four-color printing presses ahead of his competitors and was one of the earliest adopters of the "Color Supplement" in the Sunday editions of his newspapers (McQueen, 2018, p. 24). The Sunday color comic strips, which began around this time, were a big hit with readers. One of the most popular comic strips at that time was Richard F. Outcault's *Hogan's Alley*, first appearing in 1895 in Pulitzer's *New York World*. A popular character in the strip, Mickey Dugan, is depicted as a young "street urchin" dressed in a large, ill-fitting night gown. When the strip was published in color, they chose yellow for the child's shirt. From that point onward, Dugan became known as "the yellow kid" (McQueen, 2018).

But that was merely the beginning. Soon "yellow kid" merchandise was everywhere, including cards, pins, dolls, ice cream, bottle openers, sheet music, and cigarettes (Wood, n.d.). The kid was so lucrative that Hearst poached Outcault from Pulitzer's paper and began publishing just the *Yellow Kid* there. However, Pulitzer hired another artist to continue on *Hogan's Alley*, using a knock-off version of "the yellow kid." The battle between the two publishers escalated with more pages given over to the yellow kid for each issue until the "battle of the yellow kids" morphed into "yellow kid journalism" and eventually became shortened to just "yellow journalism." There are three conflicting versions of the origin story, each attributing the coinage of the term to Charles Dana, editor for the *New York Sun*; US senator Edward Oliver Wolcott; or Ervin Wardman, editor of *New York Press*. Joseph Campbell argues for Wardman in his excellent book *Yellow Journalism: Puncturing the Myths, Defining the Legacies* (Campbell, 2001).

However, deciding who coined the term "yellow journalism" remains mostly beside the point; it is the evolution and spread of the concept and its connotations during that time that interest us here. Regardless of who first said it, the lessons remain the same. What began as a way to entice more readers to their newspapers, due to the subsequent excesses of their transparent grab for more readers through increasingly questionable business practices and possible ethical transgressions, the yellow press becomes a stereotype and label indicating the *kind* of news they were peddling, characterized by the use of lurid headlines and fake interviews, coupled with sometimes outlandish images and drawings of the imaginary. Historically, the reputation derived from this kind of work, and the main source of their popularity and success, eventually serves to tarnish the reputations of all involved even as they revel in their notoriety and profitability (Campbell, 2001).

SOME GOOD FROM THE BAD: THE RISE OF JOURNALISTIC STANDARDS AND THE RIGHT TO PRIVACY

The yellow journalism era could also be characterized as a push and pull between sensationalism and the growing backlash against it, resulting in new moral and ethical standards for journalism that proved durable and long-standing. Indeed, one great irony of the yellow journalism era is that one of its greatest drivers and proponents, Joseph Pulitzer, is now valued more for his role in helping to establish the first school of journalism at Columbia University and the namesake prizes he funded "as an incentive to excellence," which celebrate the best in journalism and literature each year (Topping, 2023).

The seeds of reform were nevertheless sown in the backlash against the over-the-top practices of the yellow press. The *New York Times* adopted its famous slogan "All the news fit to print" in 1896, as a way to distinguish itself from the yellow press and as a marketing tool to attract readers in a crowded field (Campbell, 2012). Editorials and editorial cartoons in these more reputable and scrupulous newspapers and magazines found great fault with the practices of these presses and attacked them through the use of stereotyping and parody of the genre. The pushback against the genre was made easier with this reliance on the highly noticeable "yellow," making the presses an easy target for criticism, pigeonholing them in the process. *Puck* magazine, as seen with L. M. Glacken's famous cartoon "The Yellow Press," for example, called out their rhetorical excesses in bright yellow, including their "Appeals To Passion," and uses of "Venom" and "Personal Grievance" to incite readers; their politicization of news in their "Attacks on Honest Officials" and "Misrepresentation" of facts; and, finally, their business model that gained attention through "Sensationalism." It was as effective as it was simple.

However, one must be careful not to place too much stock in overvilifying the yellow newspapers themselves, despite their excesses, and should resist seeing them as the primary representatives of a bygone era that provides no tether to past or future practices. While the worst of their practices were curtailed to a certain degree in the courts of public opinion, consumer backlash, and competitor attacks on their brand of journalism, the forms of fake news, hoaxes, propaganda, and misinformation merely shifted to new containers in the coming decades. Campbell finds, too, that "newspapers recognized as representative of the yellow press . . . tended to retain some of those features" (2001, p. 153) throughout the twentieth century and even the more conservative newspapers adopted some of their innovations—especially the use of large headlines, images, and the Sunday supplements with comics and illustrations in color (2001, p. 151). The yellow press shifted, quite easily and quite readily it seems, into tabloid papers, and later into radio shows and television specials that continued to peddle lurid and sensational "news" up to the present. Elvis might really have left the building in a UFO, according to the *National Enquirer*, and true crimes of serial killers may be popular on streaming platforms, but the past serves as prologue to these and any other kind of sensational story, whatever its media container happens to be.

THE MIXED LEGACY OF YELLOW JOURNALISM

Ultimately, yellow journalism's overall legacy is a mixed and ironic one. Yellow journalism with its negative reputation for exaggeration, sensationalism, and ethical transgressions has long been seen as playing a central role in instigating the Spanish-American War in Cuba in 1898. Yet despite peddling lurid and fake stories about other topics, and even boasting "How do you like the journal's war?" as the *New York Journal* published in May 1898, these presses had, in fact, very little to do with starting a war (Campbell, 2001, p. 97). Indeed, as Campbell reveals, the famously damning telegram story where Hearst is purported to exclaim, "You furnish the pictures, and I'll furnish the war," appears to be entirely fabricated. Instead it is a legend born more of wishful thinking and factual misconceptions than an accurate story, despite how fitting of a lesson it might be. The irony of a false narrative about newspapers peddling fake news is not lost on this writer.

Yet further interest abounds, for we see reflected in this urge to believe a beautiful story at the expense of the truth the long line of "aesthetic fallacies," as Campbell (2001, p. 86) calls them, occurring throughout our written histories from Herodotus to the Middle Ages and beyond. The Cuba story has been repeated so often in the legitimate press that it is still taken as fact in some circles. But the wider point is that the story tells a moral and ethical point in pithy statement, not unlike a fable or even a fairy tale. Sometimes, in other words, a story is so good it just *has* to be true.

Just as importantly, though much less ironic, the moral and ethical backlash combating the worst information excesses, "the grossest railleries and libels, instead of honest statements and fair discussions," as New York City mayor and former judge William Jay Gaynor described it in 1910, was ultimately aided by changes in the law itself (Borchard, 2019). The concept of a right to privacy—one that has been very clearly definitive and directly applicable for our own era—was derived from the reforms of this era as a way to protect people from "the prying eyes of yellow journalists and gossip-mongers" (Gajda, 2009, p. 1045). Indeed, the basis of Americans' current bundle of rights to privacy is derived from this time period and remains no less relevant even if the medium and the level of invasiveness has changed.

The article "The Right to Privacy" published by Warren and Brandeis in the *Harvard Law Review* in 1890 lays the foundation for our current legal conceptions of privacy, spurred in part by what they called the "evil of invasion of privacy by the newspapers" (Warren and Brandeis, 1890). They explain that "inventions and business methods" from the time compel them to protect persons and secure "the right to be let alone." This right, as they see it, was especially encroached upon by "Instantaneous photographs and newspaper enterprise" and "numerous mechanical devices [that] threaten to make good the prediction that 'what is whispered in the closet shall be proclaimed from the house-tops'" (Warren and Brandeis, 1890). These new conceptions of a person's right to their own autonomy as well as right to not be exposed were driven, in reality, by the newest technologies dominating the time, especially photography, faster printing methods, and better methods of distribution. Aided by the unscrupulous practices of the newspaper publishers, the spread of information becomes nearly uncontrollable from a privacy perspective. The courts subsequently begin to hold the media responsible for breaches or invasions of privacy (Gajda, 2009). Finally, the newspaper business itself began to reform its own practices. By 1910 the first code of ethics in journalism was adopted by the Kansas State Editorial association, condemning "fake illustrations, fake interviews, and fake news dispatches" (McQueen, 2018, p. 28), and the following decades saw these codified throughout the country. Importantly, despite the excesses, in tandem with the law and internally through editorial and industry ethics, the newspaper business found a way to reform its earlier uncontrolled practices.

It is a common refrain that technology moves much faster than our laws and ethics can to deal with or mitigate their immediate impacts. That the yellow journalism era seems so similar to our own is not entirely coincidental. To paraphrase Twain, the past doesn't repeat itself, but it does frequently rhyme. And in that rhyming, similarities may stem from a number of overlapping factors affecting societies and people in the same way even if they exist in different eras. First, there is the issue of reach. The circulation of newspapers during this time attained significantly larger numbers to impact and alter public opinion about current events beyond the regions they represented. New York City newspapers began to reach broader regions, affecting national attitudes. Additionally, the speed with which news traveled had greatly increased as a result of this simultaneously wider yet denser circulation. The amount of information circulating among people also began to increase; newspapers could print far more than ever due to decreased costs in manufacturing paper. Hearst's attempt to match the information published in a single issue at half the price of Pulitzer's newspaper is a prime example of how innovations and competition greatly cheapened reader access to information.

Images began to be published, including the political cartoon—which contributes to the overall amount and type of information being shared in a smaller space. The development of color greatly enhanced the visual pleasures of readers and stimulated interest but came to define both the genre of newspaper as well as the era of journalism itself. Overall, the design of modern newspapers, including the large headline, use of pictures, and the Sunday supplement, was drawn heavily from the yellow presses. The influence was so pronounced that Pulitzer's grandson could boast one hundred years later that the world had "adopted" his methods (Campbell, 2001, p. 151).

Still, these relatively minor adjustments in technology ultimately had a great impact on the culture through the ways in which information could be shared and spread to others. These types of changes were writ large in the newspaper era, yet also served as the base for the coming of mass media communications in the form of radio and television.

RADIO DAYS: NEW TECHNOLOGIES, OLD PROBLEMS

Radio and television are just as important for mass communications as the printing press, speeding up not only the transmission of ideas and information within texts but also with images, still and moving, and sound. Radio was invented in the 1890s, with the first broadcast occurring in 1895, but did not become a significant medium for mass culture until the early 1920s. The impact of radio during this time was notable in all aspects of culture, including, not least, the arts. And it is in the arts where we find an important historical event that can help to illuminate the ways that new technologies impact people as well as drive some of the negative aspects of information sharing, including false narrative, fake news, and conspiracy theory.

The most well-known "fake news" incident of the radio era occurred on October 30, 1938, with Orson Welles's broadcast of *The War of the Worlds*. The realistic portrayal involved clever interruptions of a music program with a fake reporter announcing that Professor Farrell of the Mount Jenning Observatory detected explosions coming from the planet Mars. An alien invasion had begun, according to the broadcast, resulting in a panic from the listening public upon its initial broadcast. Many had apparently tuned in to the show after CBS's opening disclaimer, missing the announcement that it was merely a radio play. The news afterward pounced on the radio play and even accused the creators of trying to intentionally fool the listeners (Schwartz, 2015). But, just like the Hearst telegram story, however, the extent of the panic was likely overstated by the media itself.

While we won't delve too deeply into the hoax itself, the broader points and themes of hoaxes and fake news remain relevant, as we saw in the previous chapter. In *The War of the Worlds* radio broadcast the dominant form of communication is coopted, like in the previous era of the newspaper hoax, and turned into a critique of the society itself. Tellingly, Welles's hoax played upon similar fears and distrust of scientific discourse and the gullibility of people to fall for the form that something appears in as much as the content itself. With the Great Moon hoax in the nineteenth century, the form adapted was the scientific digest, written to popularize scientific discoveries; in the case of *The War of the Worlds*, nascent UFO sightings culture mixed with radio broadcast forms that provided instant news and information to people. In this case the technology has as much an impact as the message.

But that technological impact can be deadly. As we will see in the next section, regarding poet and propagandist Ezra Pound. In his work we see the unique combinations of art and culture, the impact of technology—especially radio—and the intermixture of a new medium, its messaging, and the amplification of false narratives.

THE CURIOUS CASE OF EZRA POUND: ARTISTS, ANTENNAE, AND LITERATURE AS NEWS

Twentieth-century literature's *enfant terrible*, poet Ezra Pound, was one of the leading proponents of the modernist movement in the arts, which sprung up largely in response to the period during and after World War I, especially the social upheavals and the technologies that made the war so horrifying. Born in 1885 in Idaho but raised in Pennsylvania, Pound ultimately had a hand in some of the most important movements in twentieth-century literature (especially imagism, vorticism, and modernism at large), working as a tireless creator, editor, mentor, collaborator, and educator for and among some of the most well-known figures of the time, including T. S. Eliot, H.D., and William Butler Yeats, to name just a few. His editorial work on the early drafts of Eliot's *Wasteland*—originally dubbed with the unwieldly Dickensian title "He do the police in different voices"—shows just how influential his vision of an image-dominated, "crystallized" poetry could be. Without Pound there may have been no *Wasteland* in the form we recognize it. He similarly aided Yeats in updating his poetry for a new audience and helped poet Hilda Doolittle not only with her pen name, as "H. D. Imagiste," but also forged her big break as a "paragon" of imagism, an early movement he started that attempted to strip away the perceived gaudiness of the previous Edwardian era still prevalent in verse in the 1910s (Pound, 1974, pp. 80–81).

Yet no matter how great Ezra Pound's reputation as a poet became, or his overall aesthetic contributions to literature in the twentieth century, he cannot be discussed without quickly running afoul of his lurch toward antisemitism and fascism, leading to his radio broadcasts for Fascist-led Italy from 1941 to 1943. He was later tried for treason *in absentia*, captured by American soldiers in Italy, then placed in a psychiatric facility, avoiding capital punishment for his treasonous wartime activities. The question of his fitness to stand trial and the declaration of his purported insanity has always remained unanswered and controversial. The evidence of how his time was spent at St.

Elizabeths Hospital, including his award-winning literary output and outside correspondence, suggests that Pound was quite far from being clinically insane (Corrigan, 1972).

Some have traced a mild antisemitism from his earliest days, influenced in part during his days at *The New Age* newspaper (Redman, 1991, p. 39), where he "absorbed the Edwardian and Georgian anti-Semitism that claimed to link usury with the Jews," a false yet persistent assumption (p. 49). But his mind took an especially dark and paranoid turn during the 1930s and 1940s, becoming ever bolder and less attached to reality (Surette, 1999). While his literary work has been seen as highly influential and significant to the modernist movement, "forever associated with complex poetry and a sophisticated political and economic ideology; a man with great critical and artistic influence," as Corrigan (1972) described it fifty years ago, much of what he wrote also veered into conspiratorial nonsense, propaganda, misinformation, and false narratives.

His famous decades-long work, *The Cantos*, has been judged generously by many as a crystallization of his vorticist/imagist aesthetics, written in extended form across multiple decades. But it is also documentation of his growing interest in sometimes outlandish economic theories and increasing antisemitic tropes as years wore on. Masimo Bacigalup, a noted critic of Pound, believes *The Cantos* "belong in those shops that sell swastikas and recordings of Mussolini's speeches" (Surette, 1999, p. 7). Indeed, as the decades wore on, it should be noted that his profascism and antisemitism did not abate once he was incarcerated at St. Elizabeths after the war (p. 7). He was nevertheless awarded Yale University's Bollingen Prize in 1948 for the work *Pisan Cantos*, which he had subsequently written while in the hospital. The irony, of course, is that Pound not only absorbed prevalent false narratives and conspiracy theories about Jewish people—starting as far back as his days writing and hanging around radical socialist newspaper *The New Age*, which mixed socialism and syndicalism in ways that Mussolini would adopt later in the 1920s (Redman, 1991, p. 18)—but he also later spread such false information and propaganda *through* the radio. Simultaneously appearing to be both victim and victimizer, Pound's broadcasts were according to Corrigan "the most interesting attempt on the part of any major American poet to actively engage in the business of molding the opinions and beliefs of the masses" (Corrigan, 1972, p. 779). Interesting may be a bit too generous, but certainly Pound became, as it were, the champion of a mass media "poetics of conspiracy."

By the time he starts his radio broadcasts in 1941, as Surette traces for us in his masterful examination *Pound in Purgatory*, Pound has fully absorbed the false narratives about Jewish conspiracies, "persuaded that World War II was an incident in the struggle against the Zionist plot for world domination," and accepts as truth the debunked *Protocols of the Elders of Zion*, a widely published hoax and forgery that describes a Jewish plan for world domination (1999, pp. 233–34). He seems to have resisted such conspiracies in years prior (mainly ignoring the paranoid fantasies of economist and writing correspondent Arthur Kitson, economist and rabid endorser of *The Protocols*) until the war's outbreak, despite the milieu of antisemitism throughout his time in England and Italy (p. 236).

Given the well-documented resistance to these theories in his correspondence with various writers and economists, we are driven to ponder: Who or *what* brought him to this point of stark transformation within a relatively short period of time? Surette suggests—and here is the crux of the matter—that *the radio broadcasts* of one Father Charles Coughlin, known as "the radio priest," were "the most important single influence" that pushed Pound over the edge from mild antisemitism into full-on conspiracy theory (1999, p. 261). It is not clear exactly when Pound encountered the man's radio broadcasts, likely in the mid-1930s, but Surette finds that "the conformity between Coughlin's attitudes and targets in his radio speeches and those newly adopted by Pound at the time he was listening to Coughlin is far too great to be attributed to coincidence" (p. 274). The descent into paranoia, partly a result of his interest in economics in which a large number of associates were heavily antisemitic, was pushed over the edge through the sharing of false narratives peddled on the radio that were subsequently mimicked by Pound himself. In all, from January 1941 through July 1943, Pound delivered hundreds of broadcasts on behalf of Fascist Italy, espousing antisemitic and anti-Roosevelt rhetoric until fleeing and going into hiding once the Fascist regime collapsed (Corrigan, 1972).

The influence of the "radio priest" is certainly one factor in Pound's push into conspiracy. Another influence is the modernists' well-documented propensity to adopt and utilize technology both in practice and in theory. Importantly, Pound is not writing in the absence of an older literary tradition; he is writing within the admonishing exhortation and literary manifesto to "Make It New," even as he paradoxically dredges up the past through translations of Greek, Japanese, and Chinese classics and refers to them in his poems (Morrisson, 2016). Pound and other literary modernists, including the contemporaneous Italian futurists, "understood science and technology as a central feature of the modern world, and in many ways key to its newness. But the terms in which they understood their own technological and scientific modernity varied greatly. Moreover, this transformational capacity of science and technology placed them at the center of a modernism in which transformation itself had to be understood in relationship to historical processes" (Morrisson, 2016).

Pound's own relationship to technology is similarly paradoxical. Steeped in modern imagery, he asserts that "artists are the antennae of their race" yet decries the radio as a "devil box" (Tiffany, 1995, p. 247); in the same vein, he writes that "literature is news that STAYS news" yet he holds "scorn for the masses" (p. 245) who he asserts will lap up mass media news unthinkingly. Both suggest that the influence of radio and his familiarity with it are pronounced yet conflicted and unresolved, leading him into a muddle of paranoid conceptions about technology, including the belief that technical inventions, especially the radio, should be seen "as new organs of the body that extend the perceptual and expressive range of the mediumistic artist" (p. 249), so that he in turn acts as both receiver and transmitter of the culture.

Within this conflicted and often confused conception of technology, coupled with the impact of religious figures like the "Radio Priest" Father Coughlin, Pound was clearly ripe for and receptive to the negative influences of conspiracy theories and false narratives. Yet to examine Pound's literature and poetry, some of which has been canonized in twentieth-century literature, without acknowledging the poisoned milieu from which it springs—some of it misguided at best and plainly cracked and dangerous at worst—is to miss the complexity of the man and to whitewash his dubious legacy as an artist and propagandist for fascism. It is a curious case of a legacy that has had no shortage of apologists in literary circles over the past century. He was an artist of profound gifts who fell, like many today do, for false ideas and phantasms in the mind. It is therefore essential to examine his work and his actions through the influence not only of fake news, misinformation, and conspiracy theories but also through the development of the technologies that helped to spread these pathologies.

His is ultimately a cautionary tale, as well, in which the promise of information and its new conceptions are conflated with new technology itself. It is a partly tragic outcome in which a mind, talented as it may have been, becomes poisoned by conspiracy theories, false narratives, and fake news born of the antisemitism of that time period and certain literary circles, but that also came to be amplified by radio, the dominant technology of mass communication.

But should we view Ezra Pound as the isolated case of a promising mind poisoned with misinformation or as an example of the wider phenomenon of propaganda and fake news spread through mass communication technologies? This is a difficult question to answer. Certainly, a publicly known artist of Pound's stature makes him seem like a unique case, for not everyone impacts the arts and letters as much as he has. Not everyone had his platform, either, or his fame and notoriety. Even now his legacy influences right-wing fascism in Italy in the form of CasaPound, a political party inspired by the poet's views on various economic theories and, of course, his antisemitism (Kenes,

2021). Yet from a wider perspective, the spread of false information through technology nevertheless impacts people in consistent ways, something that is still occurring, formerly with the likes of Rush Limbaugh, and today with Alex Jones, QAnon, Tucker Carlson, and others with similarly divisive views that impact people negatively. The wider impacts of spreading negative information will be examined in the next section of this book and accounts for the differences between individuals and their larger communities.

THE RISE OF THE FAIRNESS DOCTRINE: FROM YELLOW JOURNALISM TO BALANCED NEWS

Running parallel to the development of the radio and a direct antidote to the kind of misinformation and one-sided, propagandist antisemitic narratives peddled by the likes of Ezra Pound and others is the implementation of what is known in the United States as the "fairness doctrine," a policy that began to gain traction and influence throughout the country during the late 1920s. The fairness doctrine took effect shortly after the creation of the Federal Radio Commission (FRC) in 1927 and was continued by its successor, the Federal Communications Commission (FCC), until the late 1980s, when it was weakened during the Reagan administration in the name of deregulation (Perry, 2017). Its history is varied and controversial, with its development and implementation waxing and waning over decades, primarily enforced from the 1950s to the 1970s, but never fully put to rest until 2011, when the FCC finally removed it from their policies. The implementation of true balance at the heart of the doctrine was often, however, more aspiration and mythmaking than reality, with significant lapses in its enforcement noted throughout its existence, and punctuated by periods with "marked by conflict, ambivalence, and contingency" (Pickard, 2018, p. 3435).

It was the case *Great Lakes Broadcasting v. Federal Radio Commission*, 37 F.2d 993 (D.C. Cir. 1930) in 1929 that established the basis for the doctrine, in which the FRC argued "public interest requires ample play for the free and fair competition of opposing views, and the Commission believes that the principle applies to all discussions of issues of importance to the public" (Perry, 2017). Entman (1990) traces two specific goals for the doctrine, the first "to provide diversity: a wide variety of facts and opinions on public issues so that Americans can discover truth and participate effectively in democracy" (p. 104). The positive aspect of diversity was then to be encouraged by the requirement that stations provide a percentage of their time to discussing and presenting ideas of public importance. The second goal, which was more defensive in nature, was "to prevent the media (or the government through the media) from controlling public opinion by limiting the circulation of ideas" (Entman, 1990). The implementation of this goal was more punitive in theory, though never enforced at the content level—they never told stations what to broadcast—and rarely at the regulatory level too, with merely six "admonitions" to stations when a typical year might bring from five to ten thousand fairness complaints (p. 105). Notably, and perhaps telling for its overall history, only one station ever lost its license because of the fairness doctrine, for broadcasting "one-sided anti-Semitic analyses of public issues" (p. 105), and Pickard (2018) notes that only one person, the conservative Christian broadcaster Carl McIntire, ever lost their license, which was revoked in 1973. Despite the rarity of enforcement, most stations complied as the threat of punitive action nevertheless decreased risk taking in broadcast media (Entman, 1990, p. 105).

Still, the impetus for this regulation was the limited number of licenses available on the radio and later television broadcast bandwidths. Such scarcity required greater regulation of views as it was feared that if one group took over a large amount of bandwidth, only one perspective might be emphasized to the detriment of everyone. The policy was then implemented through various rules enforced by the FRC and later the FCC, including the obligation to provide more than one side of an issue as well as to refrain as an organization from expressing their own opinions on and perspectives about an issue. The 1969 Supreme Court ruling in *Red Lion Broadcasting Co. v. Federal Communications Commission* further cemented the doctrine in American culture, stating that the equal representation of ideas "is the right of the viewers and listeners, not the right of the broadcasters, which is paramount" (*Red Lion Broadcasting Co. v. FCC, 1969*). The decision stipulated that a broadcaster in Pennsylvania must allow airtime for a response from an author attacked during a radio program hosted by the Reverend Billy James Hargis. The result was a tempering of one side's unregulated accusations and the excessive haranguing of an author who previously had no recourse to reply.

Despite the favorable ruling by the Supreme Court, by the 1980s much of the discourse around the fairness doctrine was centered much more on the negative incentives toward the diversity of viewpoints, which led the FCC to eventually conclude that its work had been successful enough to guarantee ongoing and multiple access to varying perspectives (Entman, 1990, p. 106). Indeed, by 1985 the FCC wrote concerning the broadcast market that "the interest of the public in viewpoint diversity is fully served by the multiplicity of voices in the marketplace today" (p. 106). In other words, they believed people would be able to obtain "quality journalism" because the broadcast media market had become a fully competitive market, with scarcity no longer a significant issue as before due to the widespread adoption of advanced mass communication technologies (especially cable news, radio, satellite, etc.). Therefore, it was decided that the public would benefit far more from the deregulation of the fairness doctrine than in its enforcement. However, in retrospect, given the incredibly slanted perspectives found online, the conclusion may have been a bit hasty. Of course, one wonders whether the doctrine would have remained as effective in the face of the current online digital information glut. The next chapter will touch upon the impact that decommissioning the fairness doctrine has had on the overall culture of broadcasting and mass media, especially in right-wing politics.

CONCLUSION: PAST IS PROLOGUE

On a final note, the periods of time examined briefly in this chapter, ranging from the era of yellow journalism to the blurry, anticlimactic end of the fairness doctrine, provide us with a general surface view of the challenges facing information users and consumers. One wonders at times how people found anything of truth, especially during these earlier eras. Yet the main threads running through these topics throughout the nineteenth and twentieth centuries remain steadily traceable through the previous centuries and decades. First and foremost, the tendency for humans to fall for the salacious and the sensational remains with us. The ideas of antisemitism, for example, crawl up through the centuries like termites, passing along not only by word of mouth but also through the spread of lies in nonneutral formats, eating at the foundations of trust and truthfulness. The desires for gossip and other lurid details about people remain of great interest for many people. The sources of information, whether they be newspapers and books or radios and televisions, merely satisfy these demands.

Yet there is also that second thread, the impact of new technologies on unsuspecting people and their societies, that makes old messages and age-old desires for them seem novel and different yet seemingly transparent and therefore ostensibly neutral in their intentions. For as we all know, the medium itself is also its message, and the message is there to perpetuate the medium. Pound's radio broadcasts, for example, not only perpetuate the novelty of the radio itself and reflect the newness and futurism of the Fascist government he was supporting but also make these old antisemitic messages seem ever new and titillating but legitimized through the new medium. It is an essential characteristic to the modernist poetry he created.

Similarly, the yellow journalism became defined, ironically, in terms of the color printing they pioneered, being both empowered yet confined by the images they peddled. The *Gestell*—which is an enframing or positionality— as Heidegger called it in his essay "The Question Concerning Technology," may explain some of this. New technology, in Heidegger's reading, "reveals" or "discloses" to us "the things it comes into contact with" (Stern, 2022).

What this means is that the technology alters the ways in which we can see the world but also cuts us off from seeing things not only as they once were but even as they are now, forcing illusion and confusion upon us. He suggests that "what is to be feared is not technology itself, but rather its mode of disclosing the world," which forces a change in us to accept the power of the new technology.

Yet we must resist these ways in which new technologies alter our ways of seeing the world and the ways in which it becomes a self-perpetuating cycle. The balance brought about in part by the fairness doctrine was merely one limited way to help fight that cycle. But as we will see in the next chapter, much of the internet's false information and fake narratives stem from our inability to move past the medium and the technology, which allows it to prey upon our very concepts of the self and our ability to perceive and conceive of a world separate from it.

REFERENCES

Borchard, G. A. (2019). *A narrative history of the American press*. Routledge.

Campbell, W. J. (2001). *Yellow journalism: Puncturing the myths, defining the legacies*. Praeger.

Campbell, W. J. (2012). Story of the most famous seven words in US journalism. BBC News. https://www.bbc.com/news/world-us-canada-16918787.

Corrigan, R. A. (1972). Ezra Pound and the Italian Ministry for Popular Culture. *Journal of Popular Culture, V*(4), pp. 767–81. https://doi.org/10.1111/j.0022–3840.1972.0504_767.x.

Creelman, J. (1901) *On the great highway: The wanderings and adventures of a special correspondent*. Boston: Lothrop Publishing.

Department of Justice. (2015). Ezra Pound radio broadcasts. *Frequently Requested Records*. https://www.justice.gov/criminal/frequently-requested-records-0.

Entman, R. M. (1990). *Democracy without citizens: Media and the decay of American politics*. Oxford University Press.

Gajda, A. (2009). Judging journalism: The turn toward privacy and judicial regulation of the press. *California Law Review, 97*(4), pp. 1039–1105. https://doi.org/10.15779/Z387M6R.

Kenes, B. (2021). CasaPound Italy: The sui generis Fascists of the new millennium. ECPS organisation profiles. *European Center for Populism Studies* (ECPS). https://doi.org/10.55271/op0010.

McQueen, S. (2018). From yellow journalism to tabloids to clickbait. In D. E. Agosto (ed.), *Information literacy and libraries in the age of fake news*. Denver, CO: Libraries Unlimited.

Morrisson, M. S. (2016). *Modernism, science, and technology*. Bloomsbury Publishing. http://ebookcentral.proquest.com/lib/csun/detail.action?docID=4605643.

Perry, A. (2017). Fairness doctrine. *The First Amendment encyclopedia.* https://www
.mtsu.edu/first-amendment/article/955/fairness-doctrine.

Pickard, V. (2018). The strange life and death of the fairness doctrine: Tracing the decline of positive freedoms in American policy discourse. *International Journal of Communication, 12*, pp. 3434–53. https://repository.upenn.edu/asc_papers/745.

Pound, E. (1934). *ABC of reading.* Yale University Press.

Pound, E. (1974). Vortex. In Jerome Rothenberg (ed.), *Revolution of the Word: A New Gathering of American Avant Garde Poetry, 1914–1945.* Exact Change.

Red Lion Broadcasting Co. v. FCC, 395 U.S. 367 (1969).

Redman, T. (1991). *Ezra Pound and Italian fascism.* Cambridge University Press.

Schwartz, A. B. (2015). The infamous "War of the Worlds" radio broadcast was a magnificent fluke. *Smithsonian Magazine.* https://www.smithsonianmag.com/history/infamous-war-worlds-radio-broadcast-was-magnificent-fluke-180955180/.

Stern, A. (2022). Escaping the algorithms. *Commonweal Magazine.* https://www
.commonwealmagazine.org/artificial-intelligence-AI-social-media-Heidegger.

Surette, L. (1999). *Pound in purgatory: From economic radicalism to anti-semitism.* University of Illinois Press.

Tiffany, D. (1995). *Radio corpse: Imagism and the cryptaesthetic of Ezra Pound.* Harvard University Press.

Topping, S. (2023). The history of the Pulitzer Prizes. *The Pulitzer Prizes.* https://www.pulitzer.org/page/history-pulitzer-prizes.

Warren, S., and Brandeis, L. (1890). The right to privacy. *Harvard Law Review, 193.* https://groups.csail.mit.edu/mac/classes/6.805/articles/privacy/Privacy_brand_warr2.html.

Wood, M. (n.d.). Selling the kid: Commodifying the kid. *The yellow kid on the paper stage.* https://xroads.virginia.edu/~MA04/wood/ykid/commodify.htm.

Chapter 6

Social Media, Online Discourse, and the New "Daily Me"

TRUTHINESS AND WHAT *OUGHT* TO BE

With apologies to Alejandro Jodorowsky's ill-fated *Dune*, *Goncharov* may be the most famous film never made. The film poster for *Goncharov* (easily found with an online search) shows 1970s-era images of Robert DeNiro, Cybill Shepherd, Al Pacino, Harvey Keitel, Gene Hackman, and John Cazale cropped and pasted together in a fairly crude collage to advertise "the greatest mafia movie ever made" by—surprise—the greatest of all mafia movie directors, Martin Scorsese. Though it is also, confusingly, a film by someone named "Matteo JWHJ 0715." Of course, only this kind of hoax could grow and proliferate on the internet so quickly and widely, with online users creating a whole universe of scenes and developing plotlines for the story, partly out of personal enjoyment and partly out of a desire to pretend, tongue-in-cheek, that it is real in order to fool others into believing the fiction (Kircher, 2022). We see in the community discourse among these various online participants the inner workings of how a hoax is born and proliferates online. While most would not believe it, especially if one knows anything about film history or even takes a glance at the poorly matched film stills in the poster, one wonders how much it would take for people to believe it were a real film. One also wonders if others will start developing their own fakes for other "should-be" movies and books (much like summer 2023's *Barbenheimer* mashups of the *Barbie* and *Oppenheimer* films) and what that says about the unfixed nature of the internet and the malleable unreality it reflects back to us.

As noted in previous chapters, medieval forgeries, legends, false narratives, and fake news could each serve the function of both wish fulfillment and moralizing. Hoaxes, too, were used to parody literary forms and genres yet also to criticize the audience's gullibility as well. While previous hoaxes focused on how information was spread, in the case of *Goncharov* the criticism addresses how media hype and the publicity machine distort and trick viewers, especially through the genre of the meme. In that sense, the fake film *Goncharov* speaks to what people think ought to exist, and that the heroes they worship—in this case Hollywood film actors and directors—*should* have created this type of film telling this type of story. Even if they didn't, those fooled by the hoax are skewered for falling for the hype in the first place. It becomes a hall of mirrors reflecting contradictions when trying to suss out the truth from lies. In this case of a fake and a parody, we are left with the near reality of truthiness, a liminal state existing almost paradoxically somewhere between the binary of true and false. The fake rests uncomfortably in between the two as a combination of aesthetic choices, wishful thinking, and social criticism.

While *Goncharov* is a harmless prank created partly in service to a satirical point about filmmaking and marketing, the revision of history and the changing of narratives has more often been the result of abuses of power—especially through propaganda—that serve the purposes of a ruling class. Here, too, the hoax film poster both parodies and mimics the form and container of information. Like Welles's *The War of the Worlds*, which mimicked the characteristics of radio reportage via the radio play, or the Great Moon Hoax of 1830, which mimicked scientific journals via newspaper reportage, it proves a wider point about the manipulative nature of its own medium. These hoaxes show how formats have the power to exploit people's tendency to fall for something based on its outward appearance rather than its actual message. Similarly, the hoax calls attention to the issues raised by the platform itself, which often has very loose regulation of its content. This chapter, then, will examine the how the loosening of such standards in traditional media along with the rise of the new platform, the internet, helped to simultaneously free up creative expression while also unleashing a new era of fabrication.

UNRAVELING FCC STANDARDS AND
THE RISE OF PARTISAN NEWS

In the previous chapter, it was noted how the print era moved in parallel with the radio and television era, though not without some interesting give and take. The newspaper industry—and later the mass media—policed itself in some areas and developed both journalistic standards as well as impacted the legal standards for privacy. The industry also largely followed the fairness doctrine set up by federal regulators in the Federal Radio Commission

(FRC) and later with the Federal Communications Commission (FCC), keeping some of the worst excesses of sensationalist journalism at bay even as the enforcement of the doctrine itself was often never more than a loose and merely symbolic deterrent. As television began to take over in the 1960s, with nearly 90 percent of Americans having access to one (Cortada, 2016, p. 379), the fairness doctrine was nevertheless a guiding and shaping force. Much of this was due to the limited number of broadcast companies and their dominant shares of the market. The three national broadcasting networks—ABC, CBS, and NBC—provided 60 percent of all programming to two hundred affiliate stations across the country (Cortada, 2016). Millions watched the same programs, received the same information, and were subject to much the same balance from the fairness doctrine that each network generally provided (Cortada, 2016). But even these mildly enforced standards began to erode over time, chafing certain partisan movements at the time, and the reputation of their enforcement and efficacy became increasingly exposed as a myth. The dismantling of these standards partly contributed, though certainly never fully caused directly, the wildness of the internet's current excesses, which make the worst of yellow journalism seem somewhat tame in comparison.

As can be seen in figure 6.1, the rise of the current political polarization roughly coincides with the diminishment of the fairness doctrine's influence on the media. While polarization was rampant during the years coinciding

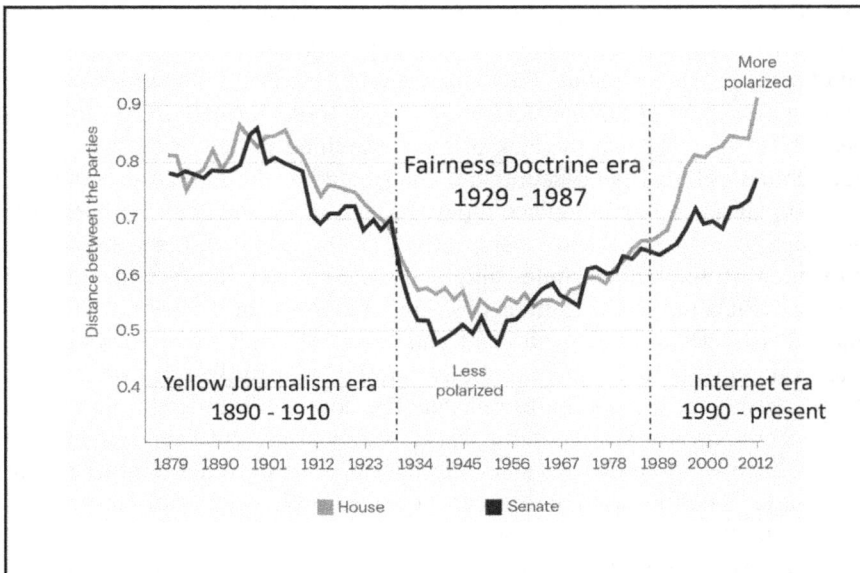

Figure 6.1.   Graph showing the level of political polarization in both the US House of Representatives and the Senate from 1879 to 2012. *Source*: Toner-Rodgers, 2021.

with the era of yellow journalism, according to Toner-Rodgers (2021), the fairness doctrine years show a significant dampening of polarization that remained largely intact for sixty years until around the late 1980s. By 1989, polarization, which already appears to be increasing from its lowest points in the 1960s and 1970s, jumps significantly, leading to the highest level of division in 2012.

But what leads to this resurgence in polarization? Tellingly, the nature of television itself had already begun changing and specializing from the 1970s onward, with the main broadcast networks gaining competition from cable television programming that strove to reach niche audiences in every type of possible subject (Cortada, 2016, pp. 379–80). The development of new media outlets, including cable and satellite television (Zelizer, 2017, p. 182), flew in the face of the fairness doctrine's primary *raison d'être*, which was that a scarcity of licenses for broadcast bandwidth necessitated fair and equal balancing of subject matter. So even before the repeal, changes were already occurring in the way in which mass media were reaching their audiences, slowly proliferating in new avenues and beginning to fragment into the "long tail" of specialized viewership.

Still, the repeal of the doctrine itself ultimately led to more dramatic changes in the media landscape (Pickard, 2018, p. 3444). While change may not have occurred overnight, it took just a few years for unfettered and fully partisan radio and television programming to take hold, ultimately disproving the FCC's assessment in the 1980s that there was sufficient diversity of perspectives and a plethora of outlets for any viewpoint to sustain objectivity and balanced representation. As Pickard finds, "the policy's absence and the rapid ascendance of similar conservative talk radio formats likely are connected," suggesting that the lack of an overarching policy of fairness likely accelerated political polarization and contributed to the limited presentation of information so commonplace today. In fact, while the doctrine itself was designed to ensure that most perspectives are represented, the conservative movement in the United States ultimately came to see it as "fundamentally hostile" (Pickard, 2018) to their positions. Later on, in the later 2000s and early 2010s, despite being dormant and essentially left for dead, the issue was brought back to life in conservative circles to instill fear in listeners that "the liberals" were planning to reinstate the doctrine in order to once again silence conservatives (Eggerton, 2011; Anonymous, 2008). As many are aware, once an issue reaches such a fraught point it becomes another victim of America's culture wars, painted as a convention in need of discarding and used as another bludgeon to attack political opponents.

In the aftermath of dropping the fairness doctrine, talk radio quickly became far more partisan and skewed in perspective, as "broadcasters understood that the regulatory obstacles toward politicized news had been dramatically lowered" and created a "new atmosphere" in the industry (Zelizer, 2017, p. 188). This quickly spread to other media. Print journalism in particular scrambled to keep their share in competition with radio and television (Zelizer, 2017). But it also involved the nascent internet as well. *New York Times* columnist Ezra Klein sums up the transformation quite well within the confines of Republican politics: "First came Rush Limbaugh and his imitators on talk radio, then Fox News (and eventually its imitators and competitors, like OANN), and then the blogs, and then digitally native outlets like Breitbart and the Daily Wire" (Klein, 2023a). Although this progression is somewhat oversimplified, the pattern nevertheless follows a similar unfolding in any range of politics across multiple coexisting platforms, including progressive media outlets, where the decline of standards also led to increasingly partisan perspectives.

Yet just as importantly, the spread of partisan ideas also helps to normalize more extreme and less generally palatable views that once existed much farther outside the mainstream, bringing them closer to the center of what is acceptable discourse. Rush Limbaugh's rise, for example "created a new market for far-out ideas," as Nicole Hemmer, historian at Vanderbilt University, states in her interview with Ezra Klein (Klein, 2023b). These fringe concepts are not isolated, either, in the new media environment. Indeed, concepts are reinforced in the minds of viewers and readers by their appearance on different programs and platforms, including radio and television, feeding into the online discourse about them. While it may seem that the various technologies currently dominating audience attention would compete with each other and fragment these audiences so that they are providing services to provide specialized "long tail" content (see Anderson, 2006), some researchers find that consolidation and overlap are occurring instead. There is in fact "a trend of convergence in the media industry," and "new media now compete with each other while cooperating with the older forms of media" (Wang and Wang, 2020, p. 197). The result is multiple levels of media use where these technologies and the messages they spread are in essence "doubly articulated" (Wang and Wang, 2020), amplifying each other despite being on different or even competing platforms and media.

So it would be a mistake to consider these types of resources primarily as competitors and drivers of audience fragmentation and Balkanization, when in fact they might actually serve to reinforce and complement each other. Wang and Wang (2020), in their study of television and internet use in China, find that audiences fragment and then coalesce again, overlapping with both technologies as media improve and offer new and updated services over time (p. 209). Video clips of broadcast television shows posted online, for example, provide new methods of meeting with their audience, who now have the time to interact among their online communities to comment and share memes, links, and other online content.

Ultimately, the implications of cross-platform interactions driving and amplifying the spread of certain information have yet to be fully explored in wider research but may be an important area to consider in terms of how fake news and false narratives are spread. It is unclear in the long run whether audiences and information consumers will continue to behave in these specific ways, but for now research is finding that audiences and information users are fragmenting and forming narrower circles while also utilizing multiple resources across platforms and media. When one encounters the same message across multiple platforms, it is possible that the likelihood of believing it increases. That is not an issue when the information encountered is factual, but it becomes a major problem if the information proves to be false.

THE GOLDEN AGE OF NEWS PARODY

However, this new age of television, radio, and internet as it morphs into cross-platform integration and content sharing has also developed into a golden age of parody, satire, and hoaxes. As we see in the definition of fake news itself, one of the primary formats and functions is the use of parody and satire in the spread of false information, but often to point out the falseness or to draw attention to something in need of criticism. In the various hoaxes touched upon in this book, ranging from the earliest hoaxes in Herodotus to the print era's elaborate newspaper pranks and Orson Welles's radio play *The War of the Worlds*—and even the recent *Goncharov* hoax—it becomes clear that mimicking the dominant forms, genres, and methods of communication are essential to fooling, as well as delighting, an audience.

Nowhere is the use of parody more apparent than satirical news shows found on television. The overall genre of news parody show has had a surprisingly long run overall and an ever-relevant impact, starting with shows like *That Was the Week That Was* in the 1960s, Weekend Update on *Saturday Night Live* (from 1975 to the present), *Not Necessarily the News* (from 1983 to 1990), *The Daily Show* (from 1996 to the present), and *Colbert Report* (from 2005 to 2014). This is an incomplete list, however, as a large number of comedy sketch shows (that is, *SCTV*) over the years have touched upon the news format with as much regularity as the topic of *Jeopardy!* or other game shows. These five shows, however, greatly overlapped and influenced each other at times, sharing "a degree of crosspollination, encouraging the understanding of individual programs as being in dialogue with previous news parody texts" (Hersey, 2013, p. 4). A number of writers worked for several of these shows, including *That Was the Week*, Weekend Update, and later *Not Necessarily the*

News. Parody host Stephen Colbert was featured on segments of *The Daily Show* before hosting the *Colbert Report* spinoff. Despite differences in time and era, each of these shows in their own way also provide clear road maps to criticizing the ways in which people viewed the world and were informed about it within the contexts of their televisions, many of whom may have been largely unaware of the excesses and absurdities inherent to the television medium itself.

Importantly, by calling out the form itself and drawing audience aware-ness to the potential for falseness to seep into the performative aspects of the medium, the parody ironically provides an outlet for dispensing truth itself. McBeth and Clemons argue that such parody shows "are not only at least as real as the mainstream news, but also that they contribute more to the type of deliberative discourse essential to genuine democracy and public policy" (McBeth and Clemons, 2011, p. 79). Parody often helps audiences become more aware of wider political points, breaking through the types of political bubbles that form around people when they are informationally deprived, or information poor as Chatman might argue. Piercing the bubble through humor and satire has long been a way to alter entrenched viewpoints (Brewer and McKnight, 2020); if you make them laugh, in other words, you can also make them see the truth.

Hersey suggests that parody news shows create "a highly useful supple-ment to traditional news outlets by often rejecting objectivity and examining existing news for illogic and conventionally modern reporting habits that undermine the presumptions of its own objectivity" (Hersey, 2013, p. 36). Again, the emphasis is on showing just how slanted the medium can be, even as it professes to its transparency and truth. What this questioning of a medium's inherent objectivity also does is emphasize the "skeptic's perspec-tive," the one who reflexively—though sometimes not entirely unreasonably either—rejects shared assumptions of fact. Nevertheless, the absurdities cut both ways in news parodies, with the targets hitting not only the readers and audiences who fall unthinkingly for the illusions posed by the media in their infotainment style of reportage but also the extreme and wild conspiracies spun by the most radical of skeptics. Stephen Colbert, for example, gifts us with the word *truthiness*, "a fake word invented by a fake person" (Meyer, 2006) that means "a quality characterizing a 'truth' that a person making an argument or assertion claims to know intuitively 'from the gut' or because it 'feels right' without regard to evidence, logic, intellectual examination, or facts" (Wikipedia contributors, 2023). The humorousness makes the point no less effective. In fact, the truth goes down far more easily this way than if someone were to say it in a serious and sententious tone. What is also important is the context of the delivery of that word, which ultimately made it more effective than if merely stating it as part of a lecture. Colbert, the ultimate clown, points out the absurdity of believing in belief yet undercuts that point by his actions of buffoonery and his transparent jabs at hypocritical self-serving rationales. The skeptic, though, may tell you that truthiness really is the way of the world, that many already state their truths without fact, and that hidden within the parody of news is the truth of news itself: that its conventions and pretensions to objectivity do not hold up under intense scrutiny and ultimately reveal their own unique absurdities and sinister conspiratorial motives.

POLITICS, SOCIAL MEDIA, AND THE MAKE-BELIEVE OF KAYFABE AND "PERFORMATIVE STUPIDITY"

On one hand there are the serious but unintentionally ridiculous stances of skeptics and conspiracy theorists—that is, flat earthers who inadvertently prove the earth is round and gravity-bound by attempting to launch themselves in rockets into the sky—who routinely expose their blind spots and deepest motivations. On the other hand, there are intentionally misleading performative skeptics—the ones who know they are lying yet persist in spreading these lies for their own advantage or to attain a different sort of goal. Such "performative stupidity" is a way of describing an important aspect of the political landscape—the rube who is really a manipulative grifter—that is not dissimilar in practice to the idea of kayfabe.

Taken from professional wrestling, the term "kayfabe" (possibly pig Latin for "fake") was spoken among wrestlers to signify when outsiders are observing and that they should each resume their roles in the act. The term speaks to the performative aspect of their work and the obligations one assumes for the role assigned to them, as all actors do when performing. Kayfabe and its relation to politics has been explored by others—Stodden and Hansen (2016) in particular—but ultimately can be described as a performance, the politics of make-believe, in which politicians, celebrities, influencers, and others—including podcasters, broadcast personalities, and the like—use social media platforms for making overstatements and deliberately transgressive opinions to stoke responses of outrage, anger, and blind emotional support in order to garner attention for themselves. They are "playing the heel" in the parlance of pro wrestling. In this sense, therefore, the purpose of much of the false information spreading online is not so much to spread an idea one whole-heartedly believes in but to spread ideas that make it *seem* like the person believes them. This manipulative aspect veers far more into conning and tricking people for personal gain rather than sincere belief.

WHY FAKE NEWS AND MISINFORMATION PROLIFERATE NOW

So while we can speculate on the causes of much of the spread of fake news and the implications of that spread, another important aspect to consider is the scale of information technology communications systems. Certainly, as seen in the early printing press eras, the spread of ideas began to occur on much larger scales than just word of mouth. More people had access to more information than ever before, and even complained about it! For them, though it seems quaint in comparison to this current Big Data era, information overload was also just as vexing and difficult to manage regardless of whether it was scrolls, codices, or books. Similarly, as radio and television increased their reach, there was further spread of information in much faster and more widespread results (Cortada, 2016, p. 379). Circulation wars during the yellow journalism era concerned tens of thousands of readers, which seems miniscule in comparison to television with Nielsen ratings routinely showing viewership in the millions of people for the most watched programs.

But these earlier figures are ultimately no match for the internet's reach, which is estimated to have over 5.16 billion users who spend at least six hours per day online (Global Digital Insights, 2023). The past thirty-three years have shown a deep shift from an initial two million online users in the early 1990s to the current number reaching nearly two-thirds (64.4 percent) of the entire world's population (Global Digital Insights, 2023). Notably, of those users more than 92 percent of them use social media sites at least monthly (Global Digital Insights). The implications for this widespread use on the spread of all information, both truthful and not, are profound and raise a number of important questions. First, what impact does the new connectivity have on people individually? What impact does it have on their immediate families? Their wider circle of friends? Their communities and nations? The impact may not scale uniformly, and so for the purposes of this study, it will examine the impact on the individual and social media, but with an eye to these wider possible impacts.

SOCIAL MEDIA AND "THE DAILY ME": POLARIZATION AND EXTREMIST POSITIONING

An increasing amount of people operating online is bound to change the tenor of human interactions and have a large impact upon wider regional, national, and international cultures, resulting in not only new understandings of others but also new conflicts and greater anxieties. Cass Sunstein suggests that the way in which people interact online gradually becomes narrowed over time and that social media provides clear comfort to users, "a comfortable anonymity," as he describes it, allowing them to become whomever they desire to be (Ogasawara, 2019, p. 61). As a result, members of online groups begin to frequent the places where they are more likely to meet like-minded people who accept their new self-image and believe they know as well as anyone else. The result is a "a communications package that is personally designed, with each component fully chosen in advance," which Sunstein calls "The Daily Me" (Ogasawara, 2019).

One's personal identity is essentially reconstituted, like adding water to a powdered soup mix, each time the person enters into the platform, assuming similar views and ideas, many of which can become more and more extreme over time. The downside of this recurring self-identification is the loss of encountering new information that might contradict their views, leading to people adhering to belief and refusing to change erroneous, hateful, or aggressive ideas. It can lead to social fragmentation and disillusion in shared governance and democratic ideals. Ogasawara traces this devolution of democratic ideals in Japanese social media, where she has found that the rise of extremism online contributed to the real-world rise of right-wing politicians like the late Shinzo Abe and his party's antidemocratic policies. She notes that Abe's Liberal Democratic Party (LDP) "shifted from conservative to ultraright, distinguishing itself from the majority right-of-centre Democratic Party" (p. 60). The LDP essentially pandered to the ultra right wing by simultaneously expanding into the internet and denigrating the more traditional mass media, with their ultimate goal of nullifying Article 9 of the Japanese constitution, which enshrines the nation's current pacifist policies and its statement on the renunciation of war (Ogasawara, 2019).

If this were an isolated incident, it might merely be a curiosity for those with keen interest in the byzantine workings of postwar Japanese politics. But the rise of extremism in a similar time frame across many countries with extreme regional and cultural differences nevertheless persists, including right-wing extremism in Canada (Crosby, 2021), numerous countries across Europe (Ugarte, 2018), Israel, Brazil, and, of course, the authoritarian regime in Russia. The overall increase in extremism finds its way into the voting population, with far-right parties now challenging more moderate democracies like those in France, Finland, and even Germany. Ugarte notes that these extremist parties have achieved their highest levels of success for elections to the European Parliament, further destabilizing the region and its fragile peace, especially in light of Russia's February 2022 invasion of Ukraine. Notably, it mirrors a similar rise in right-wing extremist groups in the United States, including the Proud Boys, Stop the Steal, and QAnon. The next section will look specifically at the role that the internet may have played in the January 6 insurrection.

JANUARY 6, 2021, AND SOCIAL MEDIA EXTREMISM: "EVERYTHING IS AN AGON"

The insurrection that took place in Washington, DC, on January 6, 2021 remains a singular and unique event in American history. At no other time, save during the Civil War, was the peaceful transfer of political power and the ideals of democracy so thoroughly and vilely trashed by its own citizens. Whether the perpetrators felt they were justified or not, the causes of it are complex and varied, some of which it is still too early to corroborate all the facts for—especially, in the absence of a trial or even an indictment as of writing this, the ultimate culpability of the former President Trump and the extent of his involvement in planning the insurrection.

It remains to be seen whether he will be held responsible for his actions or whether his role in it can even be completely revealed and documented. However, the main issues remain clear. Political violence was instigated by former President Donald Trump based on a combination of his lies about the integrity of the election itself, which stoked supporters' anger; the behind-the-scenes planning by at least many members of his circle, if not him, to circumvent the constitution by pressuring Vice President Pence to select "alternative" electors; the actions taken to find ways to circumvent the election results; and the role that online social media played in spreading false information related to Stop the Steal and similar antidemocracy sentiment. Candidate Trump in 2015–2016 and the administration itself from 2017 onward laid the groundwork for the antiestablishment mood by instilling deep distrust in mainstream news outlets and by constructing a worldview in which "everything is an agon" (Menand, 2023), a black-and-white, zero-sum struggle for supremacy in which anything goes, including fabricating the truth and justifying violence to uphold that fabrication.

In the notes circulated among the January 6 committee members, titled *Social Media & the January 6th Attack on the US Capitol Summary of Investigative Findings*, some of the findings mirror those observed by Ogasawara, Ugarte, and others. The authors of the report write, "While social media platforms may contribute to polarization generally, January 6th was driven by the radicalization of a smaller subset of users. On Facebook, Stop the Steal content, like QAnon and militia content, is associated with a relatively small, homogenous group of users" (*Social media*, 2023, p. 117). Such users, though a minority of like-minded individuals similar to online Japanese right-wingers, converged and plotted ways to protest the election results both peacefully and, ultimately, violently (*Social media*, 2023).

Yet the implication, too, is that the failure to stop the violence was in part due to the fact that these social media companies and their platforms "were exploited in tandem" by the protesters, which then "enabled the mobilization of extremists on smaller sites" (*Social media*, 2023, p. 6). The combination of major platforms and smaller websites that may have held fewer numbers but more extreme users resulted in a more widespread call to action against the election results. At the same time, the platforms themselves, including Twitter/X, did not listen to their own employees, who had been warning that the rhetoric of violence was escalating yet "bent their rules to avoid penalizing conservatives . . . out of fear of reprisals" (Zakrewski et al., 2023). The inaction on the part of the platforms themselves to curb the rising antidemocratic rhetoric contributed to the political violence that spilled over into the real world, as protesters marched along Pennsylvania, Constitution, and Madison Avenues and then forcefully broke into the United States Capitol building. It is incredibly disconcerting that the root causes of political violence still remain unexamined and underregulated.

The overall deference given to the former president as a company policy at Twitter/X was one of the reasons for the failure to prevent the violence. According to reported testimony, even though Trump was but one of hundreds of millions of accounts on the Twitter platform, his was the only one not allowed to be reviewed by mid-ranking site administrators (Zakrewski et al., 2023). The software used to monitor account activity, "which allowed moderators to establish a history and share notes about an account's past tweets and behaviors," was subsequently blocked from their use (Zakrewski et al., 2023). As a result, those who might normally have seen and reported violent rhetoric contained in Stop the Steal–related tweets were unable to see the full extent of the negative impact. Ultimately, though, it is the combination of various factors that led to the violence on January 6, 2021. Social media platforms were being used for these violent ends even as they were unable or unwilling to curb such behavior.

However, former President Trump, who was removed by Twitter and then Facebook in 2021, days after the insurrection, has since been reinstated on both Twitter (November 19, 2022) and Facebook (early 2023). His reinstatement is indicative of how social media platforms still fail to hold themselves accountable for their role in the insurrection. The lack of self-reflection from these tech companies is astounding, but not nearly as bad as the lack of accountability from the public and the government that is supposed to represent everyone's best interests.

WHERE IT GOES FROM HERE

Running parallel to the development of mass media and information technologies as well as their gradual loosening and abandonment of fairness and balance principles is the impact that these technologies have had upon the sense of privacy that grew out of the reforms of the yellow journalism era. The power that IT companies now possess has become even greater through the use of various nudging and tweaking techniques utilized in online platforms. They keep users coming back for more even as these companies track behaviors and use that data for their own advantage. The rise of surveillance with the use of online social media data tracking technologies should not be a surprise. The internet makes it easy to keep tabs on what people are writing and thinking; webcam and built-in microphone technologies are also making it easier to see exactly what they are doing and hear exactly what they are saying. The conflation of these issues raises the stakes significantly, and one would be remiss to also forget that with the rise of all these technologies, the change in human behavior is an important factor to observe.

If these last several chapters have shown anything, it is that information technology impacts people in similar ways even if the size, speed, and scope have changed. The technology merely amplifies the behaviors that users already exhibit or keep repressed. In some ways it is incredibly difficult to keep truth fixed and reality immutable when it is in human nature to prefer meaningful—if not true—narratives. If these narratives sometimes turn out to be false, we tell ourselves that they really ought to be true: like life on Mars, yellow journalists starting wars, or the divinity of Alexander the Great. It is also difficult to avoid falling for the tricks of hoaxes when we want to believe them, especially when we place so much stock in the container the message comes in. In the past, a message was usually coming directly from another person, who we could judge as trustworthy or not based on our past interactions with them. We may not have moved past that original behavior, even if the conveyer of the message is now paper, radio waves, or electronic pulses sent through fiberoptic wire.

REFERENCES

Anderson, C. (2006). *The long tail: Why the future of business is selling less of more.* Hachette Books.

Anonymous. (2008). Editorial: Fairness doctrine much ado about nothing. *Knight-Ridder/Tribune Business News.*

Brewer, Paul R., and McKnight, J. (2020). How satire helps science: Climate change, gene editing, and vaccine use aren't laughing matters—but joking about them can change minds. *National Geographic, 237*(6), p. 19.

Cortada, J. W. (2016). *All the facts: A history of information in the United States since 1870*. Oxford University Press.

Crosby, A. (2021). Policing right-wing extremism in Canada: Threat frames, ideological motivation, and societal implications. *Surveillance & Society, 19*(3), pp. 359–63. https://doi.org/10.24908/ss.v19i3.15007.

Eggerton, J. (2011). GOP dredges up fairness doctrine. *Broadcasting & Cable, 141*(10), p. 12.

Global Digital Insights. (2023). Digital around the world. *DataReportal*. https://datareportal.com/global-digital-overview.

Hersey, C. (2013). *Nothing but the truthiness: A history of television news parody and its entry into the journalistic field*. ProQuest Dissertations Publishing, 2013.

Kircher, M. M. (2022). The fake Scorsese film you haven't seen. Or have you? *New York Times*. https://www.nytimes.com/2022/11/22/style/goncharov-scorsese-tumblr.html.

Klein, E. (2023a). Three reasons the Republican Party keeps coming apart at the seams. *New York Times*. https://www.nytimes.com/2023/01/15/opinion/mccarthy-republicans-coming-apart.html.

Klein, E. (2023b). Transcript: Ezra Klein interviews Nicole Hemmer. The Ezra Klein Show. *New York Times*. https://www.nytimes.com/2023/01/20/podcasts/transcript-ezra-klein-interviews-nicole-hemmer.html.

McBeth, M. K., and Clemons, R. S. (2011). Is fake news the real news? The significance of Stewart and Colbert for Democratic discourse, politics, and policy. In A. Amarasingam (ed.), *The Stewart/Colbert effect: Essays on the real impacts of fake news*. McFarland & Company, Incorporated Publishers.

Menand, L. (2023). When Americans lost faith in the news. *The New Yorker*. https://www.newyorker.com/magazine/2023/02/06/when-americans-lost-faith-in-the-news?utm_source=pocket-newtab.

Meyer, D. (2006). The truth of truthiness. *CBS News*. Wayback Machine. https://web.archive.org/web/20131116045748/http://www.cbsnews.com/stories/2006/12/12/opinion/meyer/main2250923.shtml.

Ogasawara, M. (2019). The daily us (vs. them) from online to offline: Japan's media manipulation and cultural transcoding of collective memories. *Journal of Contemporary Eastern Asia, 18*(2), pp. 49–67. https://doi.org/10.17477/jcea.2019.18.2.049.

Pickard, V. (2018). The strange life and death of the fairness doctrine: Tracing the decline of positive freedoms in American policy discourse. *International Journal of Communication, 12*, pp. 3434–53. https://repository.upenn.edu/asc_papers/745.

Social media & the January 6th attack on the U.S. Capitol summary of investigative findings. (2023). *Washington Post*. https://www.washingtonpost.com/documents/5bfed332-d350-47c0-8562-0137a4435c68.pdf?itid=lk_inline_manual_3.

Stodden, W. P., and Hansen, J. S. (2016). Politics by Kayfabe: Professional wrestling and the creation of public opinion. http://static1.1.sqspcdn.com/static/f/332308

/26781726/1452481855523/wrestfin.pdf?token=rq1phFIu3%2Bd2hD1Qnz%2BvGVl47wU%3D.

Sunstein, C. (2001). *Republic.com.* Princeton, NJ: Princeton University Press.

Toner-Rodgers, A. (2021). *The shape of polarization: A topological data analysis of congressional voting patterns.* https://bookdown.org/atonerro/topology-polarization/.

Ugarte, B. A. (2018). The far right in western Europe: From the margins to the mainstream and back? *Cuadernos Europeos de Deusto, 59*, pp. 75–97. https://doi.org/10.18543/ced-59–2018pp75–97.

Wang, P., and Wang, X. (2020). The evolving audience network during media environment transition: A longitudinal study of cross-platform use in China. *Journal of Broadcasting & Electronic Media, 64*(2), pp. 193–214. https://doi.org/10.1080/08838151.2020.1762024.

Wikipedia contributors. (2023). Truthiness. Wikipedia, The Free Encyclopedia. https://en.wikipedia.org/w/index.php?title=Truthiness&oldid=1145747644.

Zakrewski, C., Lima, C., and Harwell, D. (2023). What the Jan. 6 probe found out about social media, but didn't report. *Washington Post.* https://www.washingtonpost.com/technology/2023/01/17/jan6-committee-report-social-media/.

Zelizer, J. E. (2017). How Washington helped create the contemporary media: Ending the fairness doctrine in 1987. In B. J. Schulman and J. Zelizer (eds.), *Media nation: The political history of news in modern America.* University of Pennsylvania Press. https://doi.org/10.9783/9780812293746.

PART III

Fake News

A Model for the Modern, Internet-Driven Phenomenon

Chapter 7

Overview of a New
Fake News Model

In the previous sections of this book, much was discussed about the wide-ranging areas that comprise the fertile ground that grows and fosters false information and fake news. Part I focused on the limitations of the human mind, the problems people face when attempting to make new usable knowledge from the information they find. Part II focused on the way that the patterns of information use and interaction mingle with human behavior across the centuries, ranging from the very beginnings of written information to the current digital information glut. All throughout this long history, patterns emerge and events rhyme, seemingly repeating in uncannily similar ways, and often following a predictable reaction whenever a new technology is introduced to a population. Of course, the technologies only change people in ways that they were already predisposed toward changing.

Part III, however, emerges from these previous discussions as a way to elucidate the ways in which the current internet-driven phenomenon of fake news spreads through our technologies. This section will delve into the construction and the meaning behind a new model for understanding and examining fake news this author designed with research partners Ahmed Alwan and Eric Garcia to describe and help understand the bundle of phenomena and information behaviors contributing to fake news. Chapter 7 specifically outlines the general overview of the model, providing the research context and definitions of fake news the model stands in contrast to. The eighth and ninth chapters will each focus on specific parts of the model, focusing first on the actors of the fake news model who create the content and second on the consumers and users of false content.

THEORIES AND DEFINITIONS OF FAKE NEWS

Before jumping right in, it is necessary to discuss briefly the need and importance of creating theoretical models. A model has been defined as a "descriptive . . . summary of a research area that joins the findings from a research study to the conceptual framework" (Cole, 2013, p. 3) and can be used to help to predict events, behaviors, or outcomes. Often the model is seen as an "interim tool or stage" within a less well-established discipline or avenue of inquiry (Cole, 2013). In this case, the fake news model is employed within the context of a research project initially completed but with further inquiry intended. Models in the library and information science field do not always suggest hypotheses to be tested, making them occasionally less valuable than those with specific queries to be tested. Nevertheless, creating a model has been an important step in the development of newer theories in information science research. In the case of Weiss et al.'s (2020) new definition for fake news, a central conception of information flow between two groups is assumed, but it is difficult to fully realize this vision without taking the idea a step further. As a result, Weiss et al. subsequently developed their own model in 2021 to help demonstrate various theories and actions taken that inform and define the concept of fake news. The result is a better visualization to help predict future behaviors for both creators and users of fake news.

The first half of this book has rather purposefully danced around the subject of fake news in some ways, refusing to fully get to defining it until now. The choice was made instead to examine the ways in which fake news and misinformation have proliferated as well as how they might have originated in historical precedents and previous methods of communication and how they manifest now in their various forms. The explorations the book has taken reviewed a long history of fake news that intertwines with the important psychological aspects of dealing with information itself. The centuries of false stories intertwine with the need for narratives that uplift and provide morals, yet the dark sides of these false stories result in abuses of power and the control of people.

FAKE NEWS DEFINED

Yet questions about fake news and misinformation have remained unanswered so far despite the deep and considered look. Are there skills people can develop along with these technologies to help them deal with the problems of false narrative and fake news? Will identifying the characteristics of fake news throughout history amount to much in terms of a definitive method of curtailing it? One wonders what can be done to better identify the complex bundle of forms and rules, each culturally derived, and personal motivations that ultimately create this rather strange phenomenon of fake news. The questions raised are a tangle and their answers difficult to extract. Herein, it is tempting to state—facetiously, of course—Dante's warning to those about to enter the gates of hell, "Lasciate ogne speranza, voi ch'intrate" ("Abandon all hope, ye who enter here"), as the book begins to delve into the complex issue of sorting fact from fiction in a world that has often decided it greatly prefers its fictions.

This section will examine fake news from a number of perspectives, starting with its expression as a genre and a description of many of its formal elements. Aïmeur et al. (2023) have found throughout the fake news research literature that there are "two major categories of fake news," each tending to remain separate and exclusive (see figure 7.1). The first category describes the *formal aspects* of the genre, the "content" basis for fake news definitions, including such things as text and multimedia that comprise the container of the information, broken further into image, video, and audio formats; text takes the form of headlines, sources, hyperlinks, and bodies of text, such as a blog. The second category describes the *intent* behind fake news, the reason for its spread, and the formats in which this might manifest. This is seen in terms of subgenres like clickbait, rumors and propaganda, hoaxes and satire, and conspiracy theories.

As suggested in Aïmeur et al.'s research, however, many of the approaches and studies taken by those investigating fake news focus on one or the other approach but generally do not incorporate both. If they do discuss both categories, they invariably blend intention and content together. The model proposed in this book, in contrast, suggests that both are essential for

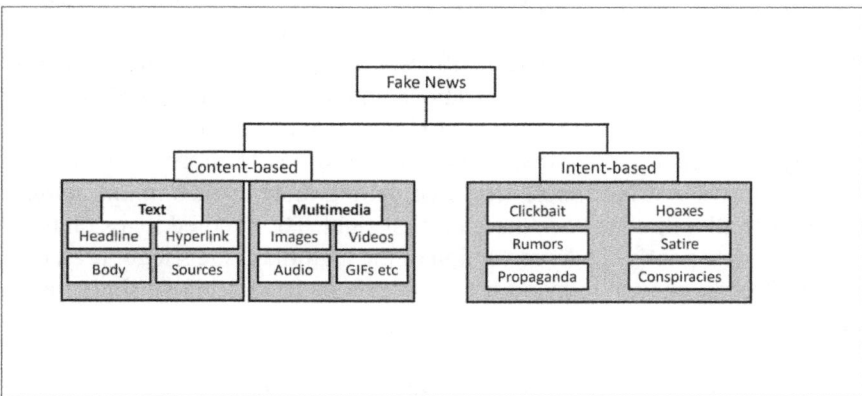

Figure 7.1.   A tree differentiating the various intent- and content-based approaches to understanding and classifying fake news. *Source*: Aïmeur et al., 2023.

understanding fake news. In other words, the content as well as the intention are equally important and can come to influence each other at times. The new model takes formal and intentional aspects of fake news a step further and focuses not only on the content that is consumed by the user or the intent that is suggested from the creator but also on the two-sided information exchange and interaction occurring between both users and creators. But before this is examined in detail, a look at each of these two broad approaches to understanding and classifying fake news is warranted.

THE FORMALIST APPROACH TO
DEFINING FAKE NEWS

Generally speaking, one of the simplest ways to describe fake news is to take it by its literal formal description, including its mimetic use of text and multimedia. In one notable definition, Golbeck et al. (2018) assert that fake news is "information, presented as a news story that is factually incorrect and designed to deceive" (p. 19); similarly, Brennen (2017) writes, "Fake news is made-up news, manipulated to look like credible journalistic reports that are designed to deceive us" (p. 180). On the surface of things, this seems to provide the easiest way to describe the phenomenon. It touches upon the fact that the fake news story is often nothing but a simple hoax with fraudulent ideas wrapped up in the trappings of legitimacy. Indeed, as we saw through the past few chapters, the hoax itself provides us with a distinct window into how people in the past came to trust the containers of the information more so than the messages themselves. The attempt at fooling an audience through mimicking form is a vital part of the genre.

One of the best examples of false stories dressed up as news occurs on sites that purposefully create URLs and logos similar to famous news outlets. ABCnews.com.co, for example, CBSnews.com.co, or washingtonpost.com. co, each take famous news organizations and spoof both their websites and their logos. Their logos are designed to intentionally deceive people who are not paying close attention to what they are viewing. The formal qualities of the container are at best poorly imitated, letting most readers in on the ruse, though not all will disbelieve these on first sight. The spoofed logos on these sites provide a poorly rendered version of the legitimate site's logo, presented just differently enough to avoid the network's trademark but so similar as to be potentially mistaken by inattentive readers.

Similarly, the story itself is presented in the same manner as many internet newspapers, even paired with an image meant to draw the eye, as well as date information and bylines similar to standard newspaper article formatting. The title "New McDonald's in Scottsdale Run Entirely by Robots"

(Jones, 2016) is intended to draw in curious readers, while the treatment of the topic focuses on the fear of losing jobs that people might harbor as a result of automation. In a mix of anger and helplessness, various people of different backgrounds are interviewed for their reactions to the prospect of a fully automated restaurant. While those reactions may be realistic, the basic premise—all the workers will be replaced with robots soon—turns out to be entirely overstated. In this regard, Golbeck et al.'s characterization of fake news as a formalized false story absolutely applies. Tellingly, the interviews seem to have been conducted by other news sources and then merely copied and inserted into the article, further exposing the work as illegitimate and untrustworthy. It is a clear example—and there are thousands of them—of how the formal elements of the news story comes to define fake news and how the container of the information lends as much credence to belief as the content. In other words, it is a news story in name only peddling false ideas purported to be real.

However, as one can see from this simplified definition of fake news, even when attempting to explain the phenomenon formally, some key elements are missing. The ultimate goal of fake news is interpreted far too narrowly when seen as merely the desire to perpetuate a hoax or promote a false idea in order to fool someone. There are issues of both intent and motivation inherent to all types of communication to consider. In this case, despite showing the conventions of a "real" news story, the intention to deceive and the ultimate goals for that deception undercut the overall meaning of the news story, forcing us to reconsider the way that meaning is created.

FAKE NEWS AS AN INTENTION

Fake news is more complex than the sum of its formal parts and resulting narrow deceptions. Others review fake news from a large array of lenses that include less formal description and more examination of the underlying and deeper intentions that drive the spread of false information. These intentions range from the desire to share a rumor that might or might not be true to satirizing the foibles of a shameless celebrity or politician. Importantly, defining fake news in this manner helps to explore the motives and meaning behind the act of creating and sharing it in the first place and may help to curb its root causes. These definitions of fake news take the form into account, certainly, but also fold in the rationales and motives for creating and sharing it.

FAKE NEWS AS PROPAGANDA/DISINFORMATION

Fake news is often viewed as a method of propaganda, which is the attempt to persuade opinions and guide action for political gain. Part II of this book documented in detail how propaganda and its tools have existed for millennia, starting with early civilizations (Taylor, 2003) and extending throughout written history, harnessing narratives to burnish images or bolster positions of established power. In a more recent era, Hintz (1940), writes that "Propaganda seeks to present part of the facts, to distort their relations, and to prove conclusions which could not be drawn from a complete and candid survey of all the facts" (p. 171). The intentions, then, are to confuse and distort, while also promoting a specific viewpoint for political considerations, which is not dissimilar from many contemporary conceptions of fake news. This is also where propaganda bleeds into disinformation, defined as a willful distortion of factual information to promote a specific end result or to sow confusion about a perceived counterviewpoint. Importantly, as Hintz (1940) points out so clearly and presciently in his writing, there is a clear distinction between education and propaganda, suggesting that there are effective approaches to neutralizing the effects of distortion of truth through learning.

However, to focus on fake news as merely an offshoot of propaganda is to overstate the case somewhat, as the term is mainly associated nowadays with war and wartime efforts at changing the hearts and minds of people at home and abroad. Sometimes propaganda is seen as a necessary evil or a means to an end that is justified by successful results. From a distance, it is easy to see the intent behind typical propaganda posters of the time. We see just how mistaken (especially racist and xenophobic wartime fearmongering) or prescient (that is, use of masks during the influenza pandemic of 1918) they really were in hindsight. The proliferation of fake news straddles both the concept of information wars and the general politicization of language and fact. In this sense, then, propaganda can only partially explain the overall phenomenon of fake news, especially as the intentions of fake news also exist far beyond the scope of stirring up confusions for political advantage.

What has changed significantly is not just the message or the motivations for distorting the message but the *medium* across which it is transmitted. In the past, propaganda was often distributed in the form of physical objects and ephemera such as pamphlets, broadsides, and posters, as Brian Schafer for the Alliance for Securing Democracy demonstrates in summary to the Alliance's yearlong observation of Russian disinformation campaigns. However, the internet is lightning quick in comparison to traditional print and television media, which can take days instead of years to circulate false stories (Schafer,

2018). The near-instant spread of false information makes it significantly more difficult to counter and contain without an equally instant response.

FAKE NEWS AS RUMOR, MISINFORMATION, AND CONSPIRACY THEORY

False information also spreads as a result of exploiting the known problems of human communication, cognition, and learning, including taking errors as fact, rumors, logical mistakes, and poor reasoning. And so while disinformation and propaganda are often seen as the willful distortion and misconstruing of facts for the sake of political or physical gain, misinformation and rumor are better seen as the unintentional errors that arise out of mistaken reasoning. This type of misguided failure to fact-check also might fall under the rubric of fake news. Someone may really believe that the earth is flat and be inspired to create a video or write an article that emphasizes this falsehood, which might be considered truthful to some. The hope for most educators is that once apprised of facts, the person changes their mind.

Yet even in cases where a conspiracy theory can be easily debunked with factual information, people nonetheless persist in believing the conspiracy. Some of this is partisan-based signaling, so-called calling cards used to distinguish between copartisans and nonpartisans on any particular issue (Smallpage et al., 2017). The extremity of these beliefs is meant to be seen as performative expressions that allow entry into an extreme club of like-minded attitudes regardless of their sincerity. The further from reality, though, the more outlandish the beliefs become. Additionally, some of the belief stems from the mistrust of power held by organizations and leads to the paranoia of extreme radical skepticism (Kramer, 1999). In this regard, conspiracy theories reveal more about the believers than the actual beliefs themselves, betraying their discomfort with who holds power over them and their discomfort with their own perceived powerlessness. Of course, a healthy understanding of reality is based on a sliding scale of how close one hews to actual fact-based reasoning. But like the problem of conflating fake news with propaganda, it would be a mistake to merely judge fake news by its function as a vehicle for unwittingly spreading false information or emotion-based opinions.

FAKE NEWS AS PARODY, SATIRE, AND POLITICAL KAYFABE

Fake news is often situated clearly within the wider phenomenon of joke and hoax news stories that imitate the form of legitimate news to fool readers.

But the intentions behind and motivations for these hoaxes and jokes vary widely. Parody in literature, for example, ridicules genre and literary conventions for the sake of gentler and more loving criticism, while satire mimics the source material in order to shine a harsher light on human behaviors. Weekend Update on *Saturday Night Live* conflates parody and satire by imitating television news conventions while also providing within this framework commentary and jokes about popular issues and public figures, both politicians and celebrities. Yet despite the trappings of the news show genre that it accurately parodies, down to the way the hosts deliver their lines and tell their stories, no one accuses *SNL* of attempting to spread fake news through the show. The notoriety of the show, for one, prevents people from taking it as a serious vehicle for delivering truthful information. Additionally, the overstated approach, outlandish punchlines, and recurring cast of satiric characters similarly provide viewers with the cues to realize that they are telling jokes.

Golbeck et al. (2018) rightfully point out that people do regularly confuse satire with fake news, often failing to see the context or understand the joke itself. This has happened with some online parody sites like *The Onion*, which uses a generally understated visual approach and subtle satire in its news stories. These have sometimes taken in well-known people and organizations, including but not limited to the Chinese newspaper *People's Daily*, Republican congressman John Fleming (LA), Fox News, and many others (Taylor, 2015; Roberson, 2022). Regardless of the content, however, the key predictor for fooling the reader stems from a failure to understand the context with a nuanced perspective. Many of those fooled by *The Onion* did not know it was a renowned satirical site, especially those based in other countries and non-English-speaking cultures. Some "jump the gun," as it were, finding fault in the story while failing to realize the implausibility of a stance. The blurred lines between reality and joke account for some of the confusion as well. Because satire and false news stories similarly copy and mimic legitimate source material, models, genres, and conventions, being able to distinguish between a joke story and a deliberately misleading false narrative requires discerning the intentions of the creators as much as understanding the format.

Similarly, fake news is more than merely a result of mistaken contexts and misunderstood jokes wrapped in the ersatz trappings of the news show genre. As mentioned in chapter 6, Stodden and Hansen suggest that politics is suffused with performative aspects of stagecraft akin to professional wrestling. They suggest that politics runs on theatrical conventions where "the accepted substitution of reality and willing suspension of belief . . . allow fans to buy into . . . fictionalized storylines" (2016, p. 1). The ultimate goal of the make-believe, or kayfabe, inherent to political discourse and its rituals is catharsis, leading many toward a convenient and accepted chance to vent frustrations about political enemies and to exult in their defeat. In the case with Donald Trump, his incessant lying and overall personal inconsistency are beside the point for his followers. It is, instead, his vanquishing of political enemies that matters far more than the truthfulness and veracity of his statements.

This fact of willful deception therefore leads us to some uncomfortable truths about fake news and false information. The receivers of falsified information *do not always see themselves as fooled victims* and neither should we assume that they are. The user of false information in these situations may know that they are being lied to and can be okay with it. In exchange for support, the resulting feeling that their leader's lies bring to them—fulfillment, catharsis, victory—matters far more than legitimacy, sincerity, or a grounding in reality. The ritual and the spectacle of political theater and the feelings they impart are what matter more.

A TECHNOLOGY OF SELF-PERPETUATION

Finally, as we review the intentions of fake news, we have to realize the issues of falseness and verifiability come embedded within the media themselves. As mentioned in previous sections in this book, the medium or container through which information is carried and conveyed to others is often most concerned with perpetuating itself as the best method in order to guarantee its survival. The old adage "the medium is the message" becomes more than a clichéd and overused expression. It is inherent in some of the false information that is perpetuated to prop up the medium itself. We have to consider that fake news is often a product of its own vessel conveying it. At the same time, that vessel also cuts and narrows the scope of the information as well, limiting contexts and hiding what might exist outside the frame, whether intentionally or unintentionally, impacting how viewers and consumers might interpret and understand the information they have encountered.

This is no more apparent than in the revelations about how Fox News in 2020, immediately after calling the presidential race for the Democrat candidate Joe Biden, began to spread lies about election fraud at the behest of Donald J. Trump—even while admitting to each other that it was false. There was, according to reportage in the *Washington Post* about the ongoing defamation suit filed by Dominion Voting Systems, "a frantic scramble as Fox tried to woo back its large conservative audience after ratings collapsed in the wake of Mr. Trump's loss" (Peters and Robertson, 2023). Fox News subsequently perpetuated false narratives and fake news in order to prevent a decline in their television ratings, which would result in damaging losses of revenues for their business model. Fake news was essentially encouraged and perpetuated through the trappings of the news broadcast by the company's desire to protect itself and its advertising revenues.

This reveals two important truths. First, facts, narrative, and information are all influenced by the containers they come in. The delivery system for the information is shaped by those who create and package the medium itself. In this case, the desire to keep viewers led them to allegedly perpetuate false narratives about a stolen election. Second, the hoaxes and parody news stories that people often fall for, despite the clues indicating their truth, are successful because they exploit one simple human truth: people often believe that the medium for a message is neutral even when it really is not. The failure to take the intrusiveness and the distortions created by the medium itself accounts for just how easy it is to fool readers and viewers so long as genre conventions are met and copied with reasonable accuracy. Once a bad actor masters the format of a medium, it can hide its intentions to fool or to shape opinion fairly easily.

A NEW DEFINITION OF FAKE NEWS: TWO SIDES OPERATE TOGETHER

The conflation of format with its level of trustworthiness brings us to the point where we must consider a new approach to defining fake news. It is not merely the form and the content but also the motives and intentions that are equally important in the concept of fake news. As shown previously, the model of "purposefully deceived reader" misses the complex tapestry of motives for creating fake news as well as the sophisticated array of audience reactions to it. As a result, it does not account for wider environmental factors and conditions that might facilitate its spread or increase its overall impact. The omission of satirical content from the concept of fake news ignores the different motivations and intentions, some of which are actually beneficial to a society, not negative. Satire and parody do not exist only to fool or trick someone, even if they often exaggerate and spell out mistruths. Instead they misstate facts in order to advocate *for* the truth. The simplest definition of fake news does not account for all the variations in motive for creating it in the first place, nor does it consider how motivation also colors its meaning overall. Indeed, this dance of information exchange requires two sides to *delegitimize* information.

THE NEED TO SEE TWO SIDES OF THE COIN

In order to accommodate the complexity, the multiple variables, and the motivations that comprise the spread and use of fake news, a new definition is proposed in which two sides are seen as essential in order to observe a full accounting of the phenomenon. To delegitimize information, both sides must in some ways agree with a falsehood, or at least agree on the reason for creating the falsehood in the first place, for it to be effectively spread. It is in this vein that Weiss et al. (2020) first proposed that fake news needs to be seen less from the perspectives of either content and form or intent and motive *but as an intertwined relationship* with moving targets and changeable purposes. A "phenomenon," in other words, "of information exchange between an actor and acted upon that primarily attempts to invalidate generally-accepted conceptions of truth for the purpose of altering established power structures" (Weiss et al., 2020). As seen in figure 7.2, the information exchange occurs between the willful agent, or "actor," and the one who consumes the information, the "acted upon."

A CENTRAL PREMISE OF FAKE NEWS

What is central to this vision of fake news is that the exchange of information between the actor and acted upon is used to alter shared values of truth. These changes can either bolster and reinforce the truth—as in the case of satire and parody—or can destabilize it in the case of disinformation and conspiracy theories. The information exchange that delegitimizes information is not solely a malicious activity tripping up the uncalculated ignorance of unwitting readers, it is also intertwined with tangible and intangible motives on

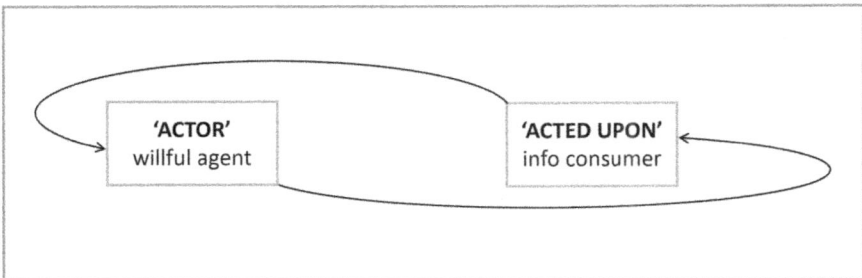

Figure 7.2. Diagram showing the basic interrelationship of information flow for the actor, who serves as agent for creating fake news, and the acted upon, who consume the information. *Source*: Weiss et al., 2021. (License: Attribution-ShareAlike 4.0 International [CC BY-SA 4.0].)

both sides of the relationship, which results in trade-offs as each side interacts and even negotiates meaning with the other.

Outcomes from spreading and consuming fake news serve a specific purpose for information consumers and may even provide desired outcomes, however arbitrary or cynical they may prove to be. This definition allows that consumers and sharers of fake news are not always fooled. They may use fake news for specific purposes that are calculated and rational, even if they run counter to trust and cooperation essential for a civil society to function. As the diagram suggests, the actor who intentionally creates fake news may in turn become acted upon just as easily as the passive consumer can become an active spreader of false information.

Notably, along these same lines, Mustafaraj and Metaxas (2017) have found in their analysis of Facebook group users that fake news would be spread by anonymous accounts infiltrating groups already conversing with each other online; people consuming information within these groups were then induced by these anonymous actors to share misinformation across their networks. The findings reveal some of the purposeful actions and motivations of fake news creators, showing the cynical realpolitik mentality of those who spread disinformation as well the motives to destabilize power structures by exploiting user trust built up within online groups and subcultures. This ability of people to move from actor to acted upon and vice versa has not been clearly identified in research and needs to be considered to fully understand the problem.

MODELING FAKE NEWS

As shown in figure 7.3, this new model of fake news focuses on the duality of the actor and the acted upon. Three principles for the model are suggested: (1) fake news is an information exchange between two sides, the actor and the acted upon; (2) the purpose of this exchange is to delegitimize or invalidate truths and trust, requiring both sides to make it work; (3) the purpose of the exchange through the false medium is to alter established power structures (to strengthen or to weaken) and requires cooperation based upon a mutually intertwined relationship.

The assumption is that the actor, performing as a willful agent, intentionally creates content for a specific purpose in mind. Such willed actions would include the choice to spread propaganda and disinformation, to repeat a rumor, to promote a theory (unfounded or untrue), or to create a parody or satire. The goals of the actor can include the desire to distort facts or to enable facts in order to alter power structures, either strengthening or weakening

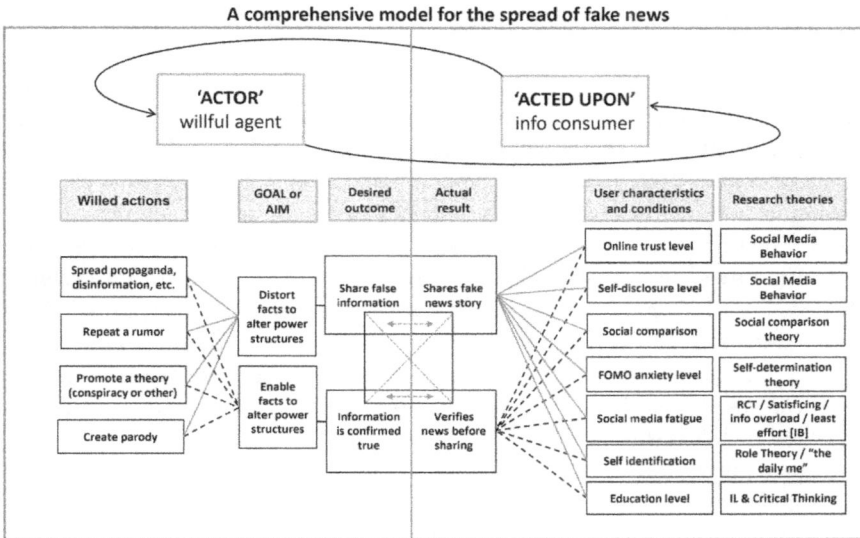

A comprehensive model for the spread of fake news

Figure 7.3.   A comprehensive model for the spread of fake news, showing dual actor/ acted upon relationship. *Source*: Weiss et al., 2021.

them. The ultimate results of these actions and goals result in either sharing false information or confirming its truth.

On the other side of things, the acted upon, who are the consumers and users of information, have the choice to take their time to verify the information or to believe it and share with others. As the model suggests, it is argued that the acted upon would show specific characteristics in their identities and behaviors that could demonstrate their likelihood of sharing fake news. Most importantly, it should be noted that the actor and acted upon may flip these roles at different times, depending upon their circumstances, aims, and purposes. As a result, by examining how producers become consumers and consumers become producers we find that fake news is applicable and relevant to *all* users of information. People using false information are not merely victims helpless at the behest of evil information predators. People, in contrast to this simplistic perspective, can be both victim and abuser, both willful hands-on proactive agents of persuasion who fool others as well as users merely reacting to the fraudulent or false information they have encountered.

QUESTIONS FOR FUTURE DEVELOPMENT

Overall, the model attempts to reconcile the problems of fake news definitions that focus too much on format and content or too much on intent and motive. Several questions and future areas of research are suggested by the model. For example, what characteristics and conditions are most evident in users likely to share fake news? What final intentions do creators of fake news have when they create a fake news story? What makes some fake news pieces more successful than others? One valuable aspect of the model is that it could be used to help determine the exact combination of factors evident between the actor and acted upon that would result in the desired outcomes of fake news. The effectiveness, in other words, of the fake news story may be better quantified by seeing how the intention behind the fake news story's creation (that is, false information is shared; a parody/satirical piece is acknowledged and understood) aligns with the reception it gets from readers and consumers (that is, the fake news story is believed and shared; the reader fails to get the joke and takes it seriously). Does the fake news, in other words, fulfill its intended goal? And how can we determine this?

From a purely formal perspective, one wonders what characteristics of fake news make it more or less likely to be shared. The mimetic nature of the fake news genre veers into the realm of hoaxes, where the imitation and forgery aspects of the original come to the fore again. Determining which factors make for an effective piece of fake news would also help researchers and policymakers develop countermeasures that might decrease its effectiveness. This could allow for systems, governments, and other organizations to better anticipate false narrative spreading in their respective areas and societies.

WHEN DOES THE "ACTED UPON" BECOME THE "ACTOR" AND VICE VERSA?

Coming back to the central exchange of information and the creation of roles, it is important to review not only the user of fake news but also the various creators of fake news. While it is possible to understand the external factors that may cause someone to consume fake news, it is not always understand *why* someone creates it. There is much less known, even, about whether creators of fake news ever come to be fooled themselves by their own creations. One may want to know what factors exist that might cause creators to become consumers and how it might be predicted based on the person's environmental and personal conditions.

The portrait of those dabbling in the false and unreal is somewhat telling. Often those delving into conspiracy theories and false narratives find that their sense of power in information may be unfulfilled. As a result they react to what appears on the surface to be marginalizing their lives and attempt to wrest control over it. As Fister points out, "those who spend their time in the library of the unreal have an abundance of something that is scarce in college classrooms: information agency. One of the powers they feel elites have tried to withhold from them is the ability to define what constitutes knowledge. They don't simply distrust what the experts say; they distrust the social systems that create expertise. They take pleasure in claiming expertise for themselves, on their own terms" (Fister, 2021). In this dynamic, creators and consumers of fake news and conspiracy theories work within overlapping grounds, feeding off each other, taking advantage of the social circles they have created and inhabited from the ground up, simultaneously consuming and producing their own knowledge, regardless of—and sometimes in spite of—its factual basis. The claiming of their own expertise on a subject is very much a pushback, too, against a perceived elitist disdain of which they are the presumed targets. Never mind that this disdain is often stimulated by the poor technique and mistake-prone reasoning that are the hallmarks of poor judgment for those inhabiting "the library of the unreal." Still, something is making these people "nibble at the edge of stale ideas," as F. Scott Fitzgerald (1925) once eloquently described it in *The Great Gatsby*.

Long before social media took over most people's online experiences, this conundrum of poor reasoning at the heart of information use and information literacy was already noticed by researchers. Pawley (2003) predicted twenty years ago that the schism between consumers of information and producers would become a major problem that LIS research would need to address, especially as it was not very well understood how "nonelite groups produce and disseminate information" (p. 446). Not making a better and more concerted effort to find out how these groups interact with information has ultimately resulted in a failure to "enlist nonelite 'consumers-as-producers' of information in processes of production and recontextualization" (Pawley, 2003). What this means is that the creation and recombination of information among those using information from a position of weakness and perceived marginalization becomes charged with conflict for its own sake and one source of the division between what people see as truthful and as conspiracies out to get them. The modern web has proven Pawley correct, it seems, as users and creators of content in these aggrieved groups spin false information, fake news, and conspiracy theories in their daily online information behaviors.

Therefore, it is vital to consider those "pivot moments" when people might possibly shift from consumers of fake news to creators and active spreaders of false information and conspiratorial narratives. If we are unable to understand those who have positioned themselves as anti-elite, and who characterize general truth as tainted and elitist, then it becomes that much more difficult to understand the causes of their behavior. This model, then, attempts to review this dynamic by examining that shift from being the acted upon and the agency-seeking actor who develops new but *counterfactual* ideas as poses against perceived power imbalances or class conflicts.

RELATIONSHIP ISSUES AND MICRO, MESO, AND MACRO WORLDS

One problem is that the relationship between the actor and acted upon is rather underdeveloped, and more research examining their interplay is necessary. At its heart, the model looks at how the desired outcomes for creating fake news might overlap and align with the actual resulting behaviors of information users. As seen in the model detail (figure 7.4), the desired outcomes for the creation of fake news split between false information being shared and information being confirmed as true. This overlaps on the opposite side with the result of the user being compelled to share the fake news story or verifying it before deciding to share. The overlaps occur when a creator of false information is able to get the user to share the false news story; similarly the creator of a false story as a parody finds that the truth is confirmed through the story and the user actually double-checks and finds out what the truth entails. It is this area of interaction between intentions and reactions that would be important to explore in the ways that people come to share or refuse to share false information.

A way to bridge the gaps between intentions desired on one side and actions taken on the other is through employing the theories of micro, meso, and macro worlds. Serpa and Ferreira (2019) suggest that "in every sociological theory, we can recognize a minimum unit (micro) and a maximum unit (macro)." The micro unit is seen as the individual within the society, acting and deciding on one's own without wider considerations, who are "actors [that] become more agentic through their interactions with others" (van Wijk et al., 2019). The micro level examines human behavior within the context of "everyday direct interaction" (Serpa and Ferreira, 2019) such as face-to-face meetings with other individuals or online communication between another person. In LIS research, using the concept of "small worlds," Chatman provides a similar look at the individual in their everyday life, arguing that it is essential for determining the behavior of information users at a micro level (Sin, 2011, p. 187).

The macro level, on the other hand, is conceived as an aggregation of people and examines the perspectives of human behavior and interaction from within "institutional contexts" that often organize, guide, or discipline the dynamics of smaller scales (van Wijk et al., 2019). This duality of perspectives, however, exists as "hypothetical poles of a scale of magnitudes, intentionalities and objective consequences of . . . action" (Serpa and Ferreira,

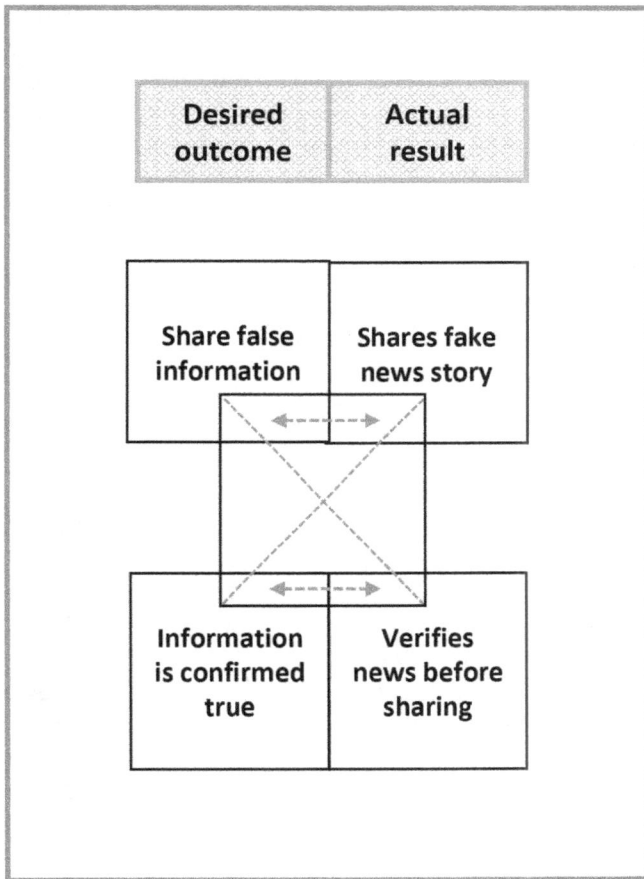

Figure 7.4. Detail of model, focusing on the meeting point between the desired outcomes of creating fake news and the actual resulting actions. *Source*: Weiss et al., 2021. (License: Attribution-ShareAlike 4.0 International [CC BY-SA 4.0].)

2019). In other words, human behavior is influenced not only at the individual level, with its attendant emotion and reflexivity, but also at the macro level, that demonstrates "how institutional contexts differ in their enabling and constraining influence on actors' actions" (van Wijk et al., 2019).

Between these two extremes there also exists an intermediate level (meso level) that serves interests less individual than the micro level and yet also less aggregated than a macro level. Van Wijk et al. describe this intermediate level in terms of "increases in interactions among diverse actors and their engagement in understanding each other's perspectives and interests and negotiating shared perspectives in 'interactive spaces'" (2019). This intermediate level can explain some of the ways in which fake news and false narratives may spread through smaller online groups and subcultures, made up as individuals but evincing influences from the small group. More importantly, researchers might come to "observe how actors' efforts can begin to jointly (re)negotiate the structures, patterns, and beliefs that constitute their social worlds and, even if tentatively and in a fragmentary manner, to co-create alternative proto-institutions with the potential to become institutionally embedded" (van Wijk et al., 2019). The meso level shows how individuals in the face of larger-scaled institutions can come to alter and change their actions and to recombine into new social worlds. As seen with fake news, and especially with Midori Ogasawara's (2019) research on online Japanese extremist groups, the issues of belief are often structured by the groups and identities a person associates with.

In LIS research, this approach of examining multiple levels in a sociological context has been utilized as well. Dow (2008) in her study on K–12 school libraries describes the three levels utilized for theories employing "a different breadth of coverage" in their approach. The first, the "micro level," examines small slices of evidence, an atomized personal examination, for example. The macro level is concerned with larger aggregates of subjects and large-scale observations of behaviors and evidence provided. The meso level, meanwhile, deals with the linkages between the two worlds and the impacts that the crossover instigates (Dow, 2008).

The concept of levels provides multiple perspectives for the review of fake news' impact on both an individual creator or user and the wider contexts and worlds in which they live. As they meet and interact, the world of an individual also exists within the wider world of larger societies; online subcultures, large as they may be, still exist as relatively smaller groups compared to the overall cultures and societies in which they live. The interaction between the two scales, the meso world, is an equally important aspect of the model. Dow further suggests that LIS as a field primarily "provides a macro level lens" for explaining social institutions and also provides "theories of diagnosis of information needs" to help provide explanations for how individuals interact with others and with information itself. Jaeger and Burnett (2010) also show that by focusing on different levels, "from the macro to the micro," researchers can find "a richer understanding of the intersections between information and the many different cultural contexts within which it is used" (p. 11).

The interactions between creator and user of fake news might be delineated by approaching the concept through this tri-leveled theoretical lens. On the macro level, one can see the aggregated behaviors of the creators and users of fake news as they exist within their larger societies and their overall impacts and potential for large-scale influence. On the micro level, one might be able to examine the issues of the individual creator as well as individual user, examine their emotions and attempts at individual agency. Finally, the meso level may be examined through the mutual but smaller groups in which each person might participate and be active within. One might see how the individual links to the greater world in terms of broader contexts, either as the creator of fake news interacting with a larger group that behaves within specific group dynamics or as an information user behaving in ways that are influenced and even bound by the larger groups developing fake news. Each of these approaches will be examined in more detail in the next two chapters, focusing on the creators of fake news in chapter 8 and the users of fake news in chapter 9.

SOME CAVEATS ON THE MODEL

Currently, there is an imbalance in the two sides of the model proposed. First, the main imbalance appears in how a person determines and identifies creators of false information. It may be in fact easier to identify users and spreaders of fake news than to identify the creators, especially if they prefer to remain anonymous in order to obscure their origins or cover up their intentions. Some of the obscurity may be related to covert political machinations, while some may be related to the social taboos of sharing this information or fear of the illegality associated with such fraudulent behaviors.

Don Fallis, who has examined extensively how disinformation works, might provide some insight into tackling this difficult area. Fallis's model suggests that disinformation is intentional misleading and effectively close to lying. In this regard, understanding the fake news creator's profile might be found within game theory related to deceptive lying. As Fallis (2015) writes, "whether a person will disinform depends on the expected costs and benefits. In particular, it depends on the costs of not being believed (weighted by the probability that this will happen) as compared with the benefits of being believed (weighted by the probability that this will happen)." As such, creating fake news might be better examined within the context of game theory where the probabilities of actions that information users will take are limited to the rules of the game. If one can get a better sense of those rules and motives dictated and bound by them, information users might also be forewarned by others who can anticipate deceptive actions, much in the same way that people are warned about the fraudulent activities of scammers, phishers, and other con artists who try to fool online users. Despite the lack of identifiable actors who create fake news, especially as they act indirectly or lurk behind the scenes, researchers might estimate and predict conditions and identify the rules of a game that foster and promote the conditions helping to proliferate levels of fake news and disinformation.

REFERENCES

Aïmeur, E., Amri, S., and Brassard, G. (2023). Fake news, disinformation and misinformation in social media: A review. *Social Network Analysis and Mining, 13*(30). https://doi.org/10.1007/s13278-023-01028-5.

Alwan, A., Garcia, E., Kirakosian, A., and Weiss, A. (2022). Fake news and libraries: How teaching faculty in higher education view librarians' roles in counteracting the spread of false information. *Partnership: The Canadian Journal of Library and Information Practice and Research, 16*(2), pp. 1–30, doi:10.21083/partnership .v16i2.6483.

Brennen, B. (2017). Making sense of lies, deceptive propaganda, and fake news. *Journal of Media Ethics, 32*, pp. 179–81.

Cole, C. (2013). "Concepts, propositions, models, and theories in information behavior research." In *The Information Behavior of a New Generation: Children and Teens in the 21st Century*, Jamshid Beheshti and J. A. Large, eds. Lanham: The Scarecrow Press, Inc.

Dow, M. I. (2008). Focus on global education: Mixed methods approach to understanding macro and micro levels of effective school libraries from an information science perspective. *International Association of School Librarianship Conference Proceedings*. doi: https://doi.org/10.29173/iasl7970.

Fallis, D. (2015). What is disinformation? *Library Trends, 63*, pp. 401–26.

Fister, B. (2021). The librarian war against QAnon. *The Atlantic*. https://www .theatlantic.com/education/archive/2021/02/how-librarians-can-fight-qanon /618047/.

Fitzgerald, F. S. (1925). *The Great Gatsby*. New York: Charles Scribner's Sons.

Golbeck, J., Mauriello, M., Auxier, B., Bhanushali, K. H., Bonk, C., Bouzaghrane, M. A., Buntain, C., Chanduka, R., Cheakalos, P., Everett, J. B., et al. (2018). Fake news vs satire: A dataset and analysis. In *Proceedings of the 10th ACM Conference on Web Science*, Amsterdam, The Netherlands, May 27–30 (pp. 17–21). New York: Association for Computing Machinery.

Hintz, W. W. (1940). Which propaganda? *College and Research Libraries, 1*(2), pp. 170–75. https://crl.acrl.org/index.php/crl.

Jaeger, P. T., and Burnett, G. (2010). *Information worlds: Behavior, technology, and social context in the age of the internet*. Taylor & Francis.

Jones, A. (2016). New McDonald's in Scottsdale run entirely by robots. *Hollywood Gazette*. https://abcnews.com.co/new-mcdonalds-in-scottsdale-run-entirely-by -robots/.

Kramer, R. M. (1999). Trust and distrust in organizations: Emerging perspectives, enduring questions. *Annual Review of Psychology, 50*(1), pp. 569–98 https://pdfs .semanticscholar.org/70b9/3a3111486496db45aa5dbb81e9d6f1776a2f.pdf.

Mustafaraj, E., and Metaxas, P. T. (2017). The fake news spreading plague: Was it preventable? Cornell University Library. arXiv, arXiv:1703.06988.

Ogasawara, M. (2019). The daily us (vs. them) from online to offline: Japan's media manipulation and cultural transcoding of collective memories. *Journal of*

Contemporary Eastern Asia, 18(2), pp. 49–67. https://doi.org/10.17477/jcea.2019 .18.2.049.

Pawley, C. (2003). Information literacy: A contradictory coupling. *The Library Quarterly: Information, Community, Policy, 73*, pp. 422–52. https://www.jstor.org /stable/4309685.

Peters, J., and Robertson, K. (2023). Murdoch acknowledges Fox News hosts endorsed election fraud falsehoods. *New York Times.* https://www.nytimes.com /2023/02/27/business/media/fox-news-dominion-rupert-murdoch.html.

Roberson, J. D. (2022). 15 times the Onion was mistaken for actual news. *Cracked.* https://www.cracked.com/article_34270_15-times-the-onion-was-mistaken-for -actual-news.html.

Schafer, B. (2018). A view from the digital trenches: Lessons from year one of Hamilton 68. *Alliance Securing Democracy, 33*, pp. 1–24. https://securingdemocracy.gmfus .org/a-view-from-the-digital-trenches-lessons-from-year-one-of-hamilton-68/.

Serpa, S., and Ferreira, C. (2019). Micro, meso and macro levels of social analysis. *International Journal of Social Science Studies, 7.* Doi: 10.11114/ijsss.v7i3.4223.

Sin, S. J. (2011). Towards agency-structure integration: A person-in-environment (PIE) framework for modelling individual-level information behaviours and outcomes. In A. Spink and J. Heinström (eds.), *New Directions in information behaviour.* Bingley, UK: Emerald Publishing.

Smallpage, S. M., Enders, A. M., and Uscinski, J. E. (2017). The partisan contours of conspiracy theory beliefs. *Research and Politics, 4*(4): pp. 1–7. https://doi.org/10 .1177/2053168017746554.

Stodden, W. P., and Hansen, J. S. (2016). Politics by Kayfabe: Professional wrestling and the creation of public opinion. http://static1.1.sqspcdn.com/static/f/332308 /26781726/1452481855523/wrestfin.pdf?token=rq1phFIu3%2Bd2hD1Qnz %2BvGVl47wU%3D.

Taylor, A. (2015). 7 times the Onion was lost in translation. *Washington Post.* https: //www.washingtonpost.com/news/worldviews/wp/2015/06/02/7-times-the-onion -was-lost-in-translation/.

Taylor, P. (2003). *Munitions of the mind: A history of propaganda from the ancient world to the present era.* Third edition. New York: Manchester University Press.

van Wijk, J., Zietsma, C., Dorado, S., de Bakker, F. G. A., and Martí, I. (2019). Social innovation: Integrating micro, meso, and macro level insights from institutional theory. *Business & Society, 58*(5), pp. 887–918. https://doi.org/10.1177 /0007650318789104.

Weiss, A. P., Alwan, A., Garcia, E. P., and Garcia, J. (2020). Surveying fake news: Assessing university faculty's fragmented definition of fake news and its impact on teaching critical thinking. *International Journal of Educational Integrity, 16*(1). https://doi.org/10.1007/s40979-019-0049-x.

Weiss, A. P., Alwan, A., Garcia, E. P., and Kirakosian, A. T. (2021). Toward a comprehensive model of fake news: A new approach to examine the creation and sharing of false information. *Societies, 11*(82). https://doi.org/10.3390/soc11030082.

Chapter 8

The "Actor" in the
Fake News Model

THE ACTOR "SPEAKS"

In the previous chapter, a new model for examining fake news was introduced, from a top-level view of the phenomenon, focusing on the importance of defining fake news not only as a consumable multimedia genre but also as a product of its creator's intentions. The model shows how the relationship between two sides, the creators and the consumers of fake news, interact and influence each other. This intertwining relationship is important to help better understand the phenomenon overall and shows how these two sides of the fake news phenomenon come to influence each other in mutually impactful ways not dissimilar to a looping effect (Vesterinen, 2022). As Gaillard et al. (2021) assert, "fake news is a co-production by the initiator and its receptive audience," and the two sides display their mutually influential impact through the spiral of creating, absorbing, and sharing false information.

Subsequently, this chapter zooms in more closely on the actor's side of the fake news model, the creators of the false narratives and misinformation that negatively influence and affect online discourse. The actor, an important codriver of the fake news phenomenon, is situated within specific but overlapping environments and shows agency in the form of willful actions that effect specific goals and catalyze desired outcomes. Those actions in turn define the actor as a novel identity in online information behavior. As the philosopher Ian Hacking posits, "all intentional acts are acts [accomplished] under a description," meaning that when a new way to describe something comes into being, "new possibilities for action come into being in consequence" (Hacking, 1999). As such, with new ways to describe the actors in a fake news model, "new realities effectively came into being" to define the fake news creator, and "our classifications and our classes conspire to emerge hand in hand, each egging the other on" (Hacking, 1999). Being aware of such looping effects can improve and enhance our understanding of explanations of these types of interactions and newly defined types of person (Vesterinen, 2022).

As with the interrelationship between actor and consumer, the actor also interrelates with fake news as a creative genre. This complex interaction of medium, actor, and actor's intention provides novel ways to describe the process of fake news. Actors exist in a real world of multifarious situations and complex contexts, mirrored in part by the information worlds within which they operate. Jaeger and Burnett (2010) provide us with their concept of multilayered information worlds where information behaviors are shaped by family and friends on one level, regional attitudes at another, and national and international organizations influencing them at the widest and most expansive level. This "coherent multi-level theory," as they describe it, illuminates how "information intersects with and is perceived and used in many different social contexts" (Jaeger and Burnett, 2010) and attempts to reconcile the "small concerns" found in Elfrida Chatman's small worlds theory and the grander scales of Jürgen Habermas's work outlining his concept of "the public sphere," which he sees as a "'space within a society,' essential to the functioning of a democracy." His conceptualization of democracy idealizes the core value of freedom as the state of being "independent both of state power and of corporate influence, within which information can freely flow and debate on matters of public, civic concern can openly proceed" (Jaeger and Burnett, 2010). Democracy's gift of freedom provides necessary room for people to act without undue pressure or influence.

As noted in the previous chapter, the use of Chatman's small worlds as well as the meso and macro worlds studied in sociology (van Wijk et al., 2019) can ultimately inform of the ways in which participants in the fake news phenomenon behave, as well as provide insight into what may motivate them. Dow's (2008) work in the K–12 arena provides a look at meso and macro scales, similar to Habermas's public sphere, within which groups of people are operating and sharing information on varying scales of interaction. Habermas extends this idea into an even broader conception, which he coins a "lifeworld," described as "that collective information and social environment that weaves together the diverse information resources, voices, and perspectives of all of the members of a society" (Jaeger and Burnett, 2010, p. 26). This information lifeworld is applicable to the areas in which the actors and acted upon interact in different levels of influence, from small individual concerns to larger public spheres, and the many steps in between. These varying levels of influence represent the complexity at the heart of the model. Both actors and the acted upon may be operating within simultaneously larger and smaller spheres of influence. The lifeworld and the varying areas that intersect within it point to the ways in which researchers might identify the information behaviors, their motivations, and the thoughts that participants in a fake news environment exhibit.

Overall this dynamic relationship between the actor and the acted upon, as seen in figure 7.3, comes to define the way that false information requires multiple participants to help it spread. While there has been significant focus on who might fall for fake news, less has been hypothesized about *who* creates it and why. Some of this is the complexity of the creative act to begin with. Anthony Giddens, in describing the development of his theory of structuration, which focuses on both the societal structures and the agents operating within them, has explained that "actors are at the same time the creators of social systems yet created by them" (Bryant, 1999, p. 2). In other words, an information world is simultaneously created by the actor, who in turn has been inhabiting this world. Such interconnectedness makes it difficult to determine at times just who is creating and developing fake news and why. Additionally, social types, which are the roles that define actors and how they are perceived within our world, can be seen as an essential part of the information worlds theory proposed by Jaeger and Burnett. Yet it is important also to see the values and behaviors these actors endeavor to show as well as delineate the boundaries that these actors operate within or transgress (Jaeger and Burnett, 2010, p. 8).

Certainly, there is something fascinating and compelling about liars and the lies they tell. Sometimes, as research suggests, lies are far more interesting and therefore shared more often than the truth (Vosoughi et al., 2018). Similarly, whether lies are told to themselves or to others, deception intrigues people, draws then in, and makes them feel complicit in something *verboten* yet thrilling. In the case of fiction, it is that compelling story told to indulge one's need for narrative sense-making. In the case of knowledge, however, it is far thornier and ever more important to acknowledge the difference between the fictional and the factual, while also realizing that language remains rooted in its ability to tell a lie and a truth simultaneously. As Camus's narrator once says self-servingly in the novel *The Fall (La Chute)*: "Don't lies eventually lead to the truth? . . . Sometimes it is easier to see clearly into the liar than into the man who tells the truth. Truth, like light, blinds. Falsehood on the contrary, is a beautiful twilight that enhances every object." One might see the outline of the truth more clearly through the strange darkening of lies than if confronted with the truth outright. Truth is usually stranger than the familiar dim but soothing narratives people comfort themselves with. Who wouldn't take comfort in the belief that the sun revolved around the earth? It made humanity feel important, unlike the truth of living in a vast universe in which we all inhabit but a tiny, fragile, and miniscule world.

Some things are also just too painful to see, perhaps. Some things do not reveal themselves unless told in soothing contrasts through lies, like the stories of heroism and mythmaking in Herodotus, for example, that show us the things as a society would like them to be. So as one looks more closely at the actor role in the relationship, certain questions begin to arise beyond just the binary of whether something—or someone—is being truthful or lying. Who, we start to ask, are the ones creating fake news? Why do they create it? What are they attempting to gain from creating fake news? What is the ultimate goal of their actions?

THE ACTOR, DEFINED AND IDENTIFIED

When thinking of actors, we tend to think of those with motives or intentions, those effecting change of some kind, creating something new, or bringing forth a willed action. In the fake news model proposed by Weiss et al. (2020, 2021), the actor is defined rather broadly as any willful agent in the fake news cycle that creates specific content that results in the presentation and sharing of false information. Yet in absence of a true profile of the actor, or a class of actors, it is unclear how to fully understand where fake news comes from. Therefore, it is important to start considering who are the people—or organizations—contributing to the fake news genre.

Some speculation on those who create fake news has been proposed among various researchers and investigators. Marianna Spring (2020), journalist for the BBC who investigates disinformation, has suggested a simple taxonomy of fake news creators. She describes five types of fake news creators—covered obliquely in our previous chapters though not stated as explicitly as this—including "jokers," "scammers," "politicians," "conspiracy theorists," and "insiders." The jokers are those, as we've seen in the past, willing to create hoaxes and jokes (cf. The Great Moon Hoax, Welles's *War of the Worlds*, the Sokal Hoax, etc.) that fool a segment of the population. The jokers create content that is capable of mimicking the forms most commonly used to spread information in order to point out the gullibility of an audience, the faults of a medium itself, or to just tell an elaborate joke for its own sake. Scammers, though working in a similar vein as jokers to fool their audiences with the verisimilitude of media formats, deceive for the sake of gaining financially from that deception. Phishing and various other types of fraudulent communications—whether emails from Nigerian princes, spoofed websites mimicking real sites, or other shady techniques—are about swindling a mark and exploiting the mark's good faith.

Numerous examples of deceptive politicians abound, some lying for vanity and personal gain and some for the sheer power and thrill it brings them.

They create fake stories about their opponents, smear them with negative associations that are not justified, or exploit weaknesses by exaggeration or misdirection. The most common examples of these fake news "hawkers," however, stem from more paranoid regimes that cling to power, employing fact erasures, propaganda, and misinformation to preserve and bolster their power through the deception of their people. Political regimes have often used fake news during wartime; recently misinformation campaigns have been documented by Thompson (2022) from the 2022 Russian invasion of Ukraine (pp. 31–34).

Certainly, if politicians and regimes are on one side of the power scale, dominating and controlling information and messages, at the other end are conspiracy theorists, who distrust power in its political and organizational manifestations. Their extreme discomfort with power drives their belief in something different, even if that belief defies the logic of reasoned thought and established, multilaterally confirmed facts. These areas include the various greatest hits of conspiracy theories such as the 9/11 truther myth, antivax, anti-GMO, fake moon landing, flat earth, and climate change denial movements (Gaillard et al., 2021). Yet conspiracy theorists and politicians often work in tandem—as with QAnon—sometimes taking up the words and false ideas of certain politicians if they share political perspectives and ideals. It results in strange bedfellows, indeed, where one group, the politicians, exploits facts to preserve or gain power, while the other group of the disenfranchised and paranoid ironically rails against misused power itself but ultimately fails to see that the abuse of power is coming from those in their own camp.

Finally, "insiders," which is a rather novel designation proposed by Spring (2020), are considered to be those credentialed (or self-credentialed) with trusted professional titles and degrees (that is, doctor, professor) yet are actually frauds. These could be the people pretending to be doctors in a skincare commercial on television, specialists in dubious vitamin advertisements, or crank researchers in uncredentialed research labs that espouse discredited views. These types are especially visible in conspiracy theorist circles covering a wide range of topics in the area of public health (especially vaccines and COVID-19), flat earth theories, and religion-based archaeology (that is, finding Noah's Ark or the Ark of the Covenant of *Raiders of the Lost Ark* fame). The issue is that their expertise is taken to be true because it is based upon a veneer of credentials or baseless research they conduct but fail to heed the criticism of peers in their discipline. These problems may also appear from time to time among legitimate academics for various reasons. Some have either fallen into extremist views on their own (that is, religious or political extremes), convinced by their beliefs—especially in the field of eugenics and race studies—or have fabricated their results to satisfy their job requirements

(Watanabe, 2020). The most notorious misinformation related to vaccines—Wakefield's 1998 study showing a link to autism—was the result of skewed data from children who were "carefully selected" for his study that was "funded by lawyers acting for parents . . . involved in lawsuits against vaccine manufacturers" (Eggertson, 2010). Wakefield is the ultimate insider, in a sense, ensconced in a position of privilege while unethically crossing the line of impartiality that to this day negatively influences some parents' decisions about vaccinations.

Clearly, multiple types of fake news "generators" have had an influence on how information spreads and can be classified, in part, by the backgrounds from which they have sprung. Many have been already alluded to, including the hoaxers and scammers, the rulers and politicians, the conspiratorially paranoid, and the confidence men selling their snake oils to the unwary. However, there is more to fake news actors and creators than just their categorization into types.

THE ACTOR AS A SUM OF INTENTIONS WITHIN ITS INFORMATION WORLDS

Instead of *who* creates fake news, it is also important to look at fake news creators and actors as the sum of their *intended actions* and their attitudes and values about information itself as they occur within their various and increasingly complex milieus. Figure 8.1 provides a detail of the actor's intentions and interactions within an information world. Although the use of types can go a long way to identify and help develop profiles of the actors generating fake news—especially if there are backgrounds and psychological profiles that might overlap—the intentions of those creating the false stories often influences their type in the first place.

Jokers, for example, are just as easily understood by their intentions and ultimate goals than any actual insight into their personal type. Disinformationists, too, who spread false information to destabilize for political gains, must be defined in part by their intentions, without which it becomes impossible to judge the meaning of these actions. Similarly, their information worlds can be incredibly varied and complex ranging from the concerns driven by smaller, everyday concerns to the "national governments, . . . supranational and non-governmental organizations, [and] the information policy environment" (Jaeger and Burnett, 2010) that impact them on the largest scales possible.

Disinformation has been broken down into several different categories, but each coincides with the intent to deceive or mislead the recipient. Note that this is most often the definition of fake news most commonly employed: "reader falls for false news story." But it is, as mentioned, more

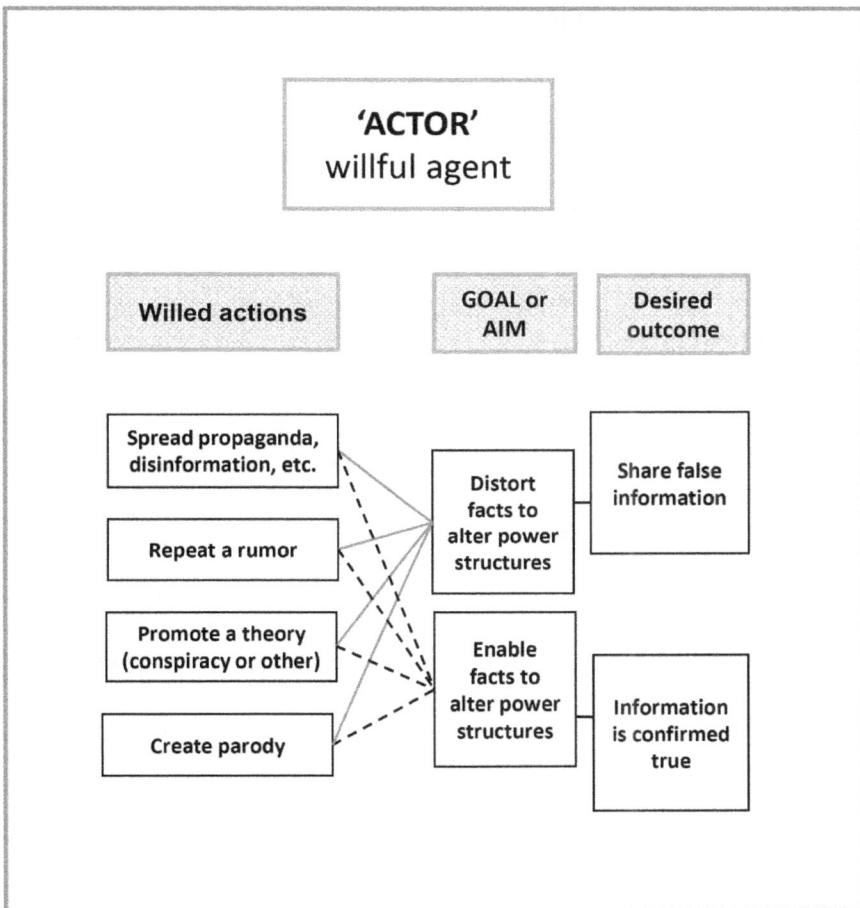

Figure 8.1. Detail of the fake news model showing the actor's actions, goals, and desired outcomes. *Source*: Weiss et al., 2021. (License: Attribution-ShareAlike 4.0 International [CC BY-SA 4.0].)

complex than this. As Fallis suggests, disinformation involves several important distinguishing aspects, including what he calls malicious lies; visual disinformation; accidental falsehoods; jokes, satire, and sarcasm; side-effect and adaptive disinformation; implausible lies; and accidental, altruistic, and detrimental disinformation (Fallis, 2015). In these various types of disinformation, the underlying intent behind them shapes its ultimate form. Malicious lies, for example, explain the intent to deceive in ways harmful to the recipient of the information, while on the other side of the spectrum altruistic disinformation is intended to protect recipients from facts deemed harmful or at least distressing to them. Satire, jokes, and sarcasm provide the lie as a method of unexpected contrasts, and the decrease of seriousness, while also attempting to point at the truth beneath the lie. In other words, the full range of human intentions, motives, and emotions may apply to the creation and dissemination of false information.

SPREADING PROPAGANDA (AND OTHER TYPES OF DISINFORMATION)

A first foray into the intentions that actors might harbor for creating fake news is related to the spreading of propaganda. As seen in chapter 6, propaganda has been part of societies for as long as politics and power have influenced them and the narratives people tell about themselves. *Who* might be spreading propaganda, however, remains a complex issue, requiring a deep study into the motivations of a society, its wielders of power, and the messages that are prioritized over others. Belloir et al. (2022), for example, believe that fake news is much closer to cyberwarfare and cyberattacks that require coordinated efforts and is "rarely created by an isolated person." The key to fighting fake news is to identify the various stakeholders and producers of disinformation. Identifying their coordinated "chain of creation" will help researchers better understand the ulterior motives for fake news being manufactured in the first place (Belloir et al., 2022). As seen with some examples from Soviet propaganda, much of it was spurred on by general opposition to the West and its widespread adoption of capitalism as the engine of societal growth and stability. The creators of propaganda may have had significant influence from the Soviet state as well as internal motivation, belief, or fear driving them. Getting to the bottom of such influences and motivations is one key to understanding the patterns underlying why people spread misinformation and fake news too.

Yet differences in time periods, living conditions, and attitudes about the powers that control their societies exist that complicate how individual motives might be clearly determined, analyzed, and recounted. The current political and social climate in Russia, for example, is significantly different from the period of Soviet control. Yet familiar anti-Western threads of thought and perspectives still persist and pervade its political philosophy. The exploitation of the societal fault line of racism in the United States has long been carried out by Russian propagandists as way to discredit American democracy and its capitalistic society (Lentz and Gower, 2011). The trend of exploiting and inflaming racial divisions that began during the Soviet Union has continued through the post-Soviet era into current online social media platforms. This reached a climax during the 2016 US presidential election campaign, as documented in the Mueller Report's findings about Russian disinformation campaigns (Mueller, 2019).

How we spot patterns, however, in propaganda techniques can help us better understand how fake news is created and what the ultimate intentions really are. As propaganda groups in Russia exploit the racial fault lines of the United States, their point is not to cry out for sincere justice for Black Americans—whether in the Soviet era or in the Putin era—but rather to incite anger and indignation between citizens, sow distrust, foment unrest, and initiate chaos among all Americans. That intention seems to be at the bottom of much of the propaganda and false narratives coming from that country. The reality of inequality in the United States is pointed out and exaggerated not for the purpose of effecting legitimate social change but for insincere, inflammatory purposes that carry forth no solutions and that attempt to demoralize those who sincerely wish for change.

PROMOTION OF A THEORY
(CONSPIRACY AND OTHER)

Similar in approach to propaganda, though not always at such a widespread scope or needing as much coordination, promoting conspiracy theories is another aim of the fake news actor. As with the British vaccine researcher Dr. Wakefield, his "insider" persona lent credence to ideas that were ultimately discredited yet persist not only among the paranoid but also well-meaning, though frightened, parents. The initial intentions of the researcher may not necessarily have been to promote the theory that vaccines cause autism; they were, instead, to find and publicize new information about their findings. That the false information was ultimately coopted by groups of people already wary of vaccines doesn't necessarily make Dr. Wakefield a prime candidate for creator of fake news and misinformation. However, it is the people who have not looked closely at his work and who nevertheless persist in believing and sharing it, as well as writing about it and perpetuating the myth, that interest us here. The recombination of his retracted false findings with the agendas and intentions of those willing to spread the discredited information make the example an incredibly powerful one to examine.

REPEATING RUMORS

Rumors, too, are a part of the creation of false narratives and fake news. Sometimes the intentions behind spreading rumors differ. As Fallis points out among disinformation types, there exist differing intentions to telling lies.

Some of these remain, as ever, deceitful and malicious. One often thinks of Iago in Shakespeare's *Othello*, who spread lies and rumors about Desdemona to exact revenge on the title character. A drama, of course, but one that rings true to our own experiences. Some, however, may be less directly harmful. In some cases the person unwittingly repeats something heard and mistakenly shares a false idea, rumor, or fake news. Rumors themselves tend to move faster than truth. The heart of the rumor mongering may be complex. Who exactly share these rumors and why? What profiles exist to help explain creating or repeating of a rumor? What motivations exist at the bottom of these rumors as well? Some of it may be intentional and directed for things like revenge. Some may be more about petty jealousies or willful ignorance of a subject.

CREATING PARODY, SATIRE, OR JOKES

Parodies and satire have a more reputable spot in the fake news world than typical disinformation, misinformation, or conspiracy theories. Obviously, the reason for this is often in the transparently conveyed intentions of whoever created the joke. Similarly, society tends to value the parody, giving it protected status as speech as well as extra protections in copyright law in the United States. The provisions for fair use in the US Code give parody an extra layer of protection against copyright infringement, as the framers of the legal structure felt that the public would be served better with such narratives derived from well-known original works. It is further seen as a transformation of the original work—in this case a metanarrative that transcends an original by forcing the audience to interrogate their own prior assumptions about a subject.

Some of the value ascribed to this genre likely stems from the realization that jokes, satires, and parodies have at their base *an obligation to the truth*. Even sarcastic comments themselves would usually fit within nonserious discourse, yet these ideas nevertheless signify someone's real intent and overall meaning behind the expression. In this regard, because the intentions are often different than outright fooling someone, parodies and satire seem to not fit entirely within the fake news model as it is most commonly defined. Yet even if a parody or satire is taken as truth, it still succeeds in eventually coming out as a hoax, further cementing the intended point of telling the truth.

THE GOALS AND AIMS OF CREATING FAKE NEWS

As figure 8.1 shows, there are also hypothesized to be two major overarching aims for creating fake news. The first major aim is to find ways to distort factual information in order to affect the power structures in which the actors inhabit. This seems on the face to be the most common motivation or aim for actors creating fake news. As seen in recently disclosed files about Russian hacking and disinformation campaigns directed against the United States, for example, the motivation is not merely to spread false stories but to weaken the power structures that hold a country's society together. The so-called Vulkan files reveal the Russian government's "tactics for automating the creation of massive numbers of fake social media accounts for disinformation campaigns" (Timberg et al., 2023). The destabilization of American discourse about itself seems to be the main aim for these campaigns. The erosion of trust seems to be the point, which is an essential component of a healthy functioning democracy.

Yet fake news can also serve to enable belief in factual information. This is most common in the creation of parodies. The parody functions not as a rebuke of truth but as a buttress helping to support truthful positions. In these instances, it should be noted, the factual information in question is not stated explicitly. Instead it is implied through the juxtaposition of overwrought, inaccurate, or outrageous claims made within the parody. This framing of the idea within the trappings of the genre, but made obvious by the ridiculousness of the content, serves to highlight what should be seen as real by implication. Instead of stating one's position outright, the parody forces the audience to confront its belief in what is true and false and eventually come to see the outrageous opinion as implausible. This helps the original idea be seen as more reasonable in contrast, buttressing truth and trust rather than eroding it.

On a final note, the differing information worlds at the heart of the actors' worlds—from individual concerns to national and international influences and cultures—need to be considered in order to understand the motivations for wanting to assist in buttressing or destabilizing the undergirding concepts and assumptions of truth and trust in a particular society. As in the case of the Vulkan files, the members of a cyberwarfare group have been directed by their superiors in a chain of command to destabilize their enemy. Yet an individual's unique motivations may also have an impact on their actions as much as the outside pressures applied to them. They may have specific pressures, both internal and external, that motivate their actions. Conversely, wider societal impacts may drive lone wolf actors' actions as well. It is in the best interest of all to find ways to differentiate between these pressures and influences occurring among all actors—whether in a group or working individually—in the fake news phenomenon.

If this all seems impossibly complex, rest assured that most would agree that the intersections existing between multiple actors or groups of actors, their respective information worlds, and their personal motivations for acting within them are inextricably bound by and simultaneously embedded within numerous variables. Isolating these may indeed be difficult—and therein lies the challenge.

DESIRED OUTCOMES, UNWITTING RESPONSES: THE INTERSECTION OF ACTORS AND CONSUMERS

The desired outcomes of fake news tend to fall within two broad areas: (1) to get information users to share and spread the false information and (2) to confirm that information alluded to in the fake news is actually true (see figure 8.1). These desired outcomes result from the aims and goals as well as the willed actions taken to instigate them. The ultimate goals of this model include determining how people can identify the creators of fake news and not only record their actions but also their intentions, while concluding whether they have been successful in those endeavors. In other words, how does one ultimately determine whether fake news has been effective or not? Of course, in order to do this, one needs to determine if the intentions of the actor have been met based on the responses and actions of the fake news consumer. One of the aspirations for this model is that it might help to determine how to create a better, more accurate profile of fake news creators.

One way to do this, first off, is to see how the desired outcomes of the fake news creator overlap with the actions of the fake news consumer, and how the results match or fail to match their desired outcomes. The trick, of course, is how to quantify this in a meaningful way and to isolate the variables that allow observers to peer into the motives and intentions of the creator. Jaeger and Burnett's information world is "designed to account for all of the elements at work in shaping the role that information plays within a society" (2010, p. 9) and recount "the possible ways to examine and quantify the phenomenon." This must include not only factual information but also information that has pathological and negative impacts on people and their societies.

In that sense, while most information behavior theories focus on the rational and intentional aspects of seeking out information and making sense of it, there is much for exploring the areas of information use that are irrational and harder to interpret as intentionally positive and aspirational actions. But the hardest thing in information science, with its foundational assumptions of rationality in information seeking and epistemological positivity in sense making, is to not only express information behavior in terms of irrational and destructive impulses, likely found in disinformation and misinformation campaigns, but to also pinpoint the variables driving the very behavior antithetical to the assumptions of information science itself.

One way to solve this issue is to at least examine the overlap of intentions created by the fake news actor and the outcomes of the users, the acted upon. If it can be determined that each side has similar intentions in both creating and sharing fake news, it might be possible to develop strategies for quantifying fake news as a shared phenomenon with shared goals on both sides. In this way the information world might be useful to help identify the "small worlds that are bound together" in various means including family, community, education, culture, and technology. One can see how information is perceived as it moves through society first by the actor who creates false narratives and fake news for specific purposes and second by the one who encounters it as the consumer (Jaeger and Burnett, 2010, pp. 9–10).

ISSUES AND UNADDRESSED PROBLEMS

The main problem with the model as it is currently devised is that the profiles of fake news actors and creators are incredibly complex and diverse. Similarly, it is difficult to ascertain the intentions and desired outcomes actors harbor when creating fake news. Motivations may be individual, but they may be, as Belloir et al. (2022) suggest, the results of coordinated group efforts. While the final results are often bifurcated into two separate types that either boost truth or disparage it, the variables that help us define actor profiles are quite profoundly complex. Identifying the ways in which the micro, meso, and macro worlds intertwine and how creators of fake news straddle these various information worlds also remains a significant challenge (van Wijk et al., 2019).

Yet to make things even more difficult, other problems have arisen as this book was being written, especially with regard to various artificial intelligence tools that promise to impact human society in deeply profound yet potentially disturbing ways. For example, large language modeling (LLM) technologies like ChatGPT, DALL-E, and Google Bard have the ability to mimic human writing, texting, and generative image making in an online environment. Additionally, according to Eloundou et al. (2023), these can "process and produce various forms of sequential data, including assembly language, protein sequences and chess games, extending beyond natural language applications alone." The technology greatly blurs the lines between the creator of the tool itself (that is, Google, OpenAI, etc.), the tool used to create something (that is, ChatGPT), and the person implementing the tool for their various purposes. Further, all of these factors are held together tenuously with just the slenderest of threads of intention. In other words, we become unsure of agency and intent when a self-acting tool makes decisions on behalf of the user who may or may not be comfortable with the final results. Who, if the content turns out to be harmful to someone, is responsible for the output? The AI creator? The AI itself? The person using AI?

It remains to be seen just how impactful this technology really will be on the development of fake images and information, but the initial lack of guardrails against malicious use of generative content appears to be exacerbating the flood of unverified and unverifiable information. The conclusions that Eloundou et al. (2023) suggest are dire, however, with "heightened economic disparity and labor disruption, which may give rise to adverse downstream effects," including, one can argue, extremism and radicalization of perspectives that lead to more misinformation and disinformation. The influence of these on the creator of fake news and, subsequently, the one who consumes fake news needs to be addressed.

Finally, complicating the understanding of the actor's role in the creation of fake news and disinformation campaigns is the fact that AI-generated content—devised for both innocent and devious ends as well as benevolent and malicious purposes—is also a business model in the information economy. This business model straddles individual desires for financial gain and societal influence and extends outward to the wider society due to the scope, reach, and speed of the technologies involved. The company Midjourney, for example, has used AI tools to generate vivid, realistic, yet nonetheless *fake* images of Donald Trump being arrested and Pope Francis wearing a puffy white Balenciaga luxury brand coat. These are mostly harmless as jokes go but potentially harmful in the wrong hands. Notably, the company allows parody images of Russian president Putin to be generated but prevents images of Chinese leaders from being made (Stanley-Becker and Harwell, 2023). Such inconsistent policy decisions appear to be based on a desire to not roil the cultural norms of certain potential markets. Furthermore, assumptions of authenticity now must be constantly questioned, even if something looks completely realistic (Maloy and Branigin, 2023). Creating this kind of verisimilitude will become a premium service for which many might pay to fool others, further complicating the influences between creators of fake news and their consumers.

REFERENCES

Belloir, N., Ouerdane, W., and Pastor, O. (2022). Characterizing fake news: A conceptual modeling-based approach. In J. Ralyté, S. Chakravarthy, M. Mohania, M.

A. Jeusfeld, and K. Karlapalem (eds.), *Conceptual modeling. ER 2022. Lecture notes in computer science*, 13607. Springer, Cham. https://doi.org/10.1007/978-3 -031-17995-2_9.

Bryant, C. G. (1999). The uses of Giddens' structuration theory. *Reihe Soziologie Institut für Höhere Studien, Abt. Soziologie, 37*. https://nbn-resolving.org/urn:nbn: de:0168-ssoar-221872.

Dow, M. I. (2008). Focus on global education: Mixed methods approach to understanding macro and micro levels of effective school libraries from an information science perspective. *International Association of School Librarianship Conference Proceedings*. doi: https://doi.org/10.29173/iasl7970.

Eggertson L. (2010). Lancet retracts 12-year-old article linking autism to MMR vaccines. *Canadian Medical Association Journal/Journal de l'Association medicale canadienne, 182*(4), E199–E200. https://doi.org/10.1503/cmaj.109–3179.

Eloundou, T., Manning, S., Mishkin, P., and Rock, D. (2023). GPTs are GPTs: An early look at the labor market impact potential of large language models. *ArXiv*. arXiv:2303.10130.

Fallis, D. (2015). What is disinformation? *Library Trends, 63*, pp. 401–26. https:// www.ideals.illinois.edu/items/92058.

Gaillard, S., Oláh, Z. A., Venmans, S., and Burke, M. (2021). Countering the cognitive, linguistic, and psychological underpinnings behind susceptibility to fake news: A review of current literature with special focus on the role of age and digital literacy. *Frontiers in Communication*. doi: 10.3389/fcomm.2021.661801.

Hacking, Ian. (1999). Making up people. In Mario Biagioli (eds.), *The science studies reader* (pp. 161–71). London: Routledge.

Jaeger, P. T., and Burnett, G. (2010). *Information worlds: Behavior, technology, and social context in the age of the internet*. Taylor & Francis Group.

Lentz, R., and Gower, K. K. (2011). *The opinions of mankind: Racial issues, press, and propaganda in the Cold War*. University of Missouri Press.

Maloy, A. F., and Branigin, A. (2023). An AI-generated "Balenciaga pope" fooled us all. How much does it matter? *Washington Post*. https://www.washingtonpost.com/ lifestyle/2023/03/27/pope-francis-coat-puffy-white-ai-fake/?isMobile=1.

Mueller, R. S. (2019). *Report on the investigation into Russian interference in the 2016 presidential election: Submitted pursuant to 28 C.F.R. §600.8(c)*. US government official edition. US Department of Justice.

Spring, Marianna. (2020). Fake news generator: Who starts viral misinformation? BBC News. YouTube. https://www.youtube.com/watch?v=UAy6PI5UtSU.

Stanley-Becker, I., and Harwell, D. (2023). How a tiny company with few rules is making fake images go mainstream. *Washington Post*. https://www.washingtonpost .com/technology/2023/03/30/midjourney-ai-image-generation-rules/.

Thompson, S. (2022). Fake news in the Polish information sphere following the Russian invasion of Ukraine in February 2022. Malmö University, Faculty of Culture and Society (KS), School of Arts and Communication (K3). Thesis. http:// urn.kb.se/resolve?urn=urn:nbn:se:mau:diva-55044.

Timberg, C., Nakashima, E., Munzinger, H., and Tanriverdi, H. (2023). The Vulkan files: Secret trove offers rare look into Russian cyberwar ambitions. *Washington*

Post. https://www.washingtonpost.com/national-security/2023/03/30/russian -cyberwarfare-documents-vulkan-files/.

van Wijk, J., Zietsma, C., Dorado, S., de Bakker, F. G. A., and Martí, I. (2019). Social innovation: Integrating micro, meso, and macro level insights from institutional theory. *Business & Society, 58*(5), pp. 887–918. https://doi.org/10.1177 /0007650318789104.

Vesterinen, T. (2021). Identifying the explanatory domain of the looping effect: Congruent and incongruent feedback mechanisms of interactive kinds. *Journal of Social Ontology, 6*(2), pp. 159–85. https://doi.org/10.1515/jso -2020–0015.

Vosoughi, S., Roy, D., and Aral, S. (2018). The spread of true and false news online. *Science* (American Association for the Advancement of Science), *359*(6380), pp. 1146–51. https://doi.org/10.1126/science.aap9559.

Wakefield, A. J., Murch, S. H., Valentine, A., Davies, S. E., Walker-Smith, J. A., Anthony, A., Linnell, J., Casson, D. M., Malik, M., Berelowitz, M., Dhillon, A. P., Thomson, M. A., and Harvey, P. (1998). Ileal-lymphoid-nodular hyperplasia, non-specific colitis, and pervasive developmental disorder in children. *The Lancet (British Edition), 351*(9103), pp. 637–41. https://doi.org/10.1016/S0140 -6736(97)11096–0.

Watanabe, T. (2020). UC Berkeley is disavowing its eugenic research fund after bioethicist and other faculty call it out. *Los Angeles Times*. https://www.latimes.com/ california/story/2020-10-26/uc-berkeley-disavows-eugenics-research-fund.

Weiss, A. P., Alwan, A., Garcia, E. P., and Garcia, J. (2020). Surveying fake news: Assessing university faculty's fragmented definition of fake news and its impact on teaching critical thinking. *International Journal of Educational Integrity, 16*(1). https://doi.org/10.1007/s40979-019-0049-x.

Weiss, A. P., Alwan, A., Garcia, E. P., and Kirakosian, A.T. (2021). Toward a comprehensive model of fake news: A new approach to examine the creation and sharing of false information. *Societies, 11*, 82. https://doi.org/10.3390/soc11030082.

Chapter 9

Consumers of Fake News

The other part of the fake news model focuses on how people interact with information and what factors may contribute to being susceptible to fake news. While the intentions of the fake news creator are often seen as stemming from a mix of individual desires and goals operating within smaller and larger contexts and information worlds, including a coordinated chain of creation, the fake news user is often characterized as an individual interacting with information on a personal scale. This way of characterizing the fake news user stems from a long tradition in library and information science that focuses on the rational actor in information seeking behavior. In many ways, rationality and intentional action are the easiest assumptions to make about information users. For the purposes of modeling human information behavior, the user is often described in terms of an individual acting in a purposeful way in order to find something that may eventually be considered information—that is, something informative that changes a person's initial state of nonknowledge into something comprehensible and useful. It is easier to visualize this process as a linear model, and much library and information science (LIS) research is devoted to this approach. Undoubtedly, some researchers complicate this approach and add variations and new variables to the linear type of information seeking and behavior model, but the underlying assumptions remain that information-seeking and human information behaviors are rational endeavors usually undertaken to satisfy personal needs that have been consciously identified and prioritized by information seekers.

Yet as explored in the beginning of this book, the actions that people take in gathering information or encountering information are often not as linear as the models describe them. People often do not understand what they are looking for. People often do not know whether they have found something or not. They are often left with a nagging, unidentifiable feeling of missing out on something. It is an urge that can go unfulfilled, like the proverbial library user who comes to a librarian, exasperated, needing help finding a book without knowing the author, title, or even subject—but who does remember that the

155

cover of the book was blue and just feels the need to find it to satisfy that irrational itch for closure. It emphasizes that such use cases are hard to pin down, harder even to research when the outcomes are in doubt. It is hardest when the desire for information is based not on reason but on emotions that are not easily articulated. Information users in these situations typically encounter less than ideal conditions that expose the vulnerabilities inherent not only to their search processes but also to the search systems they use in libraries (that is, electronic catalogs) and in their daily lives (that is, open web search engines), leaving an opening for false narratives and fake news to take root.

In contraposition to the actor, the acted upon exists in a more complex situation, less easily defined by specific intentions to deceive than a creator of false information. One can often spot the motives and intentions of a liar, especially in the contexts they have created and roles they have adopted. But with the information user, who is sometimes a target and victim of fake news and sometimes an active and willing participant, those intentions may be much less obvious and far more nuanced. The exploration of the subject turns to a number of important theories across various fields in order to help us understand the unique perspectives, proclivities, and vulnerabilities of fake news consumers.

The hypothesis, though, is somewhat simple: it is believed that there are identifiable characteristics observable in people that may make them more or less susceptible to a belief in false narratives, misinformation, and fake news. Importantly, in light of often contradictory ways of describing it, fake news is defined as the "phenomenon of information exchange between an actor and acted upon that primarily attempts to invalidate generally-accepted conceptions of truth for the purpose of altering established power structures" (Weiss et al., 2020). Based on this idea, it is further hypothesized that users of fake news would likely evince specific behaviors and conditions that increase or decrease their likeliness to share fake news or to verify information through fact-checking. The question becomes, then, what combination of factors between the "actor" and the "acted upon" most align the desired outcomes with actual results? What users, in other words, are *least* or *most likely* to share fake news or verify true information?

THE INFORMATION USER

Turning back to the model (see figure 9.1), the focus is now on the information user, where various influences and theories are posited to link them to the aims and goals of fake news creators. The user, in this model, is envisioned as playing a role in choosing to either consume and then pass along fake news to others or to verify and act accordingly (that is, abandon the information,

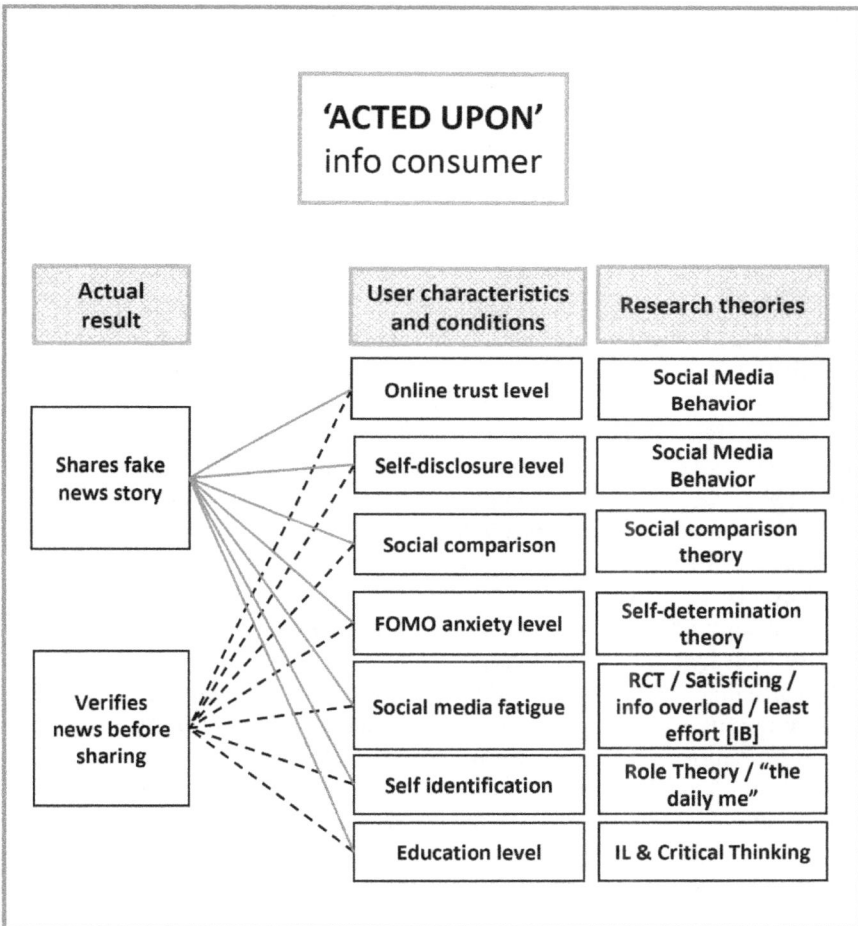

Figure 9.1.   Detail of fake news information model showing the characteristics and conditions and associated research theories for information consumers. *Source*: Weiss et al., 2021. (License: Attribution-ShareAlike 4.0 International [CC BY-SA 4.0].)

confirm and share, warn others of its falseness, etc.). It is believed that there are generally two results when one encounters fake news. Either one shares that fake news or one verifies information prior to that and determines whether it is true or false. That result, then, overlaps with the intentions of the fake news creators. Understanding the links between intention and actual outcomes is where the impact of fake news could be better determined. If one is able to predict the likelihood of sharing fake news or fact-checking it, one might be able to curtail the spread of the fake news by examining the conditions under which the information user exists. The model also helps to visualize a specific set of personal characteristics for each information user, including a range of personal motivations and feelings, education levels, self-created roles or identities, and the like. Each characteristic essentially determines whether users are more or less likely to pass along fake news to others.

To fully understand this dynamic and this profile of an information user, it is proposed that the following factors may help to determine the likelihood of an information user sharing fake news: (1) the level of trust one shows others online, (2) the amount of self-disclosed information one is comfortable sharing with others online, (3) the amount of social comparison one makes with others online, (4) the level of fear of missing out (FOMO) anxiety one feels online, (5) the amount of social media fatigue one has suffered at a specific time, (6) the way in which one creates their self-identification in online groups, and (7) one's overall education level.

The first five of these seven characteristics listed are noted in a 2019 study conducted by Talwar et al., who developed their model to examine the propensity for users to share information. They focused specifically on theories in the communications and psychology disciplines to hypothesize that these characteristics are linked directly to "sharing fake news and authenticating fake news before sharing online" (Talwar et al., 2019). Their research, which will be examined in more detail shortly, finds support in varying degrees for each of their hypothesized criteria.

In particular, Talwar et al. find several important foundational facts about information users that can help researchers develop better portraits of online user information behavior. Users who evince a high level of online trust, for example, tend to take more risks in sharing information with others, believing more readily that the information they have received or are relaying to others is accurate. They trust more implicitly that information does not have to be fact-checked. Similarly, users with a higher level of self-disclosure online— that is, they provide many personal details and share more of their identities—are more likely to share fake news online, a reflection perhaps of their desire to share whatever subjects and ideas they are currently interested in. FOMO is also seen as a factor in sharing fake news online. FOMO is a noted characteristic for those who share gossip online, which can often overlap with rumors and false narratives. The impetus is ultimately to avoid appearing to fall behind what others have already moved on to, especially trends, fashions, and popular events. Finally, issues related to social media fatigue suggest that personal feelings of information overload—which LIS researchers have studied deeply among information users for some time—can contribute to sharing faulty information. Authentication and verification itself, ironically, add to the fatigue; as a result, people sometimes share unverified information on social media due to their fatigue as a shortcut to remaining active online but with less of the attendant emotional and physical effort. The positive associations they have found, as well as the implications of their associations found in these specific characteristics of information users, provide a very useful approach to begin examining how fake news comes to be accepted and spread among people online. This helps to establish a baseline to both predict information user behavior related to fake news as well as to develop an outline of an information user's characteristics.

Two criteria later added by Weiss et al. in 2021 include "self-identification" and "education level," which stem from their own research in reviewing how teaching faculty at a university conceptualize fake news. The criteria are employed in an endeavor to illuminate two information user character-istics not addressed by Talwar et al. The first addition proposes that one's own personal identification and social identity created in relation to others within a culture or subculture may contribute to the sharing of fake news. The radicalization of opinions, especially in online chat rooms of like-minded individuals, can increase the sharing of fake news and escalate the spread of false narratives. Second, one's level of education should also be an indicator of one's likelihood of sharing fake news. Education, it should be noted, is defined here not merely in terms of degrees attained or levels of schooling reached but also in terms of a person's familiarity with the tenets and prac-tices of information literacy itself. Information literacy is a major aspect of library and information science research and practice and is used to frame how information users might become more proficient in using information academically and professionally.

Each of the seven criteria listed has been extensively researched and cited in the literature of multiple disciplines. These areas, described in more detail shortly, focus specifically on theories related to social media behavior, infor-mation fatigue, social comparison, self-determination, and rational choice. It is believed that these factors can be utilized to create more predictable pro-files of who are the likely consumers of fake news by focusing not only on personal attributes but also on specific interpersonal conditions and attitudes. When addressed in the aggregate, the factors may determine whether one has an underlying susceptibility to falling for fake news. Addressing a person's unique problem areas might alleviate the spread of fake news by "nipping it in the bud," so to speak, by treating the root personal causes of the behavior rather than the surface symptoms or external conditions.

FACTOR ONE: LEVEL OF ONLINE TRUST

Mayer et al. (1995) provide a clear path toward studying the level of online trust an information user might demonstrate through their "integrative model of organizational trust," which envisions ability, benevolence, and integrity as the main pillars of trust in an organization or group. They find that the more trust a person holds within a group, the greater risk they will take on behalf of that organization. "Trust is," they argue, "the 'willingness to take risk,' and the level of trust is an indication of the amount of risk that one is willing to take" (Schoorman et al., 2007, p. 346). The issue remains, though, of how much trust one manifests in a group that works with false information. DuBois et al. (2011), Grabner-Kräuter and Bitter (2013), Krasnova et al. (2010), and Grosser et al. (2010) each have examined trust as a major factor in the consumption and sharing of information online. These aspects include a focus on social capital theory, one's personal privacy risks involved, and the spreading of both rumor and gossip. People are more willing to share information with each other so long as they feel they can trust the members of the group, despite the great personal risk when interacting with barely known and anonymous users online.

Determining the level of trust in sharing information becomes an important indicator of whether information users would be more or less willing to verify information they encounter. If verification is seen as a less risky move, and even a nonstarter among those who are extremely trusting of others, one might argue that trust in the information coming from source "x" results in ironically *more* risky behavior and therefore less likelihood of doing the prudent thing by verifying information encountered. As Talwar et al. suggest, online trust and fake news sharing can be predicted, and "social media users having high trust in the information and news shared . . . are likely to share fake news with others and are less likely to authenticate the news before sharing" (p. 75). This predictable outcome provides a base to understand how fake news can proliferate despite other personal and environmental factors.

Similarly, in library and information science research, trust has been examined by Wenger using the concept of "communities of practice" (Davies, 2006; Wenger, 1998), which rely on mutual engagement "when members . . . build trust and relationships with one another through regular interactions" (Davies, 2006, p. 105). Relationship building in online social media is of special interest here. Researchers may be able to find important insight in how trust is formed by the ways in which people form bonds and relationships with others online. The level of such activity might also be quantified to understand better what the threshold level of trust would need to be in order for someone to be more or less likely to share false information within a group online. Along these lines, Rodríguez-Pérez and Canel (2023) recently examined whether a person's resilience against fake news and misinformation can be identified and then predicted by examining "other intangible assets" in the media such as "legitimacy and trust" that others might harbor for specific reputable news outlets. They find, interestingly, that trust in online environments does *not* contribute to a characteristic "resilience to misinformation"

(Rodríguez-Pérez and Canel, 2023). This should come as no surprise, perhaps, given that it is trust itself that ironically seems to reduce a person's vigilance in fact-checking against false information. The more trusting we are about the groups and platforms we use online, the less likely we may be to fact-check information found passing through them, and the less likely we are to be resilient to its deleterious effects.

FACTOR TWO: SELF-DISCLOSURE

In addition to the amount of trust one shows online—and partly related to the amount of risk one is willing to take online—"self-disclosure" refers to how much personal information a person is willing to share with others. In one sense, sharing personal information about oneself overlaps with the desire to be popular and gain personal attention. As a result, it is argued that the desire to gossip and to share information that may be false are interrelated. Indeed, people may be more interested in the sharing of information itself and the attention it brings them than they are concerned with whether something is true or false (Talwar et al., 2019, p. 76). As a result, it can be hypothesized that the people who "indulge in more self-disclosure are less likely to authenticate news before sharing, and be more inclined to share fake news" (Talwar et al., 2019). This approach, then, requires one to inquire of people whether or not they "indulge" in revealing and sharing more about themselves than others.

In library and information science, information users' tendencies to share information with others have been studied to some degree as far back as the early 2000s. Rioux's information acquiring and sharing (IA&S) and sharing information found for others on the web (SIF-FOW) models suggest that if users find information "perceived as useful or desirable . . . [that] would also address the information needs of someone they knew," they would be likely to share this information (Rioux, 2005). The personal motives for this sharing of information may change, but it is likely that the user is driven in some aspect by a desire to seem helpful and likable by others. Information science has focused on this desire for likability and willingness to share but may not be as focused on whether this information is true or false. The assumption may be that shared information has already been verified, or it doesn't matter overall for the theory, but this may be faulty. Indeed, the spread of fake news might be decided by and hinge upon such desires to both impress as well as to help fellow information users. In that sense, again, an entirely rational and linear approach to understanding information users is not always applicable. Desiring to please others may provide a motive, but it is not one that is fully rational with a clearly attainable goal. One might very well imagine the information user sharing a false story out of their desire to impress rather than their desire to inform, much like a friend who has recommended a book veering into conspiracy theories or false narratives.

FACTOR THREE: SOCIAL COMPARISON

Social comparison addresses the universal tendency of people to compare themselves to others. Social comparison is a long-standing theory that has existed since the 1950s and has been used extensively in psychology and sociology, hypothesizing that people are constantly evaluating not only their abilities in comparison to others but also their opinions and personal perspectives (Festinger, 1954; Cramer, et al., 2016; Wert and Salovey, 2004). The online environment appears to have exacerbated this tendency even further, with social media platforms providing "new and exciting means" for people to engage in social comparison (Talwar, 2019, p. 76). If one person were to encounter information online shared by another, it is possible that their engagement with that information could be influenced by a person's comparing themselves to the sharer of that information. In other words, the sharer of the information may indeed impact whether a person believes it or comes to reject it based upon their personal feelings of self-comparison.

While this certainly overlaps in some ways with trust and self-disclosure levels, it also provides a unique perspective in that it acknowledges how other people are perceived by the information user and considers whether fake news might be a function of whether or not you respect another person's opinion, skills, or activities. In information behavior, social positioning theory research focuses on the social status as well as the professional occupation of the information user (Sundin and Hedman, 2005, p. 294). One might argue that a successful friend who shares their anti-vaccination ideas with others might more successfully advocate for that information than if the person were less well respected or less successful in comparison.

Though social positioning does not seem to address comparisons directly, social capital, as proposed by Nan Lin, may present a more promising overlap as it endeavors to explain how users may be more or less likely to engage in social comparison and subsequent information seeking than others (Johnson, 2005, p. 325). The theory illuminates why, due to obstacles in their social structure, people in some social groups end up being less able to get the information they need than others (ibid. p. 324). This may have direct impact on whether they attempt to verify the information they encounter. If members of a certain social structure tend to downplay verification, people within that group may be more likely to act in a similar fashion.

FACTOR FOUR: FEAR OF MISSING OUT

FOMO covers the anxieties that arise in people when they engage in social media or are witnesses to events they feel are largely happening beyond their control. FOMO speaks to the nagging suspicions and personal confirmations that others, elsewhere, are consistently engaging in more meaningful and important activities, often at the expense of the anxious person. It is characterized, in some ways, by a deep-down fear of helplessness and alienation, a heightened vulnerability and a resulting recklessness to make up for experiences that are perceived as lost. FOMO itself has roots in self-determination theory, which focuses on how a person's senses of autonomy, competence, and relatedness inform their motivation and engagement in tasks. FOMO is further defined in research as the mix of a recurring anxiety and deep suspicion—especially evident among those on social media—that others, especially friends or acquaintances, are having more rewarding experiences than they (Deci and Ryan, 1985), impacting their motivation and engagement in various activities. Blackwell et al. (2017) find that FOMO was a predictor of greater social media use and addiction beyond a person's general personality traits or their attachment styles. FOMO is also linked to online users' increased sharing of gossip and personal information and is seen as a contributing factor to acting more recklessly online (Buglass et al., 2017). Each of these findings suggests that FOMO contributes to the negative behaviors associated with fake news and false information.

Self-determination theory has also been applied to LIS research via Ryan and Deci (2000), who find that information seekers are more motivated when they feel competent and acting in a manner that they believe makes the best use of their faculties. Conversely, any negative feedback or external pressures that inhibit personal agency can result in demotivating users to complete information seeking tasks (Watters and Duffy, 2005, p. 244). Self-determination informs the concept of FOMO very well, helping to explain how and why people may wind up sharing false information out of their anxiousness rather than spending a brief time verifying facts. As Talwar et al. suggest, "decreased self-regulation," central to the problem of FOMO itself, "is less likely to motivate them to make any effort to authenticate news before sharing." Users with a high sense of FOMO anxiety are therefore less likely to verify information before sharing it with others due to the desire to not only avoid the negative feelings of being left out but also to ensure the feeling that they are "part of the action," that they are seen as staying abreast of the most current news, ideas, concepts, or experiences.

FACTOR FIVE: SOCIAL MEDIA FATIGUE

Social media fatigue is believed to arise from an information user's extended overexposure online, defined partly as a subjective experience for the user that encompasses a wide array of emotions, including "anger, disappointment, tiredness, exhaustion, and reduced energy" (Ravindran et al., 2014). The continuous use of social media and time spent online is thought to increase a person's social media fatigue and contribute to their sharing of fake news due to these feelings of exhaustion and reduced energy. The amount of time spent on a specific task for verifying information, it could be argued, would be reduced as a result of the person's lack of desire or energy. The results of such fatigue include an exacerbation of feelings that can overwhelm information users.

However, social media fatigue might be just as easily examined using the theories and approaches honed through decades of library and information science research. LIS research has focused on the types of information problems that users have faced for as long as they have utilized information resources, though under different names than social media fatigue. In fact, the concepts may be long reaching and historically identifiable. These include information overload (Blair, 2010; Eppler and Mengis, 2004); the general behavior of satisficing, which means accepting, in the face of too much information or too many choices, something as "good enough" while acknowledging that it is not perfect (Prabha et al., 2007); and the long-observed behavior known as "the principle of least effort," where people have been shown to expend as little energy as possible looking for information and utilize the easiest or most well-established routes and pathways to finding it (Zipf, 1949).

Certainly, social media fatigue, information overload, satisficing, and the least effort principle show evidence of significant overlap, not only in user behavior but also in the results of that behavior (for example, reduced interaction with information, demotivation for information searching, desire to eliminate choices, etc.). Using these theories as a framework, the hypothesis can be tested whether people experiencing information overload and social media fatigue are more likely to share fake news as a result of these demotivating factors and conditions. The research would need to examine, however, whether this occurs due to a person's level of physical and mental tiredness, the general principle of the information user's tendency to make the least possible effort to search for something, or the satisficing that results from attempting to reconcile large amounts of information to meet very specific ends within limited periods of time. LIS research is well poised to help strengthen our understanding of how and why information users may be more or less likely to share false information and fake news. It provides a promising entrance into examining the individual and their potential to share fake news rather than taking the time and spending the energy to authenticate and verify that information.

ADDITIONAL FACTORS: SELF-IDENTIFICATION AND EDUCATION ATTAINMENT

The first five criteria described are well documented by Talwar et al. and promise to show links to how certain behaviors and personality traits could contribute to the spread of fake news among information users and the "acted upon." However, two other criteria that impact information behavior and outcomes need to be addressed as well. First, in factor six, the information user's self-identification or "role" within a society can contribute to their proclivity to share fake news, which again speaks to the micro, meso, and macro worlds referenced previously in chapters 7 and 8. The macro world examination would allow us to investigate the larger scale of the wider society upon the fake news user; meso world levels could be examined by those smaller subgroups and personal networks within which people operate and develop their online identities; the micro world level would show the individual emotions and personal development, through various actions. Additionally, in factor seven, an information user's overall education levels can also have an impact on whether or not someone will share fake news. An investigation of LIS research assumptions of and library-centered pragmatic approaches to information literacy will be interrogated.

FACTOR SIX: SELF-IDENTIFICATION, ROLES, AND SOCIAL POSITIONING

Self-identification theory posits that information users online constantly change and develop their internal sense of self and, in turn, alter their outward personal identifications and actions presented to others. Role theory has been suggested as a way to better categorize and understand information users' different approaches to information seeking (Prabha et al., 2007). It is surmised through this theory that the role a person has assumed (that is, university student, faculty member, layperson, expert, etc.) can contribute to whether that person continues to search for more information or stops, even if results are insufficient. Roles, they find, "provide behavioral guidelines, prescriptions or boundaries in the form of expectations" (Prabha et al., 2007) such that motivations and desires to continue are impacted by the role's normative values.

The person who self-identifies as an expert in a field, for example, and internalizes the norms that this role assumes may be more likely to continue searching out of professional obligation, while conversely a student with fewer expectations for subject mastery may stop sooner. Weiss et al. (2020) similarly suggest that roles can influence information behavior by noting that the teaching faculty studied at their university may have been less willing to admit personal susceptibility to fake news due to their pride in assuming the role of "professor." Professional pride may certainly influence the interpretation of one's own actions, making it seem harder to fully determine whether confidence in one's own abilities is warranted or not.

The advantage of examining social positioning is that it allows for more complexity in developing user identities, assuming that online information users "are active developers of their identities" (Given, 2005, p. 335). As a result of this active development of identity, one might imagine that it plays an important role in the ways people share fake news. An information user's identity or role may correspond with their willingness to share certain types of false information, rumors, or conspiracies. Similarly, the role within a specific group also impacts whether someone will share a false story. Ogasawara finds that the creation of personal identities within smaller online subcultures impacts users' willingness to share information between others in their group. Japanese right-wing online groups (*Neto-uyo*) are known to share factually incorrect news stories providing distorted perspectives that help to solidify political stances and attitudes important to them. Consequently, those within that same group or a similarly minded community are more willing to believe this information and share it with others within the group. Those who exist in such online bubbles are similarly known to disbelieve any information that comes from outside their groups, similar to cult members who deny perspectives unacknowledged by their cult. It is therefore an essential component of the fake news model to examine the ways in which people assume roles within their daily lives in the broader society (that is, by family, race, and profession) as well as within smaller subcultures (that is, online groups and chat rooms, etc.) and the ways in which these roles impact or modify their information sharing behavior.

FACTOR SEVEN: EDUCATION LEVEL

A person's level of education may also influence the likelihood of sharing fake news. Certainly, the more educated and more well versed a person is in a certain topic can provide resilience to or immunity against spreading false information, though it is no ultimate guarantee as plenty of well-educated people can fall for fake news or come to believe false narratives. While education levels and research skills vary among all people, Weiss et al. (2020) find that subject mastery can potentially diminish the impact of fake news. The weaker research methods of undergraduate students, for example, show how fake news can take root, in comparison to the deep background knowledge and robust fact-checking habits of professors, researchers, and scholars that arrive as a result of years of professional study and practice. A higher level of educational attainment has been associated with less sharing of fake news, as the informed person is more likely to be able to identify false claims and subsequently refute them. Allcott et al. (2019) and Flynn et al. (2017) assert that those who are less educated may lean more toward readily accepting misinformation than individuals who have some form of education and are more able to discern fact from fiction.

Information poverty, as outlined by Elfrida Chatman (1996), may also have an adverse effect on a person's overall ability to navigate and question information. Though an environmental factor, it impacts how likely people are to ask questions about things they do not know. Those in information-poor situations are less likely to seek out advice or find out information that they may truly have a need for—this is especially evident in the inertia seen in people that do not seek out information about medical conditions and health care (Chatman, 1996). In contrast, those in more highly educated circles are shown to rely on networks of friends and colleagues, who often serve as information brokers for them, and exist in so-called information grounds that help them cope with and better process unvetted information and rumors (Williamson, 1998). So the impact of education on information users is not merely related to individuals, but it also stems from the connections and networks people become associated with through the fruits of learning itself, including professional organizations and more diverse social circles.

Librarians for their part have generally placed a greater amount of emphasis on championing education for its ability to minimize the use of fake news and mitigate its effects. Primary focus has zeroed in on the use of information literacy standards devised by the Association of College and Research Libraries (ACRL) through its *Framework for Information Literacy for Higher Education* (Batchelor, 2017; De Paor and Heravi, 2020; Gardner and Mazzola, 2018). The ACRL framework provides a useful scaffold and overlying structure for librarians to advocate for information literacy as a general set of principles that can address a wide range of student-centered needs and to teach them pragmatic skills for utilizing information in their daily activities. Students, it is argued, benefit from information literacy instruction through learning various philosophies, principles, guidelines, and habits for interacting with and utilizing information ethically and with facility, with a focus on "critical and higher order of thinking" (Hsieh et al., 2021). Students also learn how to incorporate these principles into the use of information in education, real-life scenarios, and in their future careers, often given in pragmatic one-shot lessons. The benefits of information literacy instruction on students appear in a wide array of areas, helping students to recognize the quality, authenticity, and credibility of the information they encounter (Hobbs, 2006; Schuster, 2007). Overall, librarians are seen, even now, as helpful providers of information literacy instruction that can be used to "help debunk and decipher fake news" in order to ultimately help the communities they serve "become critical and savvy information consumers" (Cooke, 2018, p. 8).

TOWARD A NEW DIRECTION

The Problem with the Primacy of Information Literacy

Though a useful set of guidelines overall, information literacy has proven at times to be somewhat problematic in its application, with significant criticism of the ACRL's information literacy framework coming from various researchers and practitioners that find information literacy instruction lacking in both results and evidence of tangible benefits (Hsieh et al., 2021). Dixon (2021) notes that students initially arrive at their respective campuses and schools with differing levels of information literacy skills. This difference in levels is shown to increase inequality between student outcomes and may even exacerbate barriers to academic success (Buzzetto-Hollywood et al., 2018; Cullen, 2003). As a general rule in the academic library profession, the main way that librarians serve their campuses is by providing this information literacy instruction through one-shot lessons to students to demonstrate how to use library resources. Such lessons are generally informed by the ACRL framework and its series of best practices and philosophies. Faix and Fyn (2020), in one notable example, provide a close reading of the ACRL framework to help apply its principles to lessons on research strategies and source evaluations in order to help dispel the impact of misinformation.

Nevertheless, librarians still report overall difficulties in putting these ideals into practice in the classroom (Hsieh et al., 2021). This method of teaching, however useful in the short term for helping students complete university coursework, relies primarily upon one-time lessons given without uniformity to classes in numerous disciplines that may irregularly request sessions. The unevenness of implementation and the wide number of variables to assess (especially student age, major, prior education, and amount of repeated library instruction) may contribute to the weak impact this form of library instruction has on student achievement (Wong and Cmor, 2011). A potentially better alternative providing longer-term, credit-bearing courses has been proposed by many librarians, but the current number of academic libraries offering these may be as low as 19 percent (Jardine et al., 2018), and enroll-ment in such courses may be but a fraction of the student body. As a result, a large-scale shift in methods to address student needs nationwide would take a significant amount of time to implement at consistent and effective levels.

As the fake news model suggests, education level plays at least some role in the information user's potential tendencies to share false information or engage in fact-checking. Despite the large amount of time dedicated to it, however, education is not the sole factor in mitigating fake news. Indeed, a university's emphasis on developing critical thinking skills combined with the narrower emphasis on information literacy within academic libraries are probably not sufficient on their own to address and solve the problem of who might share fake news and why. Given the wider contexts and personal characteristics that the model proposes as well as some of the inherent flaws to the one-shot lesson approach to information literacy, it should not be dif-ficult to see why.

Broadening the discussion a little further, determining credible resources (for example, the steps some take to find respectable sources), a founda-tional skill for information users, is often undermined by online information itself. It often lacks the necessary contextual underpinnings in the form of well-documented metadata to help verify it by tethering it to established pat-terns of fact (Cooke, 2017). Similarly, information literacy itself can fall short in helping individuals effectively identify credible sources, especially if the very idea of a governing authority itself is under constant question by groups espousing alternative perspectives or unproven narratives (Bluemle, 2018). As a result, if too much focus is given on a specific factor at the expense of other factors, any progress that might be made against fake news—even as some overall benefit is derived from information literacy instruction itself—may ultimately be elusive. Librarians must, therefore, begin to rethink how information literacy may be better used to counteract the urge to share fake news while also keeping an eye to the larger contexts. To do this, information literacy and education levels must be seen as but one of seven equally impor-tant factors that contribute to the larger effort pinpointing the vulnerabilities that lead to sharing false information while also encouraging the behaviors and conditions that lead to verifying information and rejecting fake news.

With these criticisms in mind, misinformation's link to information lit-eracy must be better explored. The model merely accounts for information literacy to a certain extent, but it is dangerous to focus too much on just one aspect when it comes to regulating and mitigating the effects of fake news. Additionally, overemphasizing information literacy—especially as it is cur-rently implemented in the one-shot lesson form—as a main cure for fake news is likely to be counterproductive given the limited and uneven exposure students have to instruction. As a result, a more complete portrait needs to be developed, which the model attempts to provide.

A DETAILED PORTRAIT OF THE FAKE NEWS USER

Ultimately, this comprehensive model of fake news is designed to provide a clearer understanding of how and why fake news, misinformation, conspiracy theories, and other false narratives spread among individual users and throughout their online networks. Muñiz-Velázquez (2023) rightfully identifies a few of the problem tendencies that bad actors exploit as "patterns of vulnerability," which involves a full range of human cognitive biases (personal internal issues), fragmented decontextualization (content and context issues), and capitalist-driven information overload (online platform issues). These vulnerabilities can impact online information users without better policies and safeguards in place.

A clear picture of fake news users incorporates, in addition to wider macroeconomic and societal vulnerability patterns, the various characteristics mentioned previously. Talwar et al. have provided a good foundation, finding positive correlations between certain behaviors and states (trust, self-disclosure, comparisons, FOMO, and fatigue) and the tendency to share fake news with others. As noted from Talwar's results, the hypothesis that these factors contribute to either authenticating information or sharing fake news online shows clear associations in the information users they surveyed. In online trust, for example, they find that lower trust levels were statistically significant in predicting whether a person would authenticate news before they shared it online. Higher levels of trust showed positive and statistically significant associations with sharing fake news. Additionally, self-disclosure demonstrated significant positive associations with both authentication and sharing fake news. FOMO demonstrates a significant positive association with sharing fake news online. This suggests that those who harbor stronger feelings of missing out will be more likely to share fake news. Social media fatigue, on the other hand, demonstrates positive associations with authentication as well as sharing fake news, suggesting two things. The act of authentication itself can bring on fatigue in the information user, while the fatigue itself can also drive people to share whatever they have without verification. There needs to be further exploration into how fatigue in information users impacts both results.

It remains to be seen what impact self-identification within groups and education levels will have on the probability a user will authenticate information or share fake news. Demographic information, certainly, may help to pinpoint a person's education levels in relation to their other information behavioral tendencies. But getting at a person's self-identification—especially if they are different than what the person might normally be considered to fall within when acting or presenting within a subculture—may be more difficult to pin down. People often have a reason not to share their views in day-to-day life, especially if they are seen as illegal, threatening, shameful, or generally looked down upon. People also have reason to hide perspectives among people they do not know well or given specific wider political conditions. The impact of negative emotions related to the disclosure of one's identity may be a significant reason people do not provide honest answers about their online identities.

MULTIPLE VIEWS OF FALSE INFORMATION, MULTIPLE "VULNERABILITIES"

Various views and definitions of fake news also contribute to its proliferation among people who encounter false information. It is a slippery concept and hard to pin down for some. Not only is it an issue of news stories distorted from their original formal intents, but it is also a format that is hard for people to define. One person's fake news may in fact be another person's foundational resource. The subjective element cannot be underestimated and needs to be explored further. While attitudes were examined by Weiss et al. (2020) about what teaching faculty think of fake news, one area that was not explored was what *students* think of it. The surveyed faculty mentioned that they believed students were more susceptible and in danger of falling for fake news due to their lack of familiarity and expertise in factual information related to subjects as well as in their abilities to utilize the tools of reason and rhetoric. They also point out that the lack of a clear definition itself can make fake news seem less important. It remains somewhat underexplored just how that lack of a clear definition might contribute to students' ability to understand reality and the differences between true and false, fact or fiction, reality or fantasy. A multifarious and unclear definition of fake news may ultimately result in exposing the multiple vulnerabilities of those who are unable to define it. Certainly, one can argue, being unaware of the complexities of fake news, including the various guises it falls under (for example, parody, hoax, propaganda, or disinformation) could contribute to different ways in which the person becomes exposed to fraud or misdirection. When people are aware of potential scams before they happen, they are less likely to fall for them.

FUTURE PROJECTS

Between 2017 and 2019 faculty members were surveyed at a master's grant-ing university and their responses analyzed to get a sense of how they defined fake news and whether they believed students as well as themselves were susceptible to it. Did they, as Muñiz-Velázquez predicts may happen, fall into clear patterns of vulnerability like other members of the society at large? In some ways, the results of the survey suggest that some faculty believe their students truly do fall into this cycle, even as they themselves believe they are largely immune to its effects (Weiss et al., 2020; Alwan, et al, 2022). To further this research, however, future directions might involve a look at stu-dents specifically, to get a sense of what factors in the model might impact them the most. While Talwar et al. show strong and clear results for certain characteristics, some show ambiguity or fail to predict certain behaviors, and so it is important to widen the scope among all these areas.

A future direction in this research might include looking at education level, in particular, and how the other variables are impacted by this. If a person is more highly educated, for example, do the deleterious effects of FOMO or trust become reduced? This should yield valuable insight into how students might be affected by other internal factors rather than purely their education attainment, which is still higher than the average person in the United States and therefore makes them atypical of the population at large. Widening the scope, then, to include those with less education, in different types of jobs, as well as those who have varied amounts of exposure to news and information online or on television would be important.

Finally, the speed at which fake news is now generated may be an important factor to consider. In what ways does the rapid spread of faked information and false narrative impact the user? Does the speed with which something is shared have a true impact on whether someone will be more or less likely to pass it along or even fall for it? Similar issues surround the rapid spread of viral shaming and how difficult it is to contain. One wonders if the related information pathology of fake news is made worse due to the speed with which it is shared? That lag in time between when the false story is shared and the resultant fact-check debunking is made available may account for some people falling for fake news. Rumor, they say, travels faster than the truth; fake news may travel just as fast.

REFERENCES

Allcott, H., Gentzkow, M., and Yu, C. (2019). Trends in the diffusion of misinformation on social media. *Research & Politics, 6*(2). https://doi.org/10.1177/2053168019848554.

Alwan, A., Garcia, E., Kirakosian, A., and Weiss, A. (2022). Fake news and libraries: How teaching faculty in higher education view librarians' roles in counteracting the spread of false information. *Partnership: The Canadian Journal of Library and Information Practice and Research, 16*(2), pp. 1–30. doi:10.21083/partnership.v16i2.6483.

Batchelor, O. (2017). Getting out the truth: The role of libraries in the fight against fake news. *Reference Services Review, 45,* pp. 143–48. 10.1108/RSR-03-2017-0006.

Blackwell, D., Leaman, C., Tramposch, R., Osborne, C., and Liss, M. (2017). Extraversion, neuroticism, attachment style and fear of missing out as predictors of social media use and addiction. *Personality and Individual Differences, 116,* pp. 69–72. https://doi.org/10.1016/j.paid.2017.04.039.

Blair, A. (2010). *Too much to know: Managing scholarly information before the modern age.* New Have: Yale University Press.

Bluemle, S. R. (2018). Post-facts: Information literacy and authority after the 2016 election. *Libraries and the Academy, 18*(2), pp. 265–82.

Buglass, S. L., Binder, J. F., Betts, L. R., and Underwood, J. D. M. (2017). Motivators of online vulnerability: The impact of social network site use and FOMO. *Computers in Human Behavior, 66,* pp. 248–55. https://doi.org/10.1016/j.chb.2016.09.055.

Buzzetto-Hollywood, N., Wang, H., Elobeid, M., and Elobaid, M. (2018). Addressing information literacy and the digital divide in higher education. *Interdisciplinary Journal of e-Skills and Lifelong Learning, 14,* pp. 77–93. https://doi.org/10.28945/4029.

Chatman, E. A. (1996). The impoverished life-world of outsiders. *Journal of the American Society for Information Science, 47*(3), pp. 193–206.

Cooke, N. A. (2017). Posttruth, truthiness, and alternative facts: Information behavior and critical information consumption for a new age. *The Library Quarterly, 87*(3), pp. 211–21. https://www.journals.uchicago.edu/doi/epdf/10.1086/692298.

Cooke, N. A. (2018). *Fake news and alternative facts: Information literacy in a post-truth era.* Chicago: ALA Editions.

Cramer, E. M., Song, H., and Drent, A. M. (2016). Social comparison on Facebook: Motivation, affective consequences, self-esteem, and Facebook fatigue. *Computers in Human Behavior, 64,* pp. 739–46.

Cullen, R. (2003). The digital divide: A global and national call to action. *The Electronic Library, 21,* pp. 247–57.

Davies, E. (2006). Communities of practice. In K. E. Fisher, S. Erdelez, and L. E. F. McKechnie (eds.), *Theories of information behaviors* (pp. 104–9). Medford, NJ: Information Today.

De Paor, S., and Heravi, B. (2020). Information literacy and fake news: How the field of librarianship can help combat the epidemic of fake news. *Journal of Academic. Librarianship, 46*(5). https://doi.org/10.1016/j.acalib.2020.102218.

Deci, E. L., and Ryan, R. M. (1985). *Intrinsic motivation and self-determination in human behavior*. New York: Plenum Press.

Dixon, J. (2017). First impressions: LJ's first year experience survey. *Library Journal*. https://www.libraryjournal.com/?detailStory=first-impressions-ljs-first-year-experience-survey.

DuBois, T., Golbeck, J., and Srinivasan, A. (2011). Predicting trust and distrust in social networks. In *Proceedings of the 2011 IEEE Third International Conference on Privacy, Security, Risk and Trust* and *2011 IEEE Third International Conference on Social Computing*, Boston, MA, USA, October 9–11 (pp. 418–24.). Boston: IEEE Computer Society.

Eppler, M., and Mengis, J. (2004). The concept of information overload: A review of literature from organization science, accounting, marketing, MIS, and related disciplines. *The Information Society, 20*(5), pp. 325–44.

Faix, A., and Fyn, A. (2020). Framing fake news: Misinformation and the ACRL framework. *Portal, 20*(3), pp. 495–508. https://doi.org/10.1353/pla.2020.0027.

Festinger, L. (1954). A theory of social comparison processes. *Human Relations, 7*(2), pp. 117–40. https://doi.org/10.1177/001872675400700202.

Flynn, D. J., Nyhan, B., and Reifler, J. (2017). The nature and origins of misperceptions: Understanding false and unsupported beliefs about politics. *Advances in Political Psychology, 38*, pp. 127–50. https://doi.org/10.1111/pops.12394.

Gardner, M., and Mazzola, N. (2018). Fighting fake news: Tools and resources to combat disinformation. *Knowledge Quest, 47*(1), p. 6.

Given, L. M. (2005) Social positioning. In K. Fisher, S. Erdelez, and L. McKechnie (eds.), *Theories of information behavior* (pp. 334–38). Medford, NJ: Information Today.

Grabner-Kräuter, S., and Bitter, S. (2013). Trust in online social networks: A multi-faceted perspective. *Forum for Social Economics, 44*(1), pp. 48–68. doi.org/10.1080/07360932.2013.781517.

Grosser, T. J., Lopez-Kidwell, V., and Labianca, G. (2010). A social network analysis of positive and negative gossip in organizational life. *Group & Organization Management, 35*(2), pp. 177–212. https://doi.org/10.1177/1059601109360391.

Hobbs, R. (2006). Multiple visions of multimedia literacy: Emerging areas of synthesis. In M. C. McKenna, L. D. Labbo, R. D. Kieffer, and D. Reinking (eds.), *International handbook of literacy and technology* (pp. 15–28). Philadelphia: Temple University.

Hsieh, M. L., Dawson, P. H, and Yang, S. Q. (2021). The ACRL framework successes and challenges since 2016: A survey. *The Journal of Academic Librarianship, 47*(2). https://doi-org.libproxy.csun.edu/10.1016/j.acalib.2020.102306.

Jardine, S., Shropshire, S., and Koury, R. (2018). Credit-bearing information literacy courses in academic libraries: Comparing peers. *College & Research Libraries, 79*(6), pp. 768–84. https://crl.acrl.org/index.php/crl/article/view/16825.

Johnson, C. A. (2005). Nan Lin's theory of social capital. In K. Fisher, S. Erdelez, and L. McKechnie (eds.), *Theories of information behavior* (pp. 323–27). Medford, NJ: Information Today.

Krasnova, H., Spiekermann, S., Koroleva, K., and Hildebrand, T. (2010). Online social networks: Why we disclose. *Journal of Information Technology, 25*(2), pp. 109–25. https://doi.org/10.1057/jit.2010.6.

Mayer, R. C., Davis, J. H., and Schoorman, F. D. (1995). An integrative model of organizational trust. *The Academy of Management Review, 20*(3), pp. 709–34. https://doi.org/10.2307/258792.

Muñiz-Velázquez, J. (2023). (Dis)Information Literacy: A Democratic Right and Duty of All Citizens. *Media and Communication, 11*(2), pp. 1–4. https://doi.org/10.17645/mac.v11i2.7029.

Ogasawara, M. (2019). The daily us (vs. them) from online to offline: Japan's media manipulation and cultural transcoding of collective memories. *Journal of Contemporary Eastern Asia, 18*(2), pp. 49–67. https://doi.org/10.17477/jcea.2019.18.2.049.

Prabha, C., Silipigni-Connaway, L., Olszewski, L., and Jenkins, L. R. (2007). What is enough? Satisficing information needs. *Journal of Documentation, 63*(1), pp. 74–89. https://doi.org/10.1108/00220410710723894.

Ravindran, T., Yeow Kuan, A. C., and Hoe Lian, D. G. (2014). Antecedents and effects of social network fatigue. *Journal of the Association for Information Science and Technology, 65*(11), pp. 2306–20. https://doi.org/10.1002/asi.23122.

Rioux, K. (2005). Information acquiring-and-sharing. In K. Fisher, S. Erdelez, and L. McKechnie (eds.), *Theories of information behavior* (pp. 169–73). Medford, NJ: Information Today.

Rodríguez-Pérez, C., and Canel, M. (2023). Exploring European citizens' resilience to misinformation: Media legitimacy and media trust as predictive variables. *Media and Communication, 11*(2), pp. 30–41. https://doi.org/10.17645/mac.v11i2.6317.

Ryan, R. M., and Deci, E. L. (2000). Intrinsic and extrinsic motivations: Classic definitions and new directions. *Contemporary Educational Psychology, 25*(1), pp. 54–56. https://doi.org/10.1006/ceps.1999.1020.

Schoorman, F. D., Roger, C., Mayer, R. C., and Davis, J. H. (2007). An integrative model of organizational trust: Past, present, and future. *Academy of Management Review, 32*(2), pp. 344–54. https://doi.org/10.5465/amr.2007.24348410.

Schuster, S. M. (2007). Information literacy as a core value. *Biochemistry and Molecular Biology Education, 35*(5), pp. 372–73. https://doi.org/10.1002/bmb.100.

Sundin, O., and Hedman, J. (2005). Professions and occupational identities. In K. Fisher, S. Erdelez, and L. McKechnie (eds.), *Theories of information behavior* (pp. 293–97). Medford, NJ: Information Today.

Talwar, S., Dhir, A., Kaur, P., Zafar, N., and Alrasheedy, M. (2019). Why do people share fake news? Associations between the dark side of social media use and fake news sharing behavior. *Journal of Retailing and Consumer Services, 51*, pp. 72–82. https://doi.org/10.1016/j.jretconser.2019.05.026.

Watters, C., and Duffy, J. (2005). Motivational factors for interface design. In K. Fisher, S. Erdelez, and L. McKechnie (eds.), *Theories of information behavior* (pp. 242–46). Medford, NJ: Information Today.

Weiss, A., Alwan, A., Garcia, E., and Garcia, J. (2020). Surveying fake news: Assessing university faculty's fragmented definition of fake news and its impact on teaching critical thinking. *International Journal for Educational Integrity, 16*(1). https://doi.org/10.1007/s40979-019-0049-x.

Weiss, A. P., Alwan, A., Garcia, E. P., and Kirakosian, A. T. (2021). Toward a comprehensive model of fake news: A new approach to examine the creation and sharing of false information. *Societies, 11*(82). https://doi.org/10.3390/soc11030082.

Wenger, E. (1998). Communities of practice: Learning as a social system. *The Systems Thinker, 9*, pp. 2–3. https://thesystemsthinker.com/communities-of-practice-learning-as-a-social-system/.

Wert, S. R., and Salovey, P. (2004). A social comparison account of gossip. *Review of General Psychology, 8*(2), pp. 122–37. https://doi.org/10.1037/1089-2680.8.2.122.

Williamson, K. (1998). Discovered by chance: The role of incidental information acquisition in an ecological model of information use. *Library and Information Science Research, 20*(1), pp. 23–40. https://doi.org/10.1016/S0740-8188(98)90004-4.

Wong, S. H. R., and Cmor, D. (2011). Measuring association between library instruction and graduation GPA. *College and Research Libraries, 72*(5), pp. 464–73. https://doi.org/10.5860/crl-151.

Zipf, G. K. (1949). *Human behavior and the principle of least effort: An introduction to human ecology*. Cambridge, MA: Addison-Wesley.

PART IV

The Impact of Digital Fake News

Chapter 10

The Impact of Fake News on Universities, Libraries, and General Education

Part IV of this book focuses on the direct and indirect impact that digital fake news has had on the various segments of a modern information-based society. Overall, the next two chapters will focus on three main areas: education, online communication, and political discourse. The previous sections of the book have examined issues in information science and the spread of information pathologies not only in individuals but also through personal networks at varying scales. Creators and users intermingle at personal scales that can expand into wider personal circles and larger networks of friends and even may exist at larger scales with national and international communications. Although the book has already examined the history and development of fake news to the present time, speculating on the ongoing and similar struggles people continue to have with authenticity and truth, these next sections will widen the scope a bit more. We will look especially at the contemporary impact of fake news on the main pillars of societal development and the creation of information's value.

Education overall has been seen as the best approach in helping people combat misinformation, disinformation, fake news, false narratives, and conspiracy theories. Yet there are times when people, in spite of their education levels and familiarity with the tools of rhetoric and critical thinking, nevertheless fall for fake news and other fraudulent ideas. For example, despite clear evidence to the contrary, 63 percent of Republican voters in the United States nevertheless continued to believe in 2023 that the result of the 2020 presidential election was fraudulent, with 48 percent of those stating quite tellingly that it was based on "suspicion only" (Durkee, 2023). On one hand, one can certainly identify why some people have chosen to believe this lie by looking at the various factors proposed in the model, including their self-identification as staunch Republicans or as members of an extremist sub-culture (for example, MAGA or similar protofascist right-wing groups). On the other hand, some ideas persist despite their constant rebuttal in the face of evidence and despite personal education levels that might have normally predicted more skepticism than shown. True believers will remain true, some-times, even if their beliefs remain based on false information.

Looking beyond individuals, larger institutions may also be influenced, impacted, and altered by the rise of fake news and misinformation. In the history of fake news and propaganda, it was seen that libraries in the Soviet Union, for example, suffered from mistrust and the loss of privacy the totali-tarian society impressed upon its subjects (cf. Rogers, 1973). The impact on the society was profound and long lasting. Currently, universities in the United States have had trouble addressing the issues of fake news on their campuses in the face of strategic disinformation that destabilizes liberal democracies, while not meeting the challenges to produce graduates able to explore counterdisinformation and counterpropaganda (Baines, 2022). In similar ways, it will be necessary to examine the wider impacts that the debasing of trust has not only on students but also in the schools and educa-tional organizations themselves. In other words, how does false information impact schools and what does that mean for teachers and educators as well as the society at large?

This chapter will examine a number of these issues, including reactions that faculty have on the topic of fake news in their universities, and the impact that libraries—especially academic libraries—are absorbing. It will also look at how some false ideas and fake narratives can persist in education, so-called zombie concepts that do not seem to go away despite efforts to eradicate them. Finally, the chapter will look at how some places or students may be more susceptible to educational inaccuracies, getting back to some of the tenets found in the comprehensive model of fake news.

FAKE NEWS AND UNIVERSITIES: A LOOK AT SURVEY DATA ON FACULTY ATTITUDES

In a survey the author and his coresearchers administered to teaching faculty at their university in 2018, it was noticed that faculty at the time held "widely divergent views and definitions" of what they considered to be fake news. Weiss et al. (2020) found that across discipline, rank at the university (that is, early career, mid-career, and late career ranks), age, and gender, there was little agreement on ideas and conceptions of fake news. While this conclusion may not be earth-shattering to point out—and some of that lack of consensus is very obvious in the way that different people will approach and interact with information in different ways—some implications to this lack of consensus are clear. In particular, a lack of consistent views and conceptions about fake news could have future impacts on students in the area of pedagogy and in critical thinking.

TROUBLE IN PINNING DOWN FAKE NEWS

Many of the respondents saw fake news as a typically misleading story created in the form of "news" (that is, "any news/facts stated without support or reference. Usually propagated by social media"; or "News that conveys information not based on facts and that favors a particular political party"). Despite the dominance of "news stories" and "news" as the primary categorization, many other respondents showed differing conceptions of fake news, ranging from propaganda, unverified information, fabricated stories, lying, and the intentional delivery of false information. Other terms used to describe fake news included "stories," "content," "articles," "misinformation," "propaganda," "informational items," "hearsay," and "opinions" (Alwan et al., 2018). While some faculty responses were very neutral in their descriptions of these stories and who creates them, many were willing to situate fake news as the products of notorious right-wing news agencies such as Fox News or Breitbart, social media platforms, and Russian misinformation bots as prime examples. Some even avoided the description of fake news itself and instead zeroed in on behaviors and categorization of others, including students who might not know much, propagandists in other countries, and even freelance writers whose work might be considered untrustworthy (Alwan et al., 2018).

This fragmented view of fake news overall provides some insight into how difficult it can be to pin down solutions to it. Among the respondents there were also differing approaches to how faculty might address the problem of fake news with students in their courses. Such strategies include specifically raising topics in class that are relevant to the discipline to discuss and analyze why they are false or what is the truth. Some mention providing a detailed discussion of the scientific method, how to analyze data results, and raise the issues of validity, reliability, and credibility in different subjects and among controversial topics such as climate change. Each of these suggests varying approaches that are often context and discipline specific yet not uniform in the conceptualization or agreement on what fake news really is. There were also stark differences of opinion about whether fake news was even a concern at all. A few faculty respondents felt that it was not their business to care whether students were interacting with fake news and stated that they never raised the issue in their classes. Some also felt that it just was not worth the time to address fake news during their classes, as other topics took more of a priority during their limited class time, or that it was truly not relevant to the courses they taught (that is, a course on research methods, etc.) (Alwan et al., 2018).

Given these widely varying definitions and responses to the phenomenon among even a tiny sample of academics, it may be necessary to develop a more consistent definition and approach to the topic of fake news. In one important aspect, it was noted that faculty attitudes toward fake news generally fell within the well-known umbrella terms of misinformation, propaganda, and rumor. There was, notably, barely any mention of parody, satire, or make-believe, which are also essential aspects to the concept of fake news. The concepts of mimicry, imitation, and parody, as we have seen previously, play important roles in how fake news is generated, contributing to how it is spread and further perpetuated, and—importantly—how it can be counteracted. Yet it remains an underexplored aspect of the genre and one that may not be widely considered by academics in general.

Without a clearer description of the nuances and complexities of the concept, it may be more difficult for faculty to find methods of combating it through traditional teaching methods. The lack of a uniform definition, for example, impacts how faculty might be inclined or disinclined to teach students certain critical thinking skills. Depending on a professor's interest or awareness of the issue, students may graduate from the same schools with differing ideas of what comprises fake news. Without a more comprehensive approach to counteracting fake news, these novice handlers of complex information may be more easily fooled. Without a more complex understanding of the concept's nuances, furthermore, it becomes harder for students to neutralize the effects of fake news especially as it appears in different forms and is derived from multifarious intentions of nebulous origin. More personal vigilance in the use of information becomes, in some sense, a *requirement* for trusted online participation.

ROLE OF RANK AND DISCIPLINE IN ATTITUDES ABOUT FAKE NEWS

One of the more unexpected revelations from this survey was that lower-ranked teaching faculty at the author's university—especially lecturers, TAs, and adjuncts—were more likely to state that they emphasized a variety of techniques to better identify fake news and verify facts, making their roles in helping to teach critical thinking very important (Alwan et al., 2022). Some context to explain this is necessary. On one hand, lecturers usually will teach lower-level and introductory courses at the university such as first-year writing, basic composition, mathematics, a "university 101" course aimed at acclimating students to college level work, and so on. Yet these courses are a small aspect of students' college careers, and many will then spend most of their time in discipline-specific courses for their majors. Faculty in varying departments and disciplines will likely hold disparate views of fake news and how—and even whether—it should be addressed.

In the case of certain sciences, where validity and reliability in data are necessities for research, discussing how to test for these concepts is deemed foundational knowledge. Other disciplines will not address it this way, yet they do come to similar ideas with an emphasis on what they term credibility and finding credible sources. One respondent mentioned that they attempt to strengthen students' critical thinking skills ("Try to expose critical thinking skills. Ask about alternatives. I.e., never attack the basis of the information, but provide a moment of—have you thought about X from a non-value, non-judgmental ways" (Alwan et al., 2018). But many respondents did not tend to think in these terms, and this might be problematic. It suggests that a more comprehensive definition of fake news may be necessary to integrate into the higher education pedagogy in order to better work across the disciplines and narrow the gaps in teaching critical thinking that sometimes occur between disciplines.

FAKE NEWS AND THE IMPACT ON LIBRARIES AND LIBRARIAN ATTITUDES

Librarians are often seen as natural allies in issues related to the spread of false information and fake news. The library's reputation as a leader in the area of information management and the primary locus for these services has been built upon centuries of practice and evolving innovations, dating back to ancient times and extending through long historical periods of ups and downs, including warfare, conflagrations, political and religious repression, and similar societal unrest. The violent destruction of libraries in historical accounts is in many ways a reflection of their value to the societies that created them as well as the symbolic natures that their existence pressed upon those who destroyed them (Knuth, 2003).

One area that fake news and misinformation impacts is in library collection development. The prevailing wisdom has been that libraries collect only the most reputable information and resources available, with recourse to collection reshaping when materials have expired, often because they are either deemed obsolete or are the result of discredited research. Collections are "the result of implicit or explicit priorities that have been identified for satisfying information needs and are the result of assumptions about the status and relevant worth of various branches of knowledge" (Kelly, 2015). Yet issues of collection development also hinge upon the perceived legitimacy of resources and their acceptance within a mainstream, resulting in collections that skew toward the philosophical center without acknowledging fringe ideas. Some, like Dilevko (2008), advocate for "including as much overlooked material as possible" to reflect the broadest of perspectives within a given subject. Still, when the ground is poisoned, much effort needs to be taken to clean it. The push, then, to cleanse collections before they are allowed in the house impacts libraries in the overall increase in labor expended on thinking about such resources yet is also a source of constant conflict for those shaping collections for their users.

The impact on libraries in terms of lost hours is immense if the vetting of information has to be increased beyond already stretched levels of labor. In that sense, the rising tide of fake news, misinformation, deep fakes, and other false narratives generated not only by people but also disruptive digital bot and AI technologies looms over the practical operations of any library. While it is important to include "overlooked material," as Dilevko describes it, the potential flood of false information seems to instill fear into librarians, and library policies often reflect this fear of being overwhelmed by mistruths by the strict collection development policies they develop and the actions they take. The increased number of takedown, withdrawal, and academic integrity statements in libraries may be a reaction to this overwhelming fear of being flooded by counterfeits, fakes, and unethically created information. Of course, falsehoods are a routine part of the information landscape, and Anderson (2017) finds that they are not in libraries entirely by accident nor due to failure to detect and remove them, but that they are also "there by design," the result of fallible evaluations as well as the progression and regression of mainstream ideas.

Another notable exception to the general rule of collecting only credible and fully vetted sources occurs when gathering information resources that have gained historical or subject discipline interest for the communities the libraries serve. Many subject archives and repositories collect ephemera and other primary source material, as in the case of the resource *Political Extremism and Radicalism: Far-Right Groups in America*, published by Gale Publishing. This collection of materials—as well as the attendant disinformation, misinformation, and fake news inherent to them—becomes useful for those looking to understand the phenomenon of hate, xenophobia, and extremist beliefs. Collections that provide access to important primary documentation need not necessarily be fully cleansed of false information to be of use. Instead honoring truth depends upon the clear contextualization of such original resources.

A similar collection created by Reveal Digital called *Hate in America: The Newspapers of the KKK* demonstrates the pitfalls of openly publishing an archive of racist, revisionist, and xenophobic materials without a clear sense of the mission or the editorial apparatus needed to concretely contextualize the information. Echterling (2019) writes, "I found no consideration for how being a producer, what Reveal Digital calls a 'participating library,' of a xenophobic newspaper database published to the open web and ingestible in commercial search engines was different from adding published xenophobic content to the library's collection." In other words, what she is essentially attempting to ask is: What *epistemological* value does a collection of hate materials actually have if it is stripped of its original local contexts and distributed as widely as any resource online? What does it contribute to overall understanding and how humans create truthful knowledge? These are hard questions that often librarians and libraries are unable to answer satisfactorily.

The lessons of these archives are twofold. First, the epistemological context within which these objects are presented must be firmly established and the critical apparatus strong enough to preserve that context so that misinformation, revisionist false narratives, and extremist views are not allowed to perpetuate. Disclaiming the viewpoints in the archive while also posting the factual counterarguments or historical accuracies diminishes the potential for the information to be abused. Yet this also requires an increase in effort and workload to make sure that context is strong enough to counteract the potentials for misuse and misinterpretation. Second, a meta-examination of the work must be conducted as an ongoing process between creator, collector, and user, where the user encounters the negative information framed for them in order to better analyze the creator's claims to reality. Original assumptions are interrogated here, which does not allow users to take the resources at face value nor as unmediated statements of fact. Red flag warnings and disclaimers from these collections, critical structures such as introductions and footnotes, and trigger warnings provide important ways to distance the information user from the false narratives of the original creators.

Current library practice follows many of the same principles that had been laid down in the past, especially with preservation of contexts, source locations, and the protection and copying of literary works themselves. Similarly, libraries have burnished their reputations over the centuries by presenting their staff as selective gatekeepers and controllers of all-important credibility and reliability. These values of credibility and reliability, however, have come to be seen as the positive values in opposition to the destabilizing problems of fake news, misinformation, and disinformation. Sullivan finds that this binary split is endemic to library and information science as a research discipline and that there is "the tendency to dichotomize the information landscape, characterizing it as either true or false, good or bad, verified or biased" (Sullivan, 2019). Certainly, many librarians describe fake news as a bad problem and harbor assumptions that not only do other librarians agree with these self-evident assertions but that everyone else does as well.

Yet this belief of a tacit agreement among all librarians is problematic, especially when assertions about the negative impacts of fake news and misinformation are treated as assumptions of fact in their research rather than as questions and hypotheticals in need of interrogation and analysis. Sullivan implies some of the reason for this lack of interrogation is that "librarians are painfully aware that there is a problem to be addressed but have not always been clear about the nature of that problem" (Sullivan, 2019). The negative perceptions surrounding fake news harbored by librarian values—often the positive characteristics of truth, rationality, and educational enlightenment—may be coloring objective analyses of the phenomenon or missing out on ways to gather actual evidence about it. And that is really what is at issue with much librarian discussion of the fake news problem: too few of the assumptions related to library preoccupations such as information literacy, information behavior, and patron needs are examined in full in relation to fake news and misinformation. Too few theories and approaches outside of information literacy and library user behavior are addressed; more need to be incorporated to better understand the totality of user experiences and user motivations.

Some of this may, in fact, stem from the desire of librarians to cheerlead on behalf of the institutions they work for, playing the role of librarian that slides subtly over time in a benign though misleading metonymic slippage to represent embodiments of the library itself: sturdy, staid, unmoving. Undoubtedly, pressure from administrators for librarians to be advocates for and liaisons to the beneficial services of any library also contributes to the ways in which librarians approach their vocations. But that attitude can color and even introduce bias into the realities of whether librarians and libraries are ready for or even capable of mitigating the impact of fake news on their patrons.

SUSCEPTIBILITY AND VULNERABILITY IN STUDENTS: HOW IL MISSES ITS OPPORTUNITY

Some of the issues related to the problem of fake news susceptibility extend to how information literacy is taught to students. Rubin (2019) provides some important discussion on how information literacy can improve a student's reaction to the fake news and "BS" that saturate our information worlds. Yet the problems of dealing with fake news go far beyond just teaching information literacy to instill trust in people. She writes that there is "a strong sentiment that librarians have an opportunity, if not duty, to join . . . the fight against fake news" (Rubin, 2019). But she finds that librarians "do not appear to understand the real danger of misinformation—or at best only understand half of it" (Rubin, 2019). In this regard, it is necessary to understand the susceptibilities and vulnerabilities being exploited in students—especially children—in order to better combat the impact of fake news. Yet without a more complex view of the needed solutions beyond just information literacy and the assumption that "something must be done" by librarians, nothing solid will be accomplished.

The ACRL's information literacy framework is often used by librarians and LIS researchers alike as a necessary and useful guide toward this goal of ethical information use. Faix and Fyn (2020), in one example of this approach, provide readers with "a close reading of the Framework to examine how librarians can apply it more fully when teaching research strategies, especially source evaluation." Yet in similar fashion to the ways in which the LIS field can underanalyze problems related to fake news, the discipline also relies too heavily on some of the underdeveloped and underexamined assumptions of the ACRL's framework to solve specific problems. While the framework provides "a concept-driven approach to information literacy" (Faix and Fyn, 2020) rather than a mere checklist of activities to help improve student information use outcomes, the proven benefits to the approach seem to be unclear.

The frames are certainly broad enough to include all aspects of information use, including information authority ("Authority Is Constructed and Contextual"), creating new information ("Information Creation as a Process"), the value inherent to information ("Information Has Value"), research methodology ("Research as Inquiry"), the nature of scholarship itself ("Scholarship as Conversation"), and even information behavior itself ("Searching as Strategic Exploration"). In describing how to use the "Authority" frame of information literacy, Faix and Fyn assert that "the knowledge practices and dispositions from 'Authority Is Constructed and Contextual' are useful for modeling critical thinking about the authority of a source" and suggest that having students "debate and vote on the most trustworthy [resource]" can help them combat fake news (Faix and Fyn, 2020). This may be true, but one wonders whether these methods have actually been tested and what, if anything, the students had gained from doing them. Clear empirical evidence supporting the efficacy of the framework's criteria is missing in this argument. The same applies for *all* the frames and the potential activities aimed at helping students deal with fake news. These are good general rules, to be sure, and interesting activities to try within a classroom, but for improvements in scholarship, research, and even library instruction *praxis*, a better assessment of the impact on students is necessary.

Alwan et al. (2022) explore the attitude of faculty members regarding the role libraries might play in helping them and their students account for and neutralize false information. They find a number of issues raised by faculty when it comes to attitudes about librarians and their ability to assist both faculty and students in neutralizing fake news. Certainly, among the faculty ranks they find that only lecturers hold a strong enough view that either libraries or librarians might play a helpful role in having students address fake news. Higher-ranking faculty seemed to only marginally accept that libraries might have an important role to play in combating fake news; they also show that there is not much awareness of librarians doing anything about it. Some even stated quite clearly that they did not use the library for this purpose. Some went a little further, explaining that they might suggest using it for credible sources and how to use them. The exceptions appeared to be those faculty that openly rely on librarians to discuss these issues or that routinely use the library as part of class assignments (that is, a bibliography or a research assignment). Nearly all faculty rarely or never discuss fake news with librarians; additionally, they did "not perceive the library as the primary entity that can assist their students with the issue of fake news" (Alwan et al., 2022). This hesitance for teaching faculty to consult with librarians on the topic could result in future difficulties for those librarians who attempt to address the issue of fake news with faculty and their students directly.

SUGGESTING NEW DIRECTIONS FOR FAKE NEWS AND LIBRARIES

It may be necessary, then, to begin broader outreach efforts and awareness programs to help change some traditionally held conceptions of what roles librarians might play in fixing the problems related to fake news. Indeed, despite not seeing librarians as primary helpers in the fight against fake news, faculty do have important insight and advice into how libraries and librarians might help them. Perhaps not surprisingly, faculty respondents in the survey provided multiple practical suggestions for outreach opportunities that librarians might adopt to improve awareness of fake news among students, including workshops, public statements, videos, social media, blogs, regular emails, and newsletters. One respondent even suggested the unique idea of holding a "fake news festival" in the lobby of the CSU Northridge University Library next to its coffee shop (Alwan et al., 2018).

Other suggestions were less frequently stated but no less interesting in revealing teaching faculty's engagement in the issue and acknowledgment of what they see as librarian strengths. A theme of communication, similar to outreach efforts, was suggested by one person, who described their idea as an antidote to the alienation (for example, "less person-to-person interaction"; Alwan et al., 2018) that they believe contributes to fake news and people's acquiescence and numbing to it. A few respondents also suggested improving library information architecture so that fake news could be readily identified and labeled for the student during a catalog or database search without them having to go through the vetting process. Similarly, many suggested better use of web guides tailored for specific courses and the broadening of information literacy and critical thinking efforts. One person suggested a fact-check service provided by the library, perhaps envisioned as a one-on-one activity that would verify resources for the students. Finally, one felt that the issues raised by fake news were part of a larger faculty imperative and that it was "a discussion that faculty need to have within their departments"; librarians were seen as potential partners, but only if faculty would stop being effectively siloed within their respective disciplines and departments (Alwan et al., 2018).

These suggestions from faculty align somewhat with Sullivan (2019), who, in his thorough critique of librarian attitudes and assumptions about their roles in counteracting fake news and misinformation, finds a few practical, if minor, approaches to improving the situation in the short term. He suggests, similar to the faculty advice to improve search platforms' information architecture, that students need to be made more aware of and given access to technology that helps them verify and authenticate images and videos. That lesson may be hard to swallow for some, as it does ultimately take the vetting process out of librarians' hands—which has been a primary reaction to the phenomenon—and further into the escalating technology cat-and-mouse disinformation wars. One can be forgiven for being wary about using *more* technology to solve a technologically driven problem.

Sullivan also suggests that the "high degree of public trust" in libraries needs to be extended beyond the physical and figurative walls of the library and outward to communities at large. The faculty survey respondent who suggested, for example, a "fake news festival" at the library's coffeeshop, as well as the one who discussed the problems of alienation in information users, mirrors this urge to meet with the public directly to address the problems of fake news. Extending these events beyond the borders of university campuses would also reach more people and may ultimately be a more effective approach to combating the root causes of fake news.

FAKE NEWS, FALSE INFORMATION, AND ZOMBIE CONCEPTS IN K–12 EDUCATION

Of course, institutions of higher education and academic libraries are hardly the only places dealing with the issues of fake news. K–12 schools also are being forced to confront the problem of fake news and false information that form not only the antithesis to their educational goals but also fuel some of the false ideas that students are unwittingly taught in school and later perpetu-ate. The challenge of fighting fake news and misinformation in K–12 schools, however, boils down to a number of complicated issues. Education is a combination of teaching endeavors, systemic organizations, and legal policy implementations, "a complex and multidimensional system," as List and Rubenstein (2019) describe it, "beholden" to a wide array of stakeholders, including parents, students, teachers, administrators, and policymakers. But due to education's central role in the lives of so many in a society, it also is susceptible to the false information, fake news, and misinformation that targets these varied stakeholders. As each have a share in the success of the school, if any one of the various stakeholders appears to fall for false informa-tion and inaccurate information, it can impact a school's ability to teach and share reliable information.

This dynamic has played out across the country at school boards that have recently devised antitrans rules, for example, based on dubious politicized problems and so-called antiwoke ideologies and legislation (Clark, 2023). Parents, for their own part, may be mistaken about certain ideas—that is, that critical race theory is taught in their school *even when it is not*—and complain or threaten school boards if spurred on by "manufactured outrage," which ultimately has an adverse effect on schools and students (Graham, 2021; Walker, 2021; Kamenetz, 2021). For their own part, students have also been shown to be susceptible to fake news. One study finds that students are easily fooled by articles that provide more evidence, even if it is false, as opposed to articles with less, though true, evidence. Additionally, students are also more potentially susceptible to false information if they have had some previous familiarity or belief about a topic (List and Rubenstein, 2019). Such counter-intuitive hacks and short-circuits into student learning are illuminating; they show not only how students are susceptible to false information but also how educators can improve outcomes once they know where vulnerabilities exist.

Surprisingly, teachers and administrators may be no less susceptible to false information when it comes to professional-related misconceptions. Sinatra and Jacobson (2019) find that some false ideas about education are difficult to eradicate or amend, especially in K–12 education. They character-ize such false ideas that persist in educational circles—that is, you are using only 10 percent of your brain; right-brain/left-brain learners; even multiple learning styles—as "zombie concepts" that never seem to die out among educators, despite evidence demonstrating how false or misinterpreted they are. In other words, these are well-worn myths about education that continue to have "widespread popular support despite little to no empirical evidence" (Sinatra and Jacobson, 2019). Such ideas include a wide array of areas in education, including "neuromyths" about the nature of how people learn, technology myths about how students use and learn with technology (that is, a generation of "digital natives"), and educational policy myths about the effectiveness of leadership and organizational methods in schools.

Many of these myths and misconceptions are hardwired even now among not just K–12 but also those in higher education as well, including assumptions about young "digital natives" being better than older generations at using digital information (Wineburg et al., 2016), that listening to classical music will increase intelligence, or more funding automatically improves learning outcomes (Sinatra and Jacobson, 2019). Some negative but unfounded beliefs about technology persist, including the belief that internet use will dumb down students, that students are not reading, and that video games instill aggressiveness and violence in those who play them. These debunked concepts persist despite being exposed as largely untrue or overstated due to several factors, including general aversion to change, the impact of cognitive dissonance, and general habits of mind that persist in people across their lives. Most importantly, the amount of mental resistance and energy inherent to changing minds can be a major source of this persistence as well (Sinatra and Jacobson, 2019).

Sinatra and Jacobson further suggest that these persistent false concepts are hard to eradicate as correcting these beliefs requires that individuals modify their conceptual, attitudinal, and epistemic ways of thinking. Furthermore, each type of modification "is difficult to achieve in its own right, but promoting change in all three is even more challenging" (Sinatra and Jacobson, 2019). The challenge, then, is to find ways to break through calcified ways of thinking to address the specific ways that one can change a person's conceptual assumptions, their basic attitudes, and their fundamental beliefs about the nature of reality itself.

MEASURING REAL-WORLD IMPACT ON STUDENTS

While much has been examined in general terms of the impact of fake news on organizations and on education's more broadly abstract bundle of actions and policies, there has not been a close look at student outcomes. So what, then, might be some of the real-world impacts of fake news on actual students? One study, in particular, provides some deep insight. The Stanford History Education Group (SHEG) made significant waves in 2016 with their study of various levels of students' interactions with fake news. They measured students' abilities to detect false information in a variety of contexts, evaluating them for age-appropriate mastery of tasks to determine what is true. However, the results of their study were very disconcerting; from middle school to college, "in every case and at every level," the researchers state, they "were taken aback by students' lack of preparation" (Wineburg et al.,

2016). They found consistent and uniformly poor performance of information evaluative tasks.

Other studies have found similar issues with student ability to verify information. Jolley et al. (2021) in developing their tool the Adolescent Conspiracy Belief Scale (ACBQ) find that adolescence appears to be a "peak time" for theorizing about conspiracies and false information, with children ages fourteen to eighteen the most likely to demonstrate characteristics of heightened paranoid conspiratorial beliefs. Interestingly, these beliefs have an impact on student attitudes, "such as an increase in prejudice and disengagement in social issues" (Jolley at al., 2021). The disengagement in issues that impact the society as a whole—that is, climate change, gun violence, and the like—could likely lead to further alienation and distrust. In that sense, the belief in false ideas and conspiracies as well as the fake news that can drive them has significant concrete impact on all stakeholders. Yet the causes of these reactions and peak times to fall for fake news and conspiracies remain understudied. Jolley et al. (2021) suggest that psychological factors and stressors may be main factors, especially if there is difficulty in regulating emotion and anxiety—which is suggested as a factor in the fake news model in chapter 9. Further investigation is surely needed to better understand the role that anxiety and the inability to regulate emotion has on sharing fake news.

A WAY FORWARD: IDENTIFYING THE RISK FACTORS IN STUDENTS AND DECEPTIVE PRACTICES

Universities, academic libraries, and K–12 schools each have specific issues related to dealing with the problems of fake news. Though generally resilient and deeply embedded in the communities they serve, K–12 schools are situated in surprisingly susceptible positions as public organizations. As each stakeholder in a school can be susceptible in its own right, the whole structure can be impacted at various points by the influx of false information. Similarly, college students, as seen in the faculty responses to the Alwan et al. (2018) survey, can still be vulnerable to the impacts of false information given the wide array of definitions, approaches, and even levels of importance ascribed to it. As a result, more robust countermeasures and approaches for students need to be implemented in schools to help promote information that is vetted, corrected, and reliable.

For schools at all levels, the biases inherent to disciplines and methods can encroach the missions to educate their students. In spite of the best efforts at making sure the most credible information at the time is taught or made available to students, there are clearly lags in this stemming from changes in knowledge, poor understanding of students' ideas about fake news, and a lack of consensus on defining fake news itself. Similarly, in K–12 schools there are inherent biases in recurring issues and attitudes, and even from persistent beliefs that are systemically supported by teachers and administrators. Assumptions made about student learning are not always perfectly supported by empirical evidence, including the issues of information literacy and the role of critical thinking in library lessons.

Yet if information literacy and critical thinking are imperfect and incomplete approaches, what strategies can be taken to improve outcomes when it comes to fake news and misinformation? As explored in the previous chapter, education is but one of several factors contributing to the likelihood of falling for fake news, incorporating both information literacy and critical thinking approaches. It is hypothesized that students with more familiarity with such approaches, or frames in the parlance of the ACRL's framework, would demonstrate improved results and resilience against fake news. However, problems in these outcomes are still observed.

To help solve these problems, List and Rubenstein (2019) propose the Likelihood of Adoption Model (LAM) as a way to gauge students' susceptibility to fake news. They see the likelihood that someone will believe false information as an overlap of both individual characteristics (such as low prior knowledge, one's existing attitudes, and a reduced need to use thinking skills) and the characteristics of the message itself (including quality of argument, superficial validity, linguistic features, specificity, comprehensibility, simplicity, and causality). The mix of personal attributes or conditions and the nature of the written work combines to make someone more or less susceptible to the message being conveyed to them. Obviously, the wider considerations of the fake news creator, as well as the other individual factors examined in chapters 7, 8, and 9, such as FOMO, etc., need to be acknowledged. But overall, this useful approach helps to show that fake news itself has inherent characteristics that can be targeted to specific individuals that evince desired attributes to fool them.

REFERENCES

Alwan, A., Garcia, E. P., and Weiss, A. P. (2018). Fake news survey data. [Unpublished].

Alwan, A., Garcia, E., Kirakosian, A., and Weiss, A. (2022). Fake news and libraries: How teaching faculty in higher education view librarians' roles in counteracting the spread of false information. *Partnership, 16*(2), pp. 1–30. https://doi.org/10.21083/partnership.v16i2.6483.

Anderson, R. (2017). Fake news and alternative facts: Five challenges for academic libraries. *Insights, 30*(2), pp. 4–9.

Baines, P. (2022). Fake news and disinformation abounds, but what can universities do? *Times Higher Education*. https://www.timeshighereducation.com/campus/fake -news-and-disinformation-abounds-what-can-universities-do.

Clark, J. (2023). Ky. Department of Education warns schools implementing anti-LGBTQ rules. Louisville Public Media. https://www.lpm.org/news/2023-04 -17/ky-department-of-education-warns-schools-implementing-anti-lgbtq-rules.

Dilevko, J. (2008), An alternative vision of librarianship: James Danky and the socio-cultural politics of collection development. *Library Trends, 56*(3), pp. 678–704.

Durkee, A. (2023). Republicans increasingly realize there's no evidence of election fraud—but most still think 2020 election was stolen anyway, poll finds. *Forbes*. https://www.forbes.com/sites/alisondurkee/2023/03/14/republicans-increasingly -realize-theres-no-evidence-of-election-fraud-but-most-still-think-2020-election -was-stolen-anyway-poll-finds/?sh=d38afe628ecb.

Echterling, A. (2019). Ethical dilemmas in collection development of open access electronic Resources. *The Serials Librarian, 76*(1 –4), pp. 141–46. DOI: 10.1080 /0361526X.2019.1571851.

Faix, A., and Fyn, A. (2020). Framing fake news: Misinformation and the ACRL framework. *Portal, 20*(3), pp. 495–508. https://doi.org/10.1353/pla.2020.0027.

Gale. (2023). *Political extremism and radicalism: Far-right groups in America*. Gale Publishing. https://www.gale.com/c/political-extremism-and-radicalism-far-right -groups-in-america.

Graham, E. (2021). Who is behind the attacks on educators and public schools? *NEA Today*. https://www.nea.org/advocating-for-change/new-from-nea/who-behind -attacks-educators-and-public-schools.

Hacking, I. (1986). Making up people. In T. C. Heller and C. Brooke-Rose (eds.), *Reconstructing individualism: Autonomy, individuality, and the self in Western thought*. Stanford University Press, 1986.

Jolley, D., Douglas, K. M., Skipper, Y., Thomas, E., and Cookson, D. (2021). Measuring adolescents' beliefs in conspiracy theories: Development and validation of the Adolescent Conspiracy Beliefs Questionnaire (ACBQ). *British Journal of Developmental Psychology, 39*: pp. 499–520. https://doi.org/10.1111/bjdp.12368

Kamenetz, A. (2021). A look at the groups supporting school board protesters nation-wide. *National Public Radio (NPR)*. https://www.npr.org/2021/10/26/1049078199 /a-look-at-the-groups-supporting-school-board-protesters-nationwide.

Kelly, M. (2015). The materials-centred approach to public library collection devel-opment: A defense. *Library Philosophy and Practice, 2015*(1), p. 1232.

Knuth, R. (2003). *Libricide: the regime-sponsored destruction of books and libraries in the twentieth century*. Praeger.

List, A., and Rubenstein, L. D. (2019). Understanding susceptibility to educa-tional inaccuracies. In P. Kendeou, D. H. Robinson, and M. T. McCrudden (eds.), *Misinformation and fake news in education* (pp. 29–54). Information Age Publishing, Incorporated.

Rogers, R. A. (1973). Censorship and libraries in the Soviet Union. *Journal of Library History, Philosophy, and Comparative Librarianship, 8*(1), pp. 22–29.

Rubin, V. L. (2019). Disinformation and misinformation triangle: A conceptual model for "fake news" epidemic, causal factors and interventions. *Journal of Documentation, 75*(5), pp. 1013–34. https://doi.org/10.1108/JD-12-2018-0209.

Sinatra, G. M., and Jacobson, N. (2019). Zombie concepts in education: Why they won't die and why you can't kill them. In P. Kendeou, D. H. Robinson, and M. T. McCrudden (eds.), *Misinformation and fake news in education* (pp. 7–27). Information Age Publishing, Incorporated.

Sullivan, M. C. (2019). Libraries and fake news: What's the problem? what's the plan? *Communications in Information Literacy, 13*(1), pp. 91–113. https://doi.org/10.15760/comminfolit.2019.13.1.7.

Walker, T. (2021). Educators "under immediate threat" in culture of fear and violence. *NEA Today.* https://www.nea.org/advocating-for-change/new-from-nea/educators-under-immediate-threat-culture-fear-and-violence.

Weiss, A. P., Alwan, A., Garcia, E. P., and Garcia, J. (2020). Surveying fake news: Assessing university faculty's fragmented definition of fake news and its impact on teaching critical thinking. *International Journal of Educational Integrity, 16*(1). https://doi.org/10.1007/s40979-019-0049-x.

Wineburg, S., McGrew, S., Breakstone, J., and Ortega, T. (2016). Evaluating information: The cornerstone of civic online reasoning. *Stanford Digital Repository.* http://purl.stanford.edu/fv751yt5934.

Chapter 11

The Impact of Fake News on Online Communication, Media, and Political Discourse

James Cortada in his extensive review of information usage throughout American history notes that by 2013 a large percent of information seekers sought and obtained news from various online platforms, including 52 percent from Twitter, 47 from Facebook, 30 from Google, and 20 from YouTube (Cortada, 2016, p. 437). Along similar lines, Pew Research found that by 2020 the percentage of Americans getting their news from digital platforms rose to 86 percent (Shearer, 2021). This sudden shift from traditional media to online media for finding news has had profound implications, affecting changes in content and its delivery as well as people's ability to comprehend and efficiently process it. Users become more susceptible to the overflow of content, simultaneously overstimulated and overwhelmed by the volume, and increasingly more willing to share it through online platforms. Content creators for their part manipulate the vulnerabilities in others to make the message's spread far more effective—and this is worldwide in its reach.

Yet the success of this medium comes at a price for not only our thinking but also our language and communication. Sartre tells us that the person who has stripped language of its meaning does so on purpose, foisting the burden of using words responsibly onto those who still believe in them (Sartre, 1995). The result is that we feel the burden of proof falling more upon those who would respect the truth rather than those who would baselessly assert its uselessness. The impact that this has on schools and students is just starting to be better understood the more the internet traffics in and profits from false information. More immediately, we find that the factually overstuffed world of the internet also fools people into thinking they know more than they actually do about any given subject (Brooks, 2023), reveling in instant recall without real memory in a perverse online reenactment of the Dunning-Kruger effect. But screen-mediated information recall does not equate discernment.

And so this chapter will examine more deeply the ways in fake news impacts users of online media, especially in the ways it increases political polarization and extremism, and how it erodes the basic premise of information to "inform" us. With this approach we can begin to ask better questions about the nature of information and communication itself. Just what is information and what does it mean "to inform" someone? What responsibilities are there when informing people? The chapter will also look at how fake news–inspired distrust and personal alienation drives increased extremism, provides a platform to raise alternative facts to the level of established truthful discourse (much like Sartre's antisemite who debases truthful language), and enables more fake news to gain a foothold in the popular imagination. One wonders whether the media and other news and informing companies have greater responsibilities than merely presenting two sides to a story. What are these responsibilities and how might they become compromised by false narratives and fake news? How can we, both as individuals and collectively, help to create and foster more *percipient* and conscientious users of information?

INFORMATION AND A BROKEN PROMISE TO "INFORM"

Information can be a slippery and complex concept. When we ask, "what is information?" we wind up with a number of potential answers and sometimes confusing conclusions. As Capurro and Hjørland (2003) suggest, "ordinary use of a term like *information* may carry other meanings than formal definitions, implying that conflicting theoretical views may arise between the explicit scientific definitions of ordinary use." The concept of information in most basic definitions refers more to a state of "novelty and relevance," or learning a new fact or idea, and "the process of knowledge transformation, and particularly to selection and interpretation within a specific context" (Capurro and Hjørland, 2003). Indeed, the ordinary sense and use of the word seems to suggest that people are reaching a state of being "informed" about something, learning a new fact or idea that is then "closely connected to views of knowledge" (Capurro and Hjørland, 2003). Complicating matters, however, is the fact that the term is also used for concepts in engineering and mathematics, as in Claude Shannon's "A Mathematical Theory of Communication," and also in physics to describe in the abstract natural phenomena distinctly unrelated to the workings of human cognition.

Tomic (2010) proposes that information as a philosophical concept is really in fact "a meta-theory" that helps various "sub-domains"—information science in particular—"deal with the phenomenon of information" itself. Tomic sees the concept information as an overarching idea, capable of being utilized in various disciplines and areas of study, but still touching upon long-standing inquiries from classical philosophical problems, including the "principles, origins and structures of knowledge"; the nature of how to understand existence; problems of the mind; linguistics, meaning, semiotics; logical reasoning and critical thinking; and ultimately the theories and ethics of truth (Tomic, 2010). Similarly, as seen in figure 11.1, Dittrich visualizes

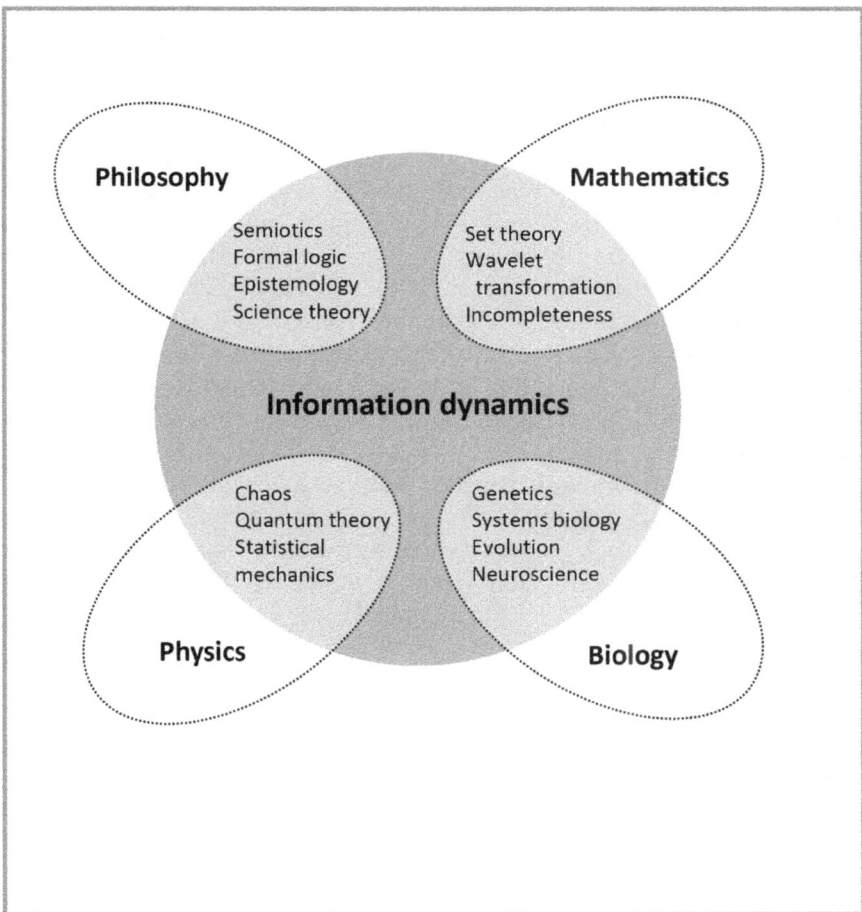

Figure 11.1. **Information as utilized in various disciplines from philosophy to mathematics and sciences.** *Source:* **Adapted from Dittrich, 2015.**

how information has become adopted by numerous sciences and disciplines, beyond philosophy itself. With its purported "flow" between entities, information acts as "an extraordinarily powerful tool to understand a vast range of phenomena on a common footing, not only in physics but also in the neighboring sciences" (Dittrich, 2015).

But this overlapping etymology, history, and widespread adoption of the word in various disciplines and uses is complicated even further by fake news and misinformation, which tends to perform as a negation or even a refutation of the implied premise of information's task of "informing" a person. It is within this antithetical activity of fake news that we find the purpose of it: to disrupt, deny, or pervert the very basis of *informing* itself. The debasement of truth by falseness also represents a play for power, a desire to supplant what is factual with the emotive "what should be" rather than what merely *is*, despite the long toil it takes to isolate whatever "it" really is. The disruption of informing morphs, perhaps, into an age where finding the novel true thing is further debased and is made secondary to the *way* in which information is moved. Thus, we are confronted by those who warn us that we are "leaving the age of the book," which seems to symbolize a time of static and trustful information, and are instead now "going through the information age towards the age of messages and messengers" (Capurro and Hjørland, 2003).

Capurro and Hjørland (2003) argue that it is technology itself that is changing our approach to information and how we learn from it. Capurro, by himself later on, also suggests that "the information age has given us not only a new alphabet but also new forms of message codification using particularly digital messengers" (Capurro, 2009, p. 137). Format, in other words, becomes just as infused with meaning and falseness as much as the words and ideas conveyed within it; format is entwined with metaphor and abstract conceptualizations. Dittrich suggests in this era, designated as an information age, similar to prior ones such as the Industrial Revolution, "that central concepts like energy and information . . . have played the role of universal metaphors, applied not only in their original field but to just about every subject that invited for scientific interpretation" (Dittrich, 2015). In that sense, we come to see the fusion of earlier ideas about information—that is, its inherent promise and inherited premise to inform and to create knowledge—and the newer conceptions of it as part of different mathematical and scientific disciplines and computer systems less interested in the message's human-derived meaning than the informational "objects" transferred within them. This divergence of the definition and conception of information itself leads to higher level of reflection on the term "beyond a restrictive humanistic view" as well as a "now de-humanized, perspective" (Capurro and Hjørland, 2003) that mix not only human communications but also technical terms (that is, production, storage, processing, information exchange, etc.) and lead to a science of information that defines itself as both "related to (computer) systems as well as to human beings" (Capurro and Hjørland, 2003).

The breakdown of information and its ability to inform, therefore, may be foundational to cultural and human behaviors due to problems with semiotics (as Eco suggests), as well as a result of technological advances, new scientific conceptions of information, and humanity's often-imperfect interactions with them. The resulting "post-truth" era, much like postmodernism, arrives in history not as a result of technology's ascendancy but as a recoil against a technocratic society busy replacing truth with power and information with technical abstraction and communicative ubiquity. Truth is compromised by digital systems, their data collection and alteration prowess, their speed of data transference, and their near-universal reach. That we live in an information age yet still suffer the same problems of cognition (that is, information overload, confirmation bias, etc.) as ever before seems to indicate that information technology does not improve lives so much as *magnify* them. The same problems of memory, misremembering, and reliance on narratives for meaning persist but seem larger and more looming when the system stretches beyond human scale, like a Mertonian "hyperobject." The change we are faced with, however, comes in the form of pervasive information technology and the ability of digital media to infiltrate all aspects of a person's life.

MEDIA CONSUMPTION, FAKE NEWS, AND ONLINE EXTREMISM

Such consumption of and by digital media platforms and the stripping of information from its contexts through problems of hyperscale has its consequences. In January 2017, for example, Kellyanne Conway, during her time serving as senior counselor to the president in the administration of Donald Trump, unintentionally though quite ironically defined an era of American politics through her coinage of the term "alternative facts." That the expression took off seems to indicate that it hit a nerve among people in the country at the time. A national mood, zeitgeist, trend, fad, whatever one calls it, is not always so succinctly expressed in such an ironic and yet truth-telling manner. Conway's glib description of what was ultimately among the earliest of thousands of lies spread through the Trump administration—as documented by the *Washington Post*'s counting of 30,000-plus lies and misstatements from the former president himself (Kessler, 2021)—hinted at the underbelly of what happens when language itself is debased, twisted, and used to serve the whims of power rather than truth itself. It is also telling that the former president—the person most often associated with false narratives and spinning lies—is also the one public figure who has single-handedly cast the most aspersions against legitimate news media outlets. In that sense, fake news is undoubtedly and intimately intertwined with politics, negative political discourse, and the even law itself.

DEMOCRATIC NORMS AND THE EROSION
OF PUBLIC TRUST FROM FAKE NEWS

Many have characterized fake news as a crisis for democracy and democratic norms and that the inability to establish truthful discourse leads into abuses of power and the erosion of democratic practices across America and the European Union (Flew, 2019; Michailidou et al., 2022). Conversely, the public sphere in the United States has tended toward buttressing the ideal of the trustworthy and pragmatic in political discourse and that democracy is uniquely able to champion it. Chambers (2021) finds that "democracy as a structural and procedural matter has a logic that pushes toward the truth" (p. 153), making its goals much more than just a guarantee of personal agency through voting. Its institutions are meant to provide space for reality to be discussed and protected. Fake news is seen, then, as disrupting democracy's basic processes to work out what is real and what is false. Certainly, as Sartre presciently predicts, debasing truth goes a long way toward destabilizing people's sense of right and wrong.

In response to this kind of perceived threat, librarians working and serving in public institutions have taken up the mantle of trying to protect and preserve the public trust in verified and verifiable news sources. Fake news is seen as a significant and "self-evident" issue (Sullivan, 2019, p. 92) that impacts democratic norms, both as a widespread issue impacting the gatekeeping of information sources themselves, as well as a problem with individual breakdowns in being informed such as education, media literacy, overuse of social media, and the like. Sullivan further suggests that "there is a pressing need for LIS professionals to engage with theories of democracy as they pertain to how informed citizens ought to be, as well as the relevant evidence about how informed those citizens have been." (p. 96). Though he laments that most in the LIS field spend far too much time "catastrophizing" over the results of fake news without providing reality-based solutions to these problems or a deep understanding of how people are actually impacted by it.

Fair enough. Yet recent studies demonstrate the negative impact that fake news has had on the erosion of belief in democracy. Reglitz (2022) finds that fake news can threaten democracies due to its ability to undermine "citizens' *epistemic* trust in each other" and ultimately reduces a person's belief in democratic institutions' legitimacy (p. 164). Similarly, Rahman and Tang (2022) outline the Russian-coined expression "firehose of falsehood," which deals in "high volume, repetitive and continuous information, no commitment to objective reality, and no commitment to consistency" (p. 155). That lack of commitment to reality and consistency is what destabilizes trust in the *demos* in democracy. If one cannot trust one's own fellow citizens over a foreign adversary, deep divisions and dysfunction will likely widen further. The disbelief in others and public institutions is further eroded by a general mistrust of information containers (that is, internet webpages) that can be edited and changed without leaving a trail of alterations.

Notably, it is also the volume and repetitiveness of the firehose of misinformation and false messaging that are key to this ability to destabilize. Buschman (2019), for example, finds that "democracy does not require a space cleared of distorting claims but spaces suited to grappling with them" (p. 221). The assumption that fake news can and should be completely eradicated within a society may be somewhat quixotic. Rather, to allow for the health of a democracy, entertaining false ideas is important to the freedoms of personal belief and discourse, yet a social framework needs to be strong enough to provide the legal and social spaces for discussing them and debunking them in an open trusted forum. The problem, then, for democracies may not be solely the specter of fake news but also the overarching inability of institutions to promote active discussion and analytical *dissection* of all ideas. Without open forums where people can state both truths and falsehoods freely, but still speak face to face so as to promote and maintain personal relationships and connections, epistemic trust will become lost. If there is a constant flood of false information that remains unchecked and unmitigated, it can overwhelm institutions' abilities to provide that space for maintaining trust.

Again, we return to the idea of information's broken promise to inform. If belief in something true is ultimately questioned, and the trust in the value of the information is lost, whether through nefarious means or a constant exposure to lies, then can we say someone has become reasonably informed? Clearly not. Still, if there is any silver lining in the issue of fake news and democracies, it is that it is "unlikely ever to be the sole cause of democratic system collapse" (Reglitz, 2022, p. 179). It would likely be secondary to wider economic and social instability. Yet the impact of fake news on democracy is still a threat. Some of those threats address those specific economic and social instabilities, including the abuse of power, the increase in political polarization and extremism, and the increased practice of spin, manipulation, and ulterior political motives.

ABUSES OF POWER, FALSE INFORMATION, AND FAKE NEWS

Fake news is seen negatively as it is most often associated with abuses of power and a built-in intention to deceive and manipulate others. As with propaganda, false information can be used to serve political powers currently in place. Additionally, the origins of that abuse of power are also tied up with leaders who normalize the behaviors that eliminate or break long-standing norms and rules (Davies et al., 2022). Such "transgressive leadership," as it has been named, is tolerated by followers far beyond the behaviors of others. Indeed, such followers are shown to clearly "downplay the severity of their leader's transgression" in exchange for political gain (Davies et al., 2022). So long as lies, falsehoods, and fake news benefit the followers of a transgressive leader, they are more willing to accept them as the price of business for their own group's successes.

Importantly, the use and spread of fake news and misinformation fits within this transgressive dynamic very well, as it allows contradictory and hypocritical beliefs and attitudes to take hold within a group. First, it allows people to believe that while others should be punished for something they believe is unethical, those within their group should not. This dynamic helps to explain, for example, current Republican downplaying of the legal indictments of their former president. Second, it fosters misinformation and fake news not solely as a tool for debasing truth but also as a tool to protect the power of leaders within their group. Third, it provides transgressing leaders room to spread lies, fake news, and misinformation without having to answer for it, while placing all the blame on those who wish to uphold social norms. The expectation of telling the truth in public discourse is dropped for their group's leader, and these followers are "more inclined to downplay" the severity of such lying (Davies et al., 2022). As a result, Donald Trump's thirty thousand documented lies are considered to be not as bad to his supporters as the few publicly documented exaggerations of former President Barack Obama or other political adversaries.

INCREASED POLARIZATION AND DISRUPTION FROM FAKE NEWS AND MISINFORMATION

Related to this acceptance of the transgressive leader is increased political polarization stemming from fake news and misinformation in political discourse. Although transgressive leaders get a pass in spreading lies that benefit their followers, fake news and misinformation campaigns also exist to exacerbate raw emotion and antagonize political enemies. As mentioned in chapter 8, Soviet-era Russian misinformation campaigns spread false narratives and fake news regarding race relations in the United States for the sake of sowing dissention and increasing political polarization (Ioffe, 2017). Contemporary examples of exploiting race and class in America were documented by Robert Mueller III in his report on Russian interference in the 2016 US presidential election (Mueller, 2019). Exposing such fractures between members of a culture through exaggerations and falsehood has increased political clashes and ramped up the so-called culture wars that pit moderately dissimilar views against each other and characterize them as wide differences. Ultimately, the aim of such polarization is to stoke feelings of anger and resentment against other groups in order to motivate people to vote for a specific party (Osmundsen et al., 2021). Of course, fake news and polarized political discourse are intended to get a rise out of partisans for the purpose of denigrating their opponents and motivating them to vote. Another benefit for politicians who polarize the electorate is that "negative feelings toward political opponents rather than positive feelings toward the in-party are the strongest predictor of fake news sharing" (Osmundsen et al., 2021). As a result, the more that false information is spread, the greater the chance that they can perpetuate a vicious cycle of polarization. Increasing the negative feelings against opponents creates a greater chance of subsequently spreading the same lies and guaranteeing support in the form of votes.

That rise in anger from using fake news also impacts other movements in political discourse, including spin and public manipulation for political party members. Another less considered motivation for creating and sharing fake news, then, is what is known as "disruption." This goal of spreading fake news is related much more to a "deep-seated discontent with the status quo" (Osmundsen et al., 2021) and stems from a desire to completely destabilize and change the prevailing social and political order of the day. Tucker et al. (2017) suggest that "social media can lend a voice to anti-system forces that actively seek to undermine liberal democracy." Such antidemocratic behaviors include spin and the use of manipulation to meet political ends that destabilize the culture and the society. Such dangers lurk just beneath the surface of the polite society that dabbles in the delegitimization of information and its promise to inform.

AWARENESS OF FAKE NEWS

Interesting things happen, too, when people become aware of manipulation in communications and more aware, specifically, of lies, hoaxes, false information, and fake news. The spillover effect of false information can cause people to second-guess their belief in social and government institutions. One recent study into the spread of fake news makes the counterintuitive finding that a greater awareness of fake news overall actually *increases the likelihood of it being shared.* It was found that credibility in news media decreases when participants, after watching the same thing, were told they saw fake news in comparison to others who were told that what they had seen was real. In a related study, people who watched a news story and then were told that it was fake decreased their levels of trust in news media, while those who were not told did not change their perceptions. Just to assert that something is fake by itself causes distrust and shows "that the social impact of fake news is not limited to its direct consequences of misinforming individuals, but also includes the potentially adverse effects of discussing fake news" (Tandoc et al., 2021).

Merely associating with lies or asserting that something is untrue destabilizes belief and certainty. This kind of spillover effect of false information causes people to second-guess their trust in institutions regardless of whether something is true or not—"poisoning the well," as the expression goes. The overall result is not only confusion about things that are true and doubts about whether information is accurate but also that it is "continuously shared among members of the public unknowingly" (Wright et al., 2021). In one experiment examining college-age students, researchers attempted to examine whether priming the students—that is, the process by which the media portrays and reproduces stereotypes and then is stimulated "or primed outside of mental awareness" to influence beliefs or behaviors—had an impact on their belief in false narratives and fake news about other people. They found, tellingly, that those participating in the experiment who were shown immigrants in a negative light (that is, as stereotypes) in a false news story exhibited more negative attitudes than those who did not see such things; conversely, those shown stories in a positive light exhibited more positive attitudes (p. 345).

Importantly, the level of shock or sensationalism in the fake news stories shown to participants actually impacted the beliefs—whether positive or negative—suggesting that the "shock value or sensationalism of the prime may also impact the level of the priming effect." This means that the level of outrageousness or emotionalizing of the content, regardless of whether it is true or false, influences a person's memory. So much so that later, when encountering similar viewpoints, they may be more receptive to accepting false concepts as true. What this suggests, then, is that the news media have great control over how information consumers process information and come to believe the narratives that these organizations broadcast. It implies that it is not merely the number of times one is exposed but also the level of excitement instilled in the viewer (Wright et al., 2021, p. 345). It is not isolated, however, to just exposure or sensationalism. The person's ethnicity, age, and gender may also each impact the likelihood of believing more extreme ideas and fake or falsified narratives.

THE DAILY ME: ONLINE EXTREMISM AS A VICIOUS CIRCLE FOR RAMPING UP FAKE NEWS

Online extremism among violent and antisocial internet subcultures may follow similar patterns of priming, sensationalism, and personal demographic attributes. Numerous studies, according to Odağ et al. (2019), especially those looking at extremist ideology among right-wing political movements and jihadism, find that they are spread across the internet both in cloaked sites as well as openly radical sites. They exploit the positive aspects of the internet, including its ease of use, speed and reach, as well as the minimal amount of censorship that exists in notably neutral sites. Younger users and those who suffer from alienation and social exclusion are seen as prime recruits for radicalization. Radicalized online groups provide such withdrawn people with "spaces for collective identification" in "virtual echo chambers" that later turn into real-world contact and group gathering (Odağ et al., 2019).

Midori Ogasawara (2019) has studied the recent online habits of right-wing and ultranationalist Japanese men (known as *Neto-uyo* in Japanese). She finds that the online environment and subcultures in various online subcommunities "reinforcing the data loops of the 'Daily Us' versus Them." Ogasawara notes that these groups are an outgrowth of anonymous online chat rooms that have organized in the real world and developed as hate groups that have begun to attack ethnic minorities in Japan, especially *zainichi* Koreans and Chinese who had been brought to Japan during the Imperial era (Ogasawara, 2019). Some of those who become radicalized are *hikikomori*, or recluses, who have few social outlets and tend to not socialize with anyone. Online chat rooms provide a need that has otherwise been stunted and left to wither among the rigid hierarchies and long-standing customs of Japanese society. The radical freedom of the internet itself coupled with the lack of social restraints that comes from anonymity has allowed for these movements to greatly increase their numbers and to effect change in right-wing Japanese politics.

The cause of this extremism involves not only the users themselves, who are often radicalized in their alienation and in turn radicalize others in vicious circles through shared online chat collectives. It also includes the way in which information technologies, especially digital social media platforms, have supplanted the more traditional ways of disseminating information. "Concepts," Ogasawara writes, "are substituted, on the level of meaning and/or language, by new ones that derive from the computer's ontology, epistemology, and pragmatics" (2019, p. 54). In other words, the technology itself alters the way in which people encounter information, making them bend to the power lurking beneath the technology and the platforms that encode the information for them, influencing through the creators' assumptions about how humans know things, create knowledge, and ultimately come to utilize this knowledge. The information encountered through computer-mediated communication channels has been fully subsumed by its medium and the platform within which it is shared and consumed. Additionally, when information is falsified to present specific viewpoints for which a person is already primed, either as a member of a group or as an attack on someone outside the group, the chance for manipulation becomes ever greater.

While Ogasawara's research focuses on specific right-wing subcultures in Japan, similar extremism, regardless of political affiliation, has been observed in numerous countries, and "the mechanisms driving radicalization processes forward on the individual level appear to be fundamentally similar across the ideologies" (Odağ et al., 2019, p. 266). Indeed, jihadism and right-wing ideological behaviors have been shown to follow very similar patterns of extremism. One of the main methods for this includes "translocal identity building" (Odağ et al., 2019). Often used in white supremacy movements (for example, Stormfront), it also applies to jihadism, Japanese *Neto-uyo* groups, and nationalist groups found all across the world. Such groups often rely on the creation of two things: (1) an in-group identity, which favors only members of a specific racial or ethnic demographic; and (2) a derogatory out-group usually composed of "ethnic and religious minorities as well as LGBTQ individuals" (Odağ et al., 2019). Ogasawara's example finds that right-wing Japanese rely primarily on virulent anti-Korean and anti-Chinese sentiments to draw their groups together. Groups in other countries worldwide rely on similar antiimmigrant sentiments, as well as antisemitism, anti-Catholicism, antiliberalism, and the like, to create adversaries and demonize them as threats.

Such radicalization, as can be surmised, also ties in with the overall issues of factual representation, the distortion of history and its revision for political purposes, and the proliferation of false narratives and fake news. In the case of Japanese *Neto-uyo*, the glory of pre–World War II Imperialist Japan retains its strong siren song, attracting members who adopt revisionist ideas about the forced sexual exploitation and slavery of Korean women (known as *comfort women* in English), the wartime atrocities of Nanking in China, or the repeal of Article 9 of the Japanese Constitution, known colloquially as the "No War" clause, which renunciates the use of military force to settle international disputes (Ogasawara, 2019). False news stories promoting these topics or discrediting opposing views to them are shared among the members of this group in order to both demonize those outside the group as well as to inculcate their ideology.

RADICALISM, DENIALISM, AND CENSORSHIP

As false narratives become entrenched within radicalized groups, what was once established as historical fact begins to fall under suspicion and attack. In numerous cases, false or misleading statements about historical facts as well as denialism and revisionist histories start to take over. From Holocaust denial to false flags and crisis actors in American mass shootings, the urge to rewrite and fantasize about unpleasant or even inconceivably horrific events remains strong. For Japanese right-wing extremists, issues related to World War II atrocities are routinely "rewritten" for the sake of their collective narrative (Ogasawara, 2019). In their eyes, "the Nanking Massacre never happened" and the comfort women were a story fabricated by those in Korea "who want to deprive Japan of its money" (Ogasawara, 2019). In America such denial occurs amid political discourse as well, leading to not only the refusal to openly discuss such subjects in American schools—including topics related to LGBTQ+, trans rights, antisemitism, and Black history—but also to the complete banning of books and materials mentioning them from school library collections (Sargent, 2023). The surge toward censoring ideas and factual information, including Holocaust education, that had once been seen as truthful obligations in the face of denialism is borne of the legacy of fake news and false narratives. Censorship is one likely consequence of the destabilization of fact created by fake news, false narratives, and revisionist histories driven by extremist viewpoints.

The causes for this spread of denial and revisionist history are numerous but follow similar patterns to behaviors for extremists, including personal demographics related to age, gender, education level, religious membership, and national participation: namely, they are usually young, male, less educated, more religious, and less active in civics (Odağ et al., 2019, p. 271). Individual situations also contribute to extremism. Candidates for extremism show higher perceptions of existential threats against them and greater belief that conflicts exist against them. Wider environmental factors contribute as well, including geography—especially in places where people feel they are unsafe from adversaries or feel outnumbered by other outgroups—and places where extremist messages and beliefs are encountered (that is, in the home, on websites online, in government propaganda, and so on) (Odağ et al., 2019).

Fear stemming from existential threats especially appears to be an important motivator in the development of extremism and its associated behaviors of denialism and acceptance of revisionist history and false narratives. One researcher finds that "the persuasive power of right-wing YouTube propaganda videos was stronger under conditions of existential threat and anxiety" (Odağ et al., 2019). Demographic fear in particular appears to drive many radical agendas, including white supremacy in the United States via its obsession with "replacement theory" and "white genocide," which are reactions to demographic decline and low birth rates (Ramakrishna, 2021) and a rise in immigrant populations. Radicalization in the Muslim world may be undergoing similar patterns with a decline in birth rates, a rise in modernization, and increased fears and anxieties as "the extreme fragility of traditional society" becomes more apparent to those experiencing these changes (Goldman, 2005).

Similarly, the COVID-19 pandemic resulted in the "interference in the behavior and health of people," causing wider anxiety and fear that in turn generated a period of "social unrest associated with violence, distrust, social disturbances, and attacks on health professionals" (Rocha et al., 2021). Some of this social unrest was both exacerbated and instigated by fake news, driven in part by strategies of denial and the assertion of false narratives that stem from the politics of fear and distrust. As Rocha et al. suggest, fake news negatively impacts societies at large and has had negative consequences on public health because "it fuels panic among people and discredits the scientific community" (2021). Ironically, it seems that the fear itself and the attendant anxiety it produces makes people even more susceptible to radicalized and extremist views found in the fake news and false information related to COVID-19; that fear and anxiety in turn become misplaced and end up fueling denialism about the virus itself.

It is clear, then, that the overlap of fake news, extremist beliefs, false narratives, and censorship have complex interrelationships among people not only within extremist groups but also in the population at large, especially when they harbor a heightened sense of perceived threats. The characteristics that encourage such extremism and belief in false narratives appear to be consistent across numerous groups, though it seems more research is needed to understand direct causes and motivations. Nevertheless, finding ways to address and neutralize these problems will be essential, especially as the technology of the internet continues evolving and "the psychology of computer-mediated communication" (Odağ et al., 2019) continues to change with it.

STRATEGIES FOR BETTER INFORMING
IN AN INFORMATION AGE

The cliché is that we live in an information age and have no real escape from the all-encompassing reality of digital culture—aside from living off the grid, of course, which has its own drawbacks. Nearly everything we do now is mediated through screens, dominated by internet communications, influenced by social media, and facilitated with digital software and tools—either through word processing, video and image editing, sound recording, and so on. Finding solely analog, nonwired artifacts and tools is getting harder each year. We are forced, then, to deal with an increased intrusiveness from digital media and a perpetual news, information, and gossip cycle. Now that there are clear dangers and problems noticed in the spread of false information and the role that radicalization plays to exacerbate this, some strategies must be developed in order to find ways to better inform all of the information users who inhabit this digital world.

This promise of better informing can be approached in several ways: first, through the press and news media itself, which still represent the most common way people receive factual information; second, through the information platforms we use; third, through the reduction of radicalization by targeting candidates deemed especially vulnerable to it; and, finally, through better defining information itself in humanistic terms, as concepts are needed to reflect personal impact and growth through knowledge, rather than in terms of engineering, computer science, mathematics, or Big Data IT and surveillance capitalism. It is, in essence, a call to return to classical philosophical questions and interrogations, as Tomic eloquently describes it; it is a call to create a renewed interest in issues of well-measured truth and veracity too often left on the wayside in favor of the ruthless efficiency of overdelivering a deluge of digital content.

INFORMED PHILOSOPHIES: OBLIGATIONS AND SEEKING TRUTH TO INFORM POWER

To begin, we need to start examining information in ways that reclaim humanistic philosophy and place the *ethical* use of it at its heart. Floridi's investigations into information ethics are an important foray into this area. The development of a philosophy of information, including a deep adherence to information ethics, is proving to be essential in the online information era. Tomic's belief is that the "wise use of information turns the philosophy of information into the unifying theory of information science" (Tomic, 2010). To move beyond the dehumanization of the technology that alienates us, we need to turn to ways that allow people to use information in ethical and "wise" ways. Renewing interest in the promise to "inform" and "be informed" is imperative. Tomic suggests the "wise use of information presupposes advanced abilities in critical thinking," which we can begin to improve in all people through education, implementation of standards, and the increased view of information as more than merely bits and bytes flowing from one system to another but also as valued and valuable content carrying important meaning for people.

INFORMED BY DEMOGRAPHICS

As mentioned previously, young men disengaged from social activities and civic organizations tend to be most the likely candidates for radicalization, extremism, and belief in false narratives and fake news related to their extremist beliefs (Odağ et al., 2019; Ogasawara, 2019). In order to alleviate these areas, it is especially important to provide clearer countermeasures against such extremism. One study from 2011 finds that the adoption of radical content was related to the following factors: "(1) self-efficacy and sensation seeking, (2) frequency of Internet use, (3) confrontation with risky behavior offline, (4) above-average psychological problems, (5) tendency to compensate the lack of social relationships in the 'real' world with online relationships" (Odağ et al., 2019). Finding ways to counter such emotional and reactionary desires for sensation and thrill seeking will be essential. Certainly, reducing internet use and finding ways to curtail risky offline behaviors are important. Addressing psychological distress and other problems becomes essential as well. Finally, as was seen in the many previous examples, personal alienation might be addressed by improving social relationships in the real world rather than allowing online relationships to dominate.

INFORMED BY THE PRESS

In previous chapters, discussion focused on the ways in which American journalism transcended the abuses of the earlier eras—especially yellow journalism—and moved toward establishing professional norms that reduce sensationalism and favor balanced and truthful reportage. Certainly, the current premise of information as a tool for informing within digital media communications stems from the press's own definition of itself as one of society's leading information institutions, dedicated—albeit in name sometimes only—to sharing truth, facts, reasoned opinions, and knowledge widely. This theory of "social responsibility" of the press prizes "ethical values such as objectivity, autonomy, and public service," advocating "that its 'principal norm' ought to be 'public enlightenment'" (Serazio, 2021).

Readers also gain from the press its "promise to inform, to announce, to instruct, and to reflect the world in all its complications" (Shaya, 2012). Readers gain from its general philosophy of sharing information in order, at its most basic functions, to inform. Taking it deeper, some view the role of the press in extremely sacred terms, where a newspaper is "the morning prayer of the bourgeoisie: . . . an act of devotion, a ritual that binds the reader to a community" (Shaya, 2012). Metaphors aside, the press often envisions itself as the medium through which a version of the truth is imparted to those who actively and sincerely seek it out. Yet the replacement of the press with a daily litany to bind the person to a community becomes frayed when the trust in the organ itself is betrayed by the false and the misleading. The damages of such lies are well documented in studies about the erosion of trust in established media, resulting in a "crisis in journalism with concomitant loss of legitimacy and authenticity" (Asak and Molale, 2020).

It takes significant time and effort to rebuild the trust that lies so easily destroy. The ubiquitous lie, mercurial and lightning fast like quicksilver, has always spread side by side with the truth through all communication technologies, whether they be through the etchings of language on stone carvings; in codices, scrolls, and parchments; or on radio, telephone, and the internet. As we see with Umberto Eco, the basics of human communication and semantic construction depend upon the interdependence of the truth and lies. Nothing, he believes, can be said meaningfully without the acknowledgment of falsehood being baked into, as it were, the whole enterprise. As such, strategies to make sure that the news remains trusted to inform, even as it facilitates the potential for deception, should be better explored. Asak and Molale, for example, suggest trying to make the truth "louder" than the lies on digital platforms and teaching journalists to improve their multitasking and online media skills (2020); they also suggest that "mainstream media must embark more on advocacy against fake news . . . to create more visibility and to continually inform and educate the public" (Asak and Molale, 2020).

From a policy perspective, Kuźmicz (2023a) proposes supporting the European Declaration on Digital Rights and Principles for the Digital Decade to help protect information users against abuses encountered online. Rights established in this declaration include the freedom of online expression, confidentiality in communications, the right to access to digital technologies, and a right to education, training, and lifelong learning. While protecting the general rights of all internet users is a good first step, the policy does not guarantee the right to access to truthful information. This stems in part from the general rule to protect people's freedom of expression and allowing varied opinions regardless of their veracity. Ultimately, however, curtailing the freedom of expression is usually seen as more detrimental to a society than the spread of false information. And so the tension between the free expression of ideas and the spread of false information will remain a central issue in the exchange of ideas and one that will likely remain unresolved in policymaking, except on a case-by-case basis to resolve actual legal disputes and damages related to slander, libel, and the invasion of privacy.

Taking things further, Lahmann (2022) proposes that a framework of responsibility should be established to curtail "transboundary disinformation," which is false information that eludes legal accountability due to the gaps in international jurisdictions. It is a problem that has become especially salient in an interconnected transnational information society. While the complexities to the change in the law itself are too involved to recount here, Lahmann concludes that "reconsidering the design and substance of the existing legal frameworks for the digital age generally and for the disinformation nexus specifically might become inevitable if lack of accountability for malicious conduct continues to prevail" (Lahmann, 2022). The end result may be the need for a system or framework that establishes attribution and the burdens of legal and ethical responsibilities, including penalties and reparations against those who are designated as spreaders and purveyors of false information nationally and across international lines. The rub, however, is that implementing international frameworks and systems can be incredibly difficult, especially in enforcing something as culturally and nationally specific as information itself.

INFORMED (ETHICALLY) BY ONLINE PLATFORMS

Some problems in the current digital information ecosystem stem from the concentration of power in disruptive information technologies and IT companies. Surveillance capitalism has been explored previously in this book with a focus on Zuboff's (2015) concept of surveillance capitalism and its hyper-concentration of capital as a result of the broken social contract between users and the IT companies that exploit their private information. Srnicek's "platform capitalism" also shines a light on the excesses and monopolistic tendencies of dominant social media platforms (2017). Most concerning, however, is that these internet-based companies have found ways to monetize the sharing of information and data about all users. It is well documented, too, that the main social media companies—that is, the FANGs (Facebook/Amazon/Netflix/Google)—benefit not from the truth spreading but from whatever information becomes the most viral. As Richter (2019) notes, "social media platforms make 'fake news' uniquely lucrative" by compensating clicks with advertising exchanges, which fuels the incentive for creating as much content as possible with as little effort or regard for its truthfulness as possible. It is the worst of all worlds: meaningless and inaccurate content vie for your attention but then fail to reward it with meaningful information or knowledge. It is no surprise, then, that fake news—which tends to be sensationalist and move more virally than true information—"fits these up-front economic incentives" (Richter, 2019).

Certainly, "the boring old truth" travels more slowly along these channels, making it less likely to "go viral" than something that shocks or titillates. In this context, where information is considered content and the number of views act as a stand-in for significance, the premise that social media can inform seems almost laughably naïve. Yet people still use information online through various platforms in order to find *something* to satisfy information needs regardless of the shortcomings of the medium. Cortada's (2016) research shows the ongoing increase in people using the internet primarily for all their information needs and the growing reliance on specific platforms (for example, Facebook, etc.) at the expense of other sources (p. 437). Their information behavior leads them to utilize the available avenues of information seeking that the IT platforms provide for them. These are, of course, not always transparent, and the search results provided can be easily manipulated for the benefit of the platform, not the user.

Some suggestions on how to combat the primacy of the medium over its user might be worthwhile to consider. Strategies may be devised to help ensure that the responsibility to inform viewers and online media consumers is met. Lobschat et al. (2021) suggest establishing a philosophy of "corporate digital responsibility" for online technology companies to promote a "set of shared values and norms guiding an organization's operations . . . related to digital technology and data." Similarly, Kuźmicz's (2023b) concept of information obligation proposes legal policies that every IT company should be required to follow. He argues that information obligation "is a key element of consumer protection, particularly in the context of innovative products" (2023b). The concept involves informing all users of how a digital information system works, any of its potential risks, and an acknowledgment of the digital rights to which a person is entitled while interacting with these systems. General Data Protection Regulation (GDPR) rules adopted by the European Union in 2016 regarding digital tracking and the use of cookies on websites are a good example of this approach to consumer protection and the overarching spirit of obligation to ethical implementation of software. However, as has been noted by many, implementation and enforcement are often too weak in protecting information users and consumers from transgressions and bad actors (Padden and Öjehag-Pettersson, 2021).

Kuźmicz further proposes developing "multilayer information obligation (MIO)," which establishes a three-layered approach to information obligation that provides consumer protections for key features of a wired product (that is, establishing its level of intrusiveness). It also establishes a need to divulge "performance information," which explains where data is processed and how the profiles of users derived from such data are used. Finally, MIO calls for detailed descriptions of a product that explain whether it is using, for example, any nonhuman elements such as applied AI techniques or applied privacy-enhancing technologies. The end result of transparency, clear intentions, and technological gatekeeping might not work on its own and therefore needs, as Lobschat et al. (2021) outline, either its adoption as a standard among all IT businesses or as a part within broader legal frameworks.

FINAL THOUGHTS

It is likely that fake news will need to be *dis*incentivized somehow to dampen its spread through information channels, be they traditional news media, message boards, or digital online platforms. Certainly, preventing the exploitation of data and information that comes from the current online user experience is essential. Additionally, the rise of extremist beliefs and behaviors needs to be addressed. Finding ways to decrease the pressures of extremist movements is an essential step in helping to reduce fake news. As Lazer et al. (2018) suggest, we might also promote more "interdisciplinary research to reduce the spread of fake news and to address the underlying pathologies it has revealed." The aim for this would be to redesign the ways that journalism is practiced in the digital information age, moving beyond the rules and norms that grew out of print journalism and early electronic media so that credibility and truthfulness are prioritized over incentivized false narratives, fake news, and misinformation.

The important steps to take in improving information environments involve greater vigilance in not merely making sure that true information is shared publicly as much as possible. For it is clear that fake news and misinformation will always be a problem. The motives to debase truth and modify facts are inherent to our languages and our thinking. Political polarization and demonizing one's political enemies remain a central part of the political and social landscape. While these problems will likely always be there, allowing transgressive leaders to overtake parties and to spread lies and strip information of its ability to inform without impunity must be addressed. In that sense, the urgency of instilling truth back into political discourse and reducing polarization are important steps to ensure prodemocratic norms and values remain in place. It is suggested, too, that sharing fake news ironically decreases trust in the sharer, and that people may tend to not share fake news due to "reputational concerns" (Osmundsen et al, 2021). Interventions, therefore, might be implemented through utilizing shame and suggesting to people that sharing unverified and noncredible information might make them look foolish. It could be a good start, then, to bring people back from the brink of their bubble madness.

REFERENCES

Asak, M. O., and Molale, T. B. (2020). Deconstructing delegitimisation of main-stream media as sources of authentic news in the post-truth era. *Communicatio, 46*(4), pp. 50–74. https://doi.org/10.1080/02500167.2020.1723664.

Brooks, D. (2023). Google isn't grad school. *The Atlantic.* https://www.theatlantic .com/ideas/archive/2023/07/illusion-explanatory-depth-humility/674624/?utm _source=pocket-newtab.

Buschman, J. (2019). Good news, bad news, and fake news. *Journal of Documentation, 75*(1), pp. 213–28. https://doi.org/10.1108/JD-05-2018-0074.

Capurro, R. (2009). Past, present, and future of the concept of information. *TripleC, 7*(2), pp. 125–41. https://doi.org/10.31269/triplec.v7i2.113.

Capurro, R., and Hjørland, B. (2003). The concept of information. *Annual Review of Information Science and Technology, 37.* http://www.capurro.de/infoconcept.html.

Chambers, S. (2021). Truth, deliberative democracy, and the virtues of accuracy: Is fake news destroying the public sphere? *Political Studies, 69*(1), pp. 147–63. https: //doi.org/10.1177/0032321719890811.

Cortada, J. W. (2016). *All the facts: A history of information in the United States since 1870.* Oxford University Press.

Davies, B., Leicht, C., and Abrams, D. (2022). Donald Trump and the rationalization of transgressive behavior: The role of group prototypicality and identity advance-ment. *Journal of Applied Social Psychology, 52*(7), pp. 481–95. https://doi.org/10 .1111/jasp.12873.

Dittrich, T. (2015). The concept of information in physics: An interdisciplinary topical lecture. *European Journal of Physics, 36.* https://iopscience.iop.org/article/10.1088 /0143-0807/36/1/015010.

Flew, T. (2019). Digital communication, the crisis of trust, and the post-global. *Communication Research and Practice, 5*(1), pp. 4–22. https://doi.org/10.1080 /22041451.2019.1561394.

Goldman, D. (2005). The demographics of radical Islam. *Asia Times.* https: //web.archive.org/web/20090423030622/http://atimes.com/atimes/Front_Page/ GH23Aa01.html.

Ioffe, J. (2017). The history of Russian involvement in America's race wars. *The Atlantic.* https://www.theatlantic.com/international/archive/2017/10/russia -facebook-race/542796/.

Kessler, G. (2021). Trump made 30,573 false or misleading claims as president. Nearly half came in his final year. *Washington Post.* https://www.washingtonpost .com/politics/how-fact-checker-tracked-trump-claims/2021/01/23/ad04b69a-5c1d -11eb-a976-bad6431e03e2_story.html.

Kuźmicz, M. (2023a). European digital rights—human rights for a digital age? *Journal of Technology and Persons with Disabilities, 11*, pp. 60–75. https:// scholarworks.csun.edu/handle/10211.3/225165.

Kuźmicz, M. (2023b). Multilayer information obligation, and why we need it. *Journal of Technology and Persons with Disabilities, 11*, pp. 43–59. https://scholarworks .csun.edu/handle/10211.3/225159.

Lahmann, H. (2022). Infecting the mind: Establishing responsibility for transboundary disinformation. *European Journal of International Law, 33*(2), pp. 411–40. https://doi.org/10.1093/ejil/chac023.

Lazer, D. M. J., Baum, M. A., Benkler, Y., Berinsky, A. J., Greenhill, K. M., Menczer, F., Metzger, M. J., Nyhan, B., Pennycook, G., Rothschild, D., Schudson, M., Sloman, S. A., Sunstein, C. R., Thorson, E. A., Watts, D. J., and Zittrain, J. L. (2018). The science of fake news: Addressing fake news requires a multidisciplinary effort. *Science (American Association for the Advancement of Science), 359*(6380), pp. 1094–96. https://doi.org/10.1126/science.aao2998.

Lobschat, L., Mueller, B., Eggers, F., Brandimarte, L., Diefenbach, S., Kroschke, M., and Wirtz, J. (2021). Corporate digital responsibility. *Journal of Business Research, 122*, pp. 875–88. https://doi.org/10.1016/j.jbusres.2019.10.006.

Michailidou, A., Eike, E., and Trenz, H. J. (2022). Journalism, truth and the restoration of trust in democracy: Tracing the EU "fake news" strategy. In M. Conrad, G. Hálfdanarson, A. Michailidou, C. Galpin, and N. Pyrhönen (eds.), *Europe in the age of post-truth politics* (pp. 53–75). Springer International Publishing AG.

Mueller, R. S. (2019). *Report on the investigation into Russian interference in the 2016 presidential election: Submitted pursuant to 28 C.F.R. §600.8(c)*. Redacted version. US Department of Justice.

Odağ, Ö., Leiser, A., and Boehnke, K. (2019). Reviewing the role of the internet in radicalization processes. *Journal for Deradicalization, 21*, pp. 261–300. https://journals.sfu.ca/jd/index.php/jd/article/view/289.

Ogasawara, M. (2019). The daily us (vs. them) from online to offline: Japan's media manipulation and cultural transcoding of collective memories. *Journal of Contemporary Eastern Asia, 18*(2), pp. 49–67. https://doi.org/10.17477/jcea.2019.18.2.049.

Osmundsen, M., Bor, A., Vahlstrup, P. B., Bechmann, A., and Petersen, M. B. (2021). Partisan polarization is the primary psychological motivation behind political fake news sharing on Twitter. *The American Political Science Review, 115*(3), pp. 999–1015. https://doi.org/10.1017/S0003055421000290.

Padden, M., and Öjehag-Pettersson, A. (2021). Protected how? Problem representations of risk in the General Data Protection Regulation (GDPR). *Critical Policy Studies, 15*(4), pp. 486–503. https://doi.org/10.1080/19460171.2021.1927776.

Rahman, R. A., and Tang, S. M. (2022). Fake news and internet shutdowns in Indonesia: Symptoms of failure to uphold democracy. *Constitutional Review (Online), 8*(1), pp. 151–83. https://doi.org/10.31078/consrev816.

Ramakrishna, K. (2021). The white supremacist penetration of Western security forces: The wider implications. *New England Journal of Public Policy, 33*(2). https://scholarworks.umb.edu/nejpp/vol33/iss2/4

Reglitz, M. (2022). Fake news and democracy. *Journal of Ethics & Social Philosophy, 22*(2), pp. 162–87. https://doi.org/10.26556/jesp.v22i2.1258.

Richter, A. (2019). Fake news and freedom of the media. *Journal of International Entertainment & Media Law, 8*(1), pp. 1–33. https://www.swlaw.edu/sites/default/files/2019-03/Fake%20News%20and%20Freedom%20of%20the%20Media%20%20Richter.pdf.

Rocha, Y. M., de Moura, G. A., Desidério, G. A., de Oliveira, C. H., Lourenço, F. D., and de Figueiredo Nicolete, L. D. (2021). The impact of fake news on social media and its influence on health during the COVID-19 pandemic: A systematic review. *Journal of Public Health, 31*, pp. 1007–16. https://doi.org/10.1007/s10389-021 -01658-z.

Sargent, G. (2023). As more schools target "Maus," Art Spiegelman's fears are deepening. *Washington Post*. https://www.washingtonpost.com/opinions/2023/06/14/art -spiegelman-maus-book-bans/.

Sartre, J. P. (1995). *Anti-Semite and Jew*. G. J. Becker (Trans.). Schocken Books.

Serazio, M. (2021). The other "fake" news: Professional ideals and objectivity ambitions in brand journalism. *Journalism (London, England), 22*(6), pp. 1340– 56. https://doi.org/10.1177/1464884919829923.

Shaya, G. (2012). The myth of the Fourth Estate. *Lapham's Quarterly*. https://www .laphamsquarterly.org/roundtable/myth-fourth-estate.

Shearer, E. (2021). More than eight-in-ten Americans get news from digital devices. *Pew Research Center*. https://www.pewresearch.org/short-reads/2021/01/12/more -than-eight-in-ten-americans-get-news-from-digital-devices/.

Srnicek, N. (2017). *Platform capitalism*. Cambridge, UK: Polity.

Sullivan, M. C. (2019). Libraries and fake news: What's the problem? What's the plan? *Communications in Information Literacy, 13*(1), pp. 91–113. https://doi.org/10 .15760/comminfolit.2019.13.1.7.

Tandoc, E. C., Duffy, A., Jones-Jang, S. M., and Pin, W. G. W. (2021). Poisoning the information well? The impact of fake news on news media credibility. *Journal of Language and Politics, 20*(5), pp. 783–802. https://doi.org/10.1075/jlp.21029.tan.

Tomic, T. (2010). The philosophy of information as an underlying and unifying theory of information science. *Information Research, 15*(4). https://informationr.net/ir/15 -4/colis714.html.

Tucker, J. A., Theocharis, Y., Roberts, M. E., and Barberá, P. (2017). From liberation to turmoil: Social media and democracy. *Journal of Democracy, 28*(4), pp. 46–59.

Wright, C., Brinklow-Vaughn, R., Johannes, K., and Rodriguez, F. (2021). Media portrayals of immigration and refugees in hard and fake news and their impact on consumer attitudes. *The Howard Journal of Communications, 32*(4), pp. 331–51. https: //doi.org/10.1080/10646175.2020.1810180.

Zuboff, S. (2015). Big other: Surveillance capitalism and the prospects of an information civilization. *Journal of Information Technology, 30*(1), pp. 75–89.

PART V

Fighting Fake News

Joining Small and Large Worlds Together

Chapter 12

Neutralizing the Pathologies of Fake News Impacting Information Behavior in Individuals

EXAMINING THE IMPACT OF SMALL WORLDS

The rate of people believing in specific conspiracies has been rising—sometimes dramatically—over the past two decades. People willing to accept that the moon landings were faked, for example, have risen from 6 percent in 1999 to nearly 12 percent in 2022, doubling among the US population the further the event recedes into memory. Similar upticks have been documented about belief in a flat earth and vaccines as vehicles for microchip delivery (Hamilton, 2022). Or take the crackpot ideas of Robert F. Kennedy Jr., scion of the Kennedy political dynasty and minor Independent candidate for the 2024 US presidential election, who still asserts that vaccines are harmful to children (Bond, 2023) and has made the issue a part of his campaign plat-form. Conspiracies are routinely touted by various "titans of industry" such as Elon Musk (Shephard, 2023), or celebrities who have publicly dabbled in things they know nothing about (that is, "chemtrails" from airplanes) but are stricken by paranoia about them (Cairns, 2016). The list of conspiracies goes on and on, mind-numbing in its sickly factless banality. But what drives individuals to adopt such "reflexive contrarianism" (Krugman, 2023) that unmoors them from reason, facts, and logical thinking? What drives a person to these extreme beliefs? Determining these factors in people's lives may help in understanding their susceptibility to unexamined beliefs and reflexive contrarianism and could help lead to important solutions for mitigating its effect in individuals.

The final part of this book, then, will address these different ways in which fake news and misinformation might be counteracted and their effects mitigated through the use of various strategies for improved thinking. It will also address a combination of factors that influence information users, including examining their narrower life contexts, their larger social worlds, and the ways in which these different circles in their lives interact with and influence each other.

The first of these factors, the small world, also known as the local world of the individual, focuses on the individual factors that influence a person, including their singular concerns and attitudes, their individual small-scale relationships within a small group of people, and the like. This chapter will examine the ways in which people might neutralize the negative effects of fake news and misinformation through efforts made as individuals. This is framed specifically in terms of the concept of the small world of the typical information user and delves into the metacognitive problem areas in information users. The end result is to both pinpoint the specific traits and characteristics that make one susceptible to fake news and false information and quantify them so that a scale of susceptibility is established to better understand the extremes of this phenomenon. What, in other words, does susceptibility to false information *look like* for an individual?

SMALL WORLDS THEORY

Broadly speaking, most information behavior research focuses on the rational search for and acquisition of information. As seen in figure 2.4, Johnson's (2009) diagram shows that the purposive acquisition of information tends to be more widely examined in library and information research than other areas of information behavior. From domains, gaps, play theory, selective exposure, and pathways, to the study of information systems and information architecture and search engines, the purposive acquisition of information is bound by the attempt to identify and describe our "known unknowns," a main concern of information science itself. It also speaks to the ways in which external manipulations, such as nudging, tracking, and system bias, can drive us or subtly guide us to seek out certain information at the expense of other things. LIS research has made much progress in these areas, helping to identify what makes for successful information retrieval under ideal conditions that assume information seekers are rational beings seeking information for a specific conscious purpose.

Yet we all know, from the various personal and social pathologies that block us in our everyday lives, that life is not lived under ideal laboratory conditions. The same goes for information behavior. We can all succumb to external manipulations of our behavior and yet are not always aware of them. We can all succumb to personal limitations, such as being unaware of our own ignorance about something or being fooled and deluded by others as well as ourselves. From fragmented social worlds, using the least effort to find something, to information poverty and our limiting social groups, as well as information and cognitive overload itself, we are influenced by more than just rationality and purpose. We can all succumb, in other words, to the irrational in information behavior. As Comes et al. (2020) point out, people live in "an increasingly fragmented and volatile information landscape" where "information is subjective and localized, of unknown origin and reliability." As a result, research may be failing to provide an accurate examination of the poor conditions information users routinely operate under as well as understanding how irrational behavior fits within such a volatile milieu online.

Along these lines, Elfrida Chatman provides an important foundational framework for understanding some of the irrational and unconscious limiting factors and pathologies that have impacted information users (Chatman, 1991; 1996; 1999). Chatman's research focuses on the concept of the small world that describes a group "where the members share similar opinions and concerns, and understand each other because of the customs and language they uniquely share" (Dankasa, 2017). While the concept of an information bubble, or an echo chamber, is not new and has lately influenced much thinking about information seekers (cf. Kuzmenko et al., 2021; Comes et al., 2020; Kirdemir and Agarwal, 2022) using only the information they know or the limited sources they might trust, Chatman focuses more on the study of specific groups of people, including prisoners, the poor, custodial workers, and marginalized women, who tended to be ignored in research. She finds some counterintuitive results in the group dynamics of these specific populations. People who are members of a small world often do "not cross the boundaries of their world to seek information" (Dankasa, 2017). Importantly, within their small worlds the ways in which information is sought after can often be bound by the rules and normative values of that group (Burnett et al., 2001). The impact on the person is seen in terms of not only one's personal characteristics but also in terms of the information environment in which they are situated (Sin, 2011, p. 187). Through the small worlds, LIS research can better understand how immediate personal environments contribute to an information seeker's ability or inability to find and interact with information.

Examining these smaller worlds of information users, and developing profiles of users within those worlds, can help to identify specific social pathologies that might prevent users from seeking things out. Chatman was especially interested in "exploring how ordinary people experience information in connection with everyday needs" (Fulton, 2005, p. 79). This led her to examine the ways in which these purported small worlds might set the boundaries of a person's behaviors within a specific group. Chatman explored areas of poverty that had impact on the information behavior of the people living within those constraints and deprivations. Examining people in various situations, such as prisoners or poor older women, provided the background to show what prevents people from seeking out specific information more regularly. It also shows how they might similarly behave looking for information based on their similar experiences, needs, wants, and values held within that subgroup.

Chatman finds, notably, that the women she researched in one group did not engage in information sharing with each other in the ways that she had expected (Hersberger, 2005, p. 76). The result of this was the development of her theory of information poverty, closely related to the limited worlds she was examining (Chatman, 1991). Ultimately, Chatman develops a wider "life in the round" theory incorporating these two important ideas, suggesting a number of principles that apply, one can argue, to the use and misuse of information, fake news, and false narratives (Chatman, 1996). She focuses especially on a number of important propositions that establish the boundaries of the person (that is, its small world) and suggests that social norms acutely impact whether someone will seek information.

A person's worldview is then established based upon the behaviors dictated by the social norms. Such a life is then taken for granted (that is, it's all-encompassing) and curtails one's need to seek out information. Most important and related to the discussion of fake news is the fact that members of a small world living "in the round," as Chatman describes it, will usually not cross their small world boundaries to seek out information. If someone does cross boundaries, they will do so only if the information is perceived as "critical" to that individual, the group considers this information relevant to them, or the person perceives that their small world is no longer helping them or functioning as they assumed it would (Fulton, 2005, p. 81). Chatman's work mirrors other disciplines—especially in sociology and psychology— that have found "individuals experience culture as fragments of information but that culture also serves to give structure to the fragments of information" (Burnett and Jaeger, 2011). The world of using information is already at its foundation very fragmented and experienced in uneven bits that arrive from different places, times, people, and so on. This reorganization of fragments into something like a narrative creates a culture that, in turn, provides both structure and stricture to make this information cohere. People come to establish knowledge and factual certainty through this interplay of information and culture. In this regard, of course, if an online subculture finds ways to devalue some bits of information or reconstructs them in ways that belie the fundamental truths and hides other important aspects that might create a different conclusion, then it provides a clear space for false narratives and misinformation to take hold. Cultural narratives, language, and personal beliefs may all conflate together and mislead people so that fact becomes blurred despite the best intentions to preserve and honor it.

All in all, the examination of the small worlds of an information user becomes an essential component of how fake news might come to proliferate among subgroups. The narrow worlds constraining information users can impact them in negative as well as positive ways. When positive, proeducational, and personal learning values are normal for a specific group, the members of that group benefit. However, when the group devalues truth or erects taboos around certain subjects, forcing individuals to avoid seeking them out or learning about them, problems in the purposive acquisition of information compound. As such, it is imperative to find ways to break through any small worlds—like the online right-wing bubbles of the Japanese *Neto-uyo*, for example—that serve as barriers to factual information and create hotbeds of fever-swamp speculation. At stake is the reformulation of shared facts and established historical narratives that can lead on one side to the creation and sharing of new truths or to false narratives and misinformation on the other side.

USING METACOGNITION TO HELP WITH FAKE NEWS AND FALSE INFORMATION

What, then, are the ways that researchers can help to bring people out of their small world influences and adopt more widespread or common practices of information interaction and behavior, aside from having their influences changed due to dramatic external circumstances (that is, a sudden disease or life-changing disaster)? It often happens that we rarely change our lives or our behaviors until something forces our hands, causing significant regret later. One suggestion to help people avoid being forced to change only during crises is to begin looking at strengthening one's metacognitive skills—a strong component of educational outcomes themselves—and improving one's awareness of how one interacts with information. The likelihood of being able to break out of negative groups or behaviors grows with an increase in education levels and one's ability to think both critically and mindfully about a subject.

As mentioned in previous sections of this book, metacognition involves teaching people to learn about learning itself and to reflect upon methods that help to strengthen such learning. If we are merely experiencing our culture in disparate and uneven fragments, then what is most necessary is the ability to *filter and integrate* what we encounter in order to make sense of it. To do so we need an overall understanding of our needs, goals, and abilities.

Metacognition meets these areas by addressing "knowledge of one's self, knowledge of the nature of a cognitive task in relation to one's own cognitive abilities, and knowledge of how and when to effectively use cognitive strategies to complete a cognitive task" (Bowler, 2011, p. 76). This can help with the development of strategies to further bolster information users coming face to face with false information, fake news, and similar pathologies in information gathering and synthesis. Notably, some researchers have found that "metacognitive knowledge compensated for a lack of system and domain knowledge" (Bowler, 2011). This suggests that even if a person knows little about any given subject at hand, their understanding of how their mind works to integrate information as well as their ability to develop a working theory of knowledge based on the information they encounter will help them to overcome gaps in factual and subject-domain knowledge.

As mentioned in chapter 9 regarding the consumers of fake news, certain personal characteristics may contribute to the greater sharing of false information, including fear of missing out (FOMO), one's level of trust exhibited while online, the level of self-disclosure about one's personal life and thoughts, the amount of social comparison one engages in, how mentally fatigued or overloaded one is, how one identifies within a group, and finally the education level that one has attained for engaging in information literacy and critical thinking practices. Addressing these areas and applying metacognitive approaches to helping information users become aware of such factors may be beneficial to help individual users come to a greater understanding of how their personal thoughts, feelings, and attitudes at any given time might make them more or less susceptible to using, falling for, or sharing fake news. Figure 12.1 provides a list of these potential metacognitive "antidotes" to the various problem areas individuals harbor when interacting with and using information.

FEAR OF MISSING OUT (FOMO)

For FOMO, people were seen to share false information more freely as a result of thinking that they were missing out from something within their group or subculture. Sharing information with others without vetting it so as to be the first one in their group to adopt something was a strong indicator of using fake news. As Talwar et al. (2019) find, the correlation between this state of being—though self-reported among survey respondents—and sharing fake news was seen as a strong factor contributing to the spread of false information. One also might surmise that living within a smaller world, as Chatman has proposed, could exacerbate the feelings of FOMO that members of a group might develop. When one considers the personal as well as the

'ACTED UPON'
info consumer

User characteristics and conditions	Possible Metacognitive Knowledge 'Antidotes'
Online trust level	• Understanding curiosity • Communicating with others
Self-disclosure level	• Awareness of place within small world • Understanding personal strengths and weaknesses
Social comparison	• Understanding personal strengths and weaknesses • Knowing that you do not know
FOMO anxiety level	• Pulling back and reflecting • Knowing that you do not know • Understanding personal strengths and weaknesses
Social media fatigue	• Understanding effort needed to adapt • Building a base
Self identification	• Awareness of place within a small world • Context in a larger world
Education level	• Understanding curiosity • Communicating with others • Understanding strengths and weaknesses • Knowing that you do not know • most other metacognitive abilities that can be learned through education / etc.

Figure 12.1. List of metacognitive knowledge "antidotes" to information users' characteristics that contribute to the sharing of fake news with others.

small group dynamic, the likelihood of individuals increasing their sharing of fake news within their group may rise especially if FOMO is a strong characteristic or normative value that is prized and rewarded among members.

Several strategies that help to improve metacognitive knowledge and abilities involve personal behaviors that block impulsive behavior. Bowler's metacognitive skills taxonomy suggests "pulling back and reflecting" (2011, pp. 110–11), which advises people to take a break, leave for some time, and then think about the topic more deeply than when engaged with something or someone online. One could suggest that if online users were to better regulate their behavior and fight off feelings of being left behind or left out, they could help curtail the spread of fake news. Similarly, the need to disengage and relax could alleviate irrational fears about missing out on what others are doing and saying, including the sharing of "hot" information that has yet to be verified. FOMO anxiety might also be reduced by addressing another metacognitive strategy of coming to "know that you do not know" (p. 109) about any given subject. Many times, the person sharing fake news may do so out of not wanting to seem ignorant in the eyes of others. Yet, ironically, sharing a fake news story usually confirms their ignorance about a subject. It betrays their state of not knowing about their own ignorance. As Bowler suggests, "information seekers are prompted by an awareness of a gap" (p. 109), but one might argue that the irrational fears in FOMO interfere with this understanding of the self. Often, if others are sharing false information, it may be the case that people are willing to override their primary awareness of whether they know or do not know something. This is worth exploring further. Related to being aware of one's ignorance is also "knowing your strengths and weaknesses," which comes as a result of self-assessment, and "the ability to critique one's own cognitive and affective states" (p. 109). Being in a state of FOMO might actually interfere with being able to critique and understand one's current mental state and may prevent one from truly understanding personal gaps in knowledge.

ONLINE TRUST

High levels of trust in others online—either among a small world group or at large—are also a potential indicator of one's likelihood of sharing fake news with others (Talwar et al., 2019). In many ways, a reliance on trust runs the basic operations of any society. Lack of trust is associated with greater conflict and disagreement, while strong civil societies, such as those found in Scandinavia, that are bolstered by high levels of trust contribute to "curtailing widespread fear, mobilizing for collective manifestations of grief and restoring a sense of normalcy" in times of crisis or division (Selle and Wollebæk, 2015, p. 274). Any time we get into a car and drive down the correct side of the street, or stop at a red light, for example, we trust that others are going to do the same. Of course, when they don't, rules and penalties exist to enforce this behavior. Similar trust in information can also keep smaller groups functioning but often without incentives to make sure the information is trustworthy. Flaws in the trust agreements between people become apparent when dealing with rumors and false information. Trust in others while online may contribute to fake news as people tend to be less likely to vet the information they have found if they blindly trust their sources of information.

To help improve outcomes related to overly trusting sources within a smaller group or in a small world, it might be helpful to teach people to communicate with others and to improve their understanding of curiosity (Bowler, 2011, pp. Papa8–11). Communicating with others works as an important part of metacognitive knowledge as it can help "to clarify points of confusion about conflicting information or it can help to unite information into a cohesive unit" (p. 108). Yet it is important to note that if groups are too small or too limited in their perspectives, such efforts at communication could backfire. In this sense, it might be important to encourage people to widen their network of relationships so as to increase the likelihood of coming across more factual rather than false information.

A better understanding of curiosity itself may also decrease the negative impact of being overly trustful online. Understanding curiosity points to "the stark choices" people need to make when confronted with information as they consider how much or how deeply they need to delve into a subject (Bowler, 2011, p. 111). Being too trusting in a source of information may diminish the curiosity one feels in pursuing the matter further. Conversely, being more aware that curiosity is curtailed in these situations might help information users to buck this tendency. As Bowler describes it, understanding curiosity is "a risk/benefit analysis that hinges on understanding how far curiosity can take you before it becomes a liability, rather than a benefit" for any given information-related task (p. 112). In some ways, feelings of high trust might be best described to information users as a red flag and that the more confident a person feels toward a particular idea, solution, or information source might be best utilized as the starting point to be more skeptical.

SELF-DISCLOSURE

Self-disclosure occurs online in the various ways people reveal personal information about themselves and also develop their own identities within online groups and subcultures. The desire to gossip and share information—whether true or not, accurate or exaggerated, disclosed fully or just partially—may be related to an increase in fake news sharing. The reason for this is that such people may be more willing to disclose any information, especially if it is "exciting and sensational," about themselves and others in order to gain popularity within their desired cohort (Weiss et al., 2021). The information behavior research model called "SIF-FOW" (sharing information found for others on the web) shows that if users find information they think others will like or find useful and make themselves look good among them in the process, they are more likely to share it (Weiss et al., 2021). The sharing of this information is meant to develop a reputation through the act of disclosing information to others they think will desire it and reciprocate with praise. One's identity is intertwined with the sharing, in other words, and the creation of reputation coincides with the presentation of one's purported beliefs and opinions.

Certainly, one way to address this issue is to make information users more aware of the impact that their small world has on them and to reconsider whether sharing information to bolster their reputations in a group is ultimately beneficial or harmful. As with curiosity, it is dependent upon an analysis of risk versus reward. Making people aware of the normative values they are operating under, and the pressures these exert on group members, may help to curtail some of this behavior. Similarly, in the metacognitive knowledge base as well, knowing one's personal strengths and weaknesses may help to diminish this behavior. The more one knows about oneself and one's desires for a reputation that is developed and burnished through sharing personalized information, the more one can analyze the motives behind this. Yet the main obstacle that self-disclosure presents in being more aware of one's strengths and weaknesses may be the urge to overestimate and overstate one's accomplishments online and simultaneously diminish one's struggles. Teaching people to become more aware of this tendency may improve one's self-honesty and contribute to more objective and clear-eyed assessment of a person's cognitive and affective state of being.

SOCIAL COMPARISON

In social comparison, which stems from long-standing theories from the 1950s, people are seen as habitually comparing their lives and themselves to other people. The introduction of social media to this dynamic, however, has exacerbated this tendency in people. Certainly, the small worlds that people inhabit are a direct impact on whether someone will engage in social comparisons with others. If others are bound to the normative values in the group, expectations may exist that pressure a person into comparing their own actions to others. Comparison increases when people view social media and see the happy surface presented to them, "a facade that highlights the fun and excitement but does not tell us much about where we are struggling in our daily lives at a deeper level" (Karim et al., 2020). If limited self-disclosure is one way to present to the world one's greatest successes, then social comparison is the receiving end of the dynamic. People will compare their current feelings to what they see on social media, often to the detriment of their mental health when what they see happens to be primarily—but unrealistically—good things (Karim et al., 2020). In terms of fake news sharing, people who compare themselves to others may be more susceptible to fake news if the people they admire or relate to in their social networks are sharing it in their group.

To combat this situation, metacognitive knowledge that addresses "knowing that you do not know" might improve some outcomes in curtailing the sharing of fake news and false information among those who engage in a significant amount of social comparisons. A lot of times people are impacted by the opinions of others that they have compared themselves to and, as with online trust, may adopt their opinions without deeply considering them. People may also consider someone else's sheen of success and be swayed by that outward image, believing false information because they think such beliefs contribute to that success. It may be that being made aware of gaps in knowledge—even awareness of that gap between image and reality in social media itself—might prevent someone from merely taking an opinion from someone else without looking more closely at it.

SOCIAL MEDIA FATIGUE

One of the more deeply explored pathologies in human information behavior is information overload, a condition that arises when a person encounters too much information to continue searching. People often face too many choices while searching for information and wind up with choice paralysis, unable to critically engage in a topic or to choose one thing over another. Other times, people will purposefully search for just enough, called *satisficing* and—quite reasonably sometimes—settle for partial or incomplete results to meet a specific information task. Social media fatigue is related to these conditions in that the person suffering from the fatigue experiences similar negative emotions, such as anger, disappointment, tiredness, and reduced energy, as a result of using social media for too long. The relationship to fake news comes from the information user's subsequent lack of energy needed to confirm or deny whether something is true or false. Being tired from overuse of information technology might result in more sharing of false information due to the information user's inability to take the time and energy to verify whether the news is true.

From the metacognitive knowledge perspective, coming to understand the time and effort required to complete a task may improve outcomes, especially as any project is "the result of sustained effort, attention to detail, and a consistent level of persistence" (Bowler, 2011, p. 112). Yet even as people are physically and mentally fatigued, many may not realize it while they are using information technology. Indeed, while many are often aware of *how* to do a task, many have trouble following through and actually doing it. If people are made aware of their state of being at the time, however, they might engage in techniques to help improve their mental focus or reduce their feelings of tiredness. It also helps for people to become more aware of just how much energy it actually takes to thoroughly investigate and conduct a fact-check. The more one practices information vetting, the less taxing it may become as an overall practice in utilizing information.

This is also related to the overall need to improve one's knowledge of a subject and the need to change course, adapt to the information one has found, and the basics of searching for something to verify information. This concept of "building a base" is essential for improving stamina in both learning and searching for information. Improving one's base of knowledge involves "strategic use of exploratory tactics to help build foundational domain knowledge" (Bowler, 2011, p. 107). The fatigue one feels while exploring new topics can give way to more general mental strength in various subject learning the more one learns and builds their base. This improvement in stamina can curtail the sharing of fake news stemming from one's sense of social media fatigue and information overload.

SELF-IDENTIFICATION

The awareness of one's small world group impacts and binds a person by what are considered the good, bad, and normative values of their group. The more one self-identifies with the radicalism of a group, for example, the less likely one is to remain situated within overall mainstream values. One feels more tension between the values and ideas of the group and the wider mainstream. Role theory and Sunstein's concept of "the daily me" contribute to the adoption of new ideas and help to demonstrate the principle that online users of information "are active developers of their identities" (Weiss et al., 2021, p. 10).

However, metacognition may be difficult to use when dealing with self-identified extremists, who seem to reject many of the good-faith advice and strategies proposed by it. In many ways, extremism is a breaking of the "connecting" strategies (Bowler, 2011, pp. 108–9) used in metacognition, a core set of skills that focus on clarifying information and the joining of various factual information together to form more coherent and broader world views. Connecting helps "to make sense of the disparate pieces of information" that people encounter. In the case of Japanese right-wing extremists, however, that connecting of Imperial Japan with atrocities in China and Korea has been broken through the use of denial and deflection. The self-identification as members of the *Neto-uyo* prohibits them from seeing connections and leads them into denial that such events ever took place, despite the massive amounts of evidence establishing them as historical fact. The connections have gone haywire, in a sense. Similarly, antisemitic Holocaust denial and anti-vaccine movements seem to devolve into refusals to connect facts in one area of history or science with other areas. To improve this situation, it is imperative to focus on the connections between events, facts, and established mainstream interpretations.

EDUCATION LEVEL

Finally, education level appears to impact the ability one has to master and wield metacognitive strategies. Those who fall for fake news tend to be less educated and may be bound by the normative rules of their small world groups, preventing them from breaking out of the self-imposed bubbles they may be operating within. Notably, information literacy and critical thinking strategies overlap with many metacognition skills, providing road maps for teaching librarians to the improve educational outcomes. The specific approaches to metacognition can be adopted by educators to better improve the ways that people handle and incorporate information into their lives. Yet information literacy and critical thinking *by themselves* cannot primarily solve the problems of fake news and misinformation. The overall individual characteristics of an individual might provide a profile of their susceptibility to falling for and sharing fake news. These characteristics, as mentioned earlier, require more specific approaches that might utilize specific metacognitive skills but also might be better alleviated through knowledge of the specific normative values of the person's small world environment.

FUTURE DIRECTIONS: VISUALIZING A QUOTIENT FOR FAKE NEWS SUSCEPTIBILITY

After identifying one's small world influences, various levels of information behavior, and attitudes regarding information use and online behavior, while examining the ways in which people might better use their metacognitive skills to improve their information seeking and processing, we can now look at the ways in which we might both pinpoint and quantify one's specific susceptibility to false information. The goal is to create in the aggregate a kind of fake news susceptibility quotient and profile, helping people see whether they have certain qualities that might be addressed to improve cognitive abilities. The following will speculate upon this currently hypothetical visualization of fake news susceptibility.

What might this individual susceptibility quotient look like? It will be important to scale it in terms of points to show the areas, as in a radar scale, where one area is more likely to be more pronounced in relation to another. So in the case of a hypothetical online user, one might gauge various levels of information user activity and come to examine their behaviors so as to visualize their susceptibility factor as in figure 12.2. On a scale of 0 to 50 (0 being not a risk factor, 50 being the highest risk factor), one can gauge the tendency of a person to engage in FOMO behavior (that is, high degree of risk = 40), their levels of online trust (highest risk = 50), their levels of self-disclosure (high risk = 40), how much social comparison they engage in (highest risk = 50), their levels of social media fatigue (moderate risk = 25), how they identify and the groups they work within (highest risk = 50), and their education levels (least educated represents highest risk = 50).

So, as an example, if there were someone who had dropped out of high school (low education levels scale higher), became a member of an online extremist right-wing group (high degree of self-identification in a group), who distrusts all but those in his group (high trust of group members), and who has high degree of social comparison (compared to others in group) and

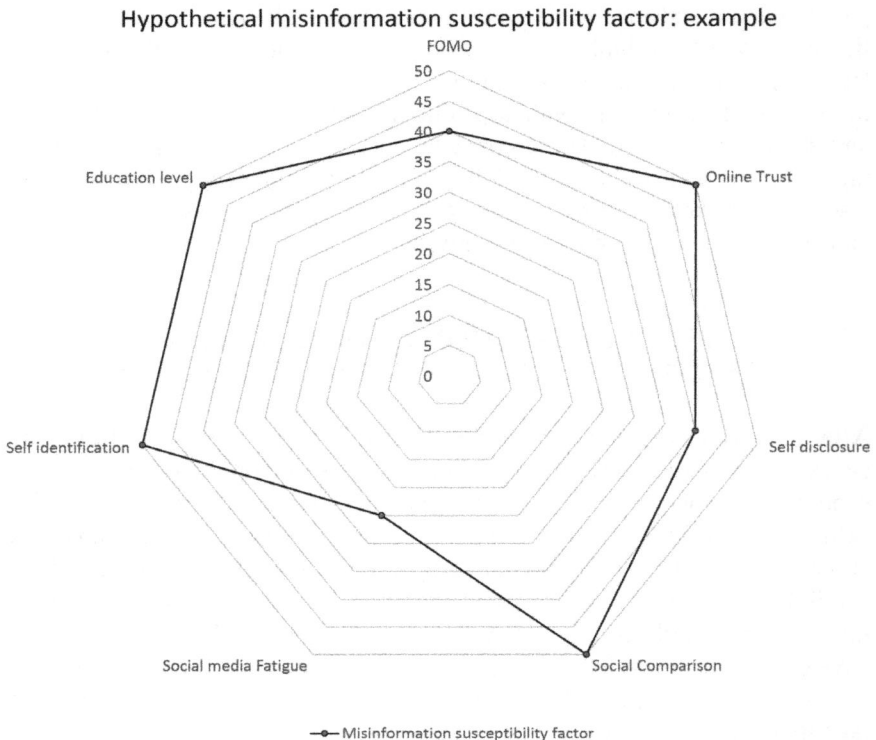

Figure 12.2.   **Hypothetical radio diagram for a misinformation susceptibility factor to aid in visualizing an individual's problem areas of sharing fake news.**

a moderately high degree of self-disclosure within his group, one might visualize the factors that contribute to his fake news sharing, as in figure 12.2. The ultimate goal for this modeling is to show the areas that need development to improve strategies for fighting fake news. Identifying personal susceptibility factors driving the spread of fake news can help improve outcomes against the spread of misinformation among specific online information users. In the end, such factors identify individual characteristics and focus on the individual's life and experiences within their small worlds, making them invaluable tools for fighting the spread of false information.

TAILORED MISINFORMATION DEPROGRAMMING

The relative lack of success in educating people about avoiding fake news and providing strategies based in information literacy approaches has been a main source of criticism among those outside of librarianship. Typical approaches to fighting fake news, like ACT UP (standing for author, currency, truth, unbiased, privilege) (Stahura, 2018), while widely adopted and cited in library and information science, might not work effectively because the authors assume, like much of LIS research, that a certain amount of rational will and intention exists in the information user. Call it the myopia of good intentions: librarians often assume patrons think just like librarians who enjoy and relish the search process they are trained in, while reveling in the purposeful, reasoned acquisition of information. Taking the efficacy of this attitude as self-evident, many librarians reason that information users are bound to improve in their interactions with fake news if they follow librarian advice and best practices.

But what if, for example, FOMO is exceptionally strong in a student? How would typical information literacy approaches deal with this irrational sensation of missing out and the impulse to share a fake news story in order to seem cool? How would FOMO impact whether a student would be willing to spend time on a strategic search, or to ponder how "authority has been constructed"? What if others in their group are using false information and they feel the pressure to also use it? It's not simply a matter of piercing the bubbles of maladaptive information behaviors with the sword of rational thinking, perfectly vetted library sources, and well-planned strategic searches. Librarians instead need to approach these problems by looking at the other pathologies, factors, and individual proclivities influencing a person and then tailor an educational approach *specifically to their weaknesses*. Indeed, the problems of misinformation may be far more complex than many information literacy approaches assume. Scholarship may well be a conversation, but when students who are novice researchers are impacted by distractions or false narratives, that conversation becomes difficult to pick up on without clear guidance.

The hypothetical next steps, therefore, would be to create educational plans that meet and address individual information pathologies contributing to the spread of fake news and the misuse of information in personal networks and at the individual level. This approach would focus on the weaknesses noted and tailors assessment of misinformation susceptibility toward the metacognitive skills seen as needed for improvement as well as development.

WHAT INTERVENTIONS ARE NECESSARY?

The tailored educational approach would emphasize areas in which a person shows weaknesses in their information interactions and could then be used to alleviate some of the pathologies that stem from them. For example, if a person shows very strong evidence of FOMO in their online activities, some suggested approaches for educating these users would be to discuss how to disengage with their friends and acquaintances on social media. Rather than trying to show good sources to go to, the educator might instead attempt to instill ways for the person to reduce their reliance on social media, and even suggest a limit in the number of hours spent online. This might help a person to stop thinking that others are more "in the know" than they are. Rather than trying to showcase the pathways to reputable sources, it might be more effective to demonstrate how social media impacts a person's moods and cognitive functions. Perhaps a new approach might be to have students discuss the influence of social media on their lives and have them, in their own words, explain the draw of it as well as the drawbacks. Being aware of one's emotional states while searching might improve user outcomes. Similar approaches might be taken with online comparisons, self-disclosure, and online trust. Each of these areas speaks to the social behaviors of interacting with others online and might need to be addressed as such. If sharing misinformation is partly a problem with behavior, then attempting to solve it with exhaustive LibGuides and other pathways to information sources or assumptions that information literacy frames can solve this may not be very effective strategies.

Personal identity is an especially difficult and even intractable part of the misinformation equation. The increase of extremism in online users often results from the fact that others in a group are thinking along similar lines. To break through this kind of bubble, educators would need to find ways to present alternative sources, but in ways that subtly shift the perspectives of such extreme thinkers. The approach might need to adopt different methods of explanation to demonstrate logical fallacies in extreme positions; or, more directly, an educator might provide an analysis of a fake news piece that demonstrates the ways in which the logic of an extremist group is altered and manipulated in order to convince unassuming readers or extremists to accept illogical conclusions without reflection.

As information overload and social media fatigue may also contribute to the spread of fake news, there also needs to be an acknowledgment of the ways that information systems tax the mental state of their users. The principle of least effort suggests that people are not that interested in "the search" as a satisfying activity. They see it as work and a closed task that ultimately becomes burdensome if needs are not met rather quickly or it becomes increasingly open ended. Much has been made of information overload in research. Approaches in tailored education could suggest that users take breaks and indulge in stepping back from systems to recover cognitive energy while also providing calm to help with increased attention to details.

What this proposed hypothetical fake news intervention strategy adds up to is essentially providing an alternative approach to addressing the problems of fake news that have less to do with assumptions of purposeful acquisition of information and more to do with irrationality and the imperfect environmental and systemic conditions that affect users. It is possible that this approach can improve individual outcomes in relation to fake news, helping users get a better sense of the external forces, internal emotional influences, and cognitive limits that impact their information behaviors. Ultimately, however, the main drawback with an individually tailored intervention in information misuse is how difficult it will be to scale up in order to address the number of online users—literally billions—so that it is effective on a wider scale.

Yet it might be better to see this approach as one side of a multisided solution. The grassroots, person-to-person approach can link up with wider contexts—both meso worlds and the larger macro worlds that people inhabit—and can thus be addressed by broader national and international policies and best practices. The next chapter will examine the wider contexts that impact the sharing of fake news and will propose ways that larger institutions can both improve and regulate the problems of false information in their wider societies.

REFERENCES

Bond, S. (2023). RFK Jr.'s presidential campaign is driven by conspiracy theories. *National Public Radio.* https://www.npr.org/2023/07/13/1187272781/rfk-jr-kennedy-conspiracy-theories-social-media-presidential-campaign.

Bowler, L. (2011). Into the land of adolescent metacognitive knowledge during the information search process: A metacognitive ethnography. In A. Spink and J. Heinström (eds.), *New directions in information behaviour* (pp. 93–126). Emerald.

Burnett, G., Besant, M., and Chatman, E. A. (2001). Small worlds: Normative behavior in virtual communities and feminist bookselling. *Journal of the American Society for Information Science and Technology, 52*(7), pp. 536–47. https://doi.org /10.1002/asi.1102.

Burnett, G., and Jaeger, P. T. (2011). The theory of information worlds and information behavior. In A. Spink and J. Heinström (eds.), *New directions in information behaviour* (pp. 161–80). Emerald.

Cairns, R. (2016). Climates of suspicion: "Chemtrail" conspiracy narratives and the international politics of geoengineering. *The Geographical Journal, 182*(1), pp. 70–84. https://doi.org/10.1111/geoj.12116.

Chatman, E. A. (1991). Life in a small world: Applicability of gratification theory to information-seeking behavior. *Journal of the American Society for Information Science, 42*(6), pp. 438–49. https://doi.org/10.1002/(SICI)1097–4571(199107)42:6 <438::AID-ASI6>3.0.CO;2-B.

Chatman, E. A. (1996). The impoverished life-world of outsiders. *Journal of the American Society for Information Science, 47*(3), pp. 193–206. https://doi.org/10 .1002/(SICI)1097–4571(199603)47:3<193::AID-ASI3>3.0.CO;2-T.

Chatman, E. A. (1999). A theory of life in the round. *Journal of the American Society for Information Science, 50*(3), pp. 207–17. https://doi.org/10.1002/(SICI)1097– 4571(1999)50:3<207::AID-ASI3>3.0.CO;2–8.

Comes, M., van de Walle, B., and Van Wassenhove, L. (2020). The coordination-information bubble in humanitarian response: Theoretical foundations and empirical investigations. *Production and Operations Management, 29*(11), pp. 2484–2507. https://doi.org/10.1111/poms.13236.

Dankasa, J. (2017). Seeking information in circles: The application of Chatman's life in the round theory to the information small world of Catholic clergy in northern Nigeria. *Journal of Information Science, 43*(2), pp. 246–59. https://doi.org/10.1177 /0165551516632659.

Fulton, C. (2005). Chatman's life in the round. In K. E. Fisher, S. Erdelez, and L. McKechnie (eds.), *Theories of information behavior* (pp. 79–82). Information Today.

Hamilton, L. (2022). Conspiracy vs. science: A survey of U.S. public beliefs. *Carsey Research National Issue Brief, 162*. Carsey School of Public Policy. University of New Hampshire. https://carsey.unh.edu/publication/conspiracy-vs-science-a -survey-of-us-public-beliefs.

Hersberger, J. (2005). Chatman's information poverty. In K. E. Fisher, S. Erdelez, and L. McKechnie (eds.), *Theories of information behavior* (pp. 75–78). Information Today.

Johnson, J. D. (2009). An impressionistic mapping of information behavior with special attention to contexts, rationality, and ignorance. *Information Processing and Management, 45*, pp. 593–604.

Karim, F., Oyewande, A., Abdalla, L. F., Chaudhry Ehsanullah, R., and Khan, S. (2020). Social media use and its connection to mental health: A systematic review. *Curēus, 12*(6). https://doi.org/10.7759/cureus.8627.

Kirdemir, B., and Agarwal, N. (2022). Exploring bias and information bubbles in YouTube's video recommendation networks. *Complex Networks & Their Applications X, 1016*, pp. 166–77. https://doi.org/10.1007/978-3-030-93413-2_15.

Kuzmenko, O., Cyburt, A., Yarovenko, H., Yersh, V., and Humenna, Y. (2021). Modeling of "information bubbles" in the global information space. *Journal of International Studies (Kyiv), 14*(4), pp. 270–85. https://doi.org/10.14254/2071–8330.2021/14–4/18.

Krugman, P. (2023). The rich are crazier than you and me. *New York Times*. https://www.nytimes.com/2023/07/06/opinion/robert-kennedy-jr-silicon-valley.html.

Selle, P., and Wollebæk, D. (2015). The complex relationship between civil society and trust. *Italian Sociological Review, 5*(3), pp. 273–91. https://doi.org/10.13136/isr.v5i3.110.

Shephard, A. (2023). What is Elon Musk building? *The New Republic*. https://newrepublic.com/article/170931/elon-musk-twitter-right-wing-conspiracy-theories.

Sin, S. (2011). Towards agency-structure integration: A person-in-environment (PIE) framework for modelling individual-level information behaviors and outcomes. In A. Spink and J. Heinström (eds.), *New directions in information behaviour* (pp. 180–209). Emerald.

Stahura, D. (2018). ACT UP for evaluating sources: Pushing against privilege. *College & Research Libraries News, 79*(10), pp. 551–52. https://doi.org/10.5860/crln.79.10.551.

Talwar, S., Dhir, A., Kaur, P., Zafar, N., and Alrasheedy, M. (2019). Why do people share fake news? Associations between the dark side of social media use and fake news sharing behavior. *Journal of Retailing and Consumer Services, 51*, pp. 72–82. https://doi.org/10.1016/j.jretconser.2019.05.026.

Weiss, A. P., Alwan, A., Garcia, E. P., and Kirakosian, A. T. (2021). Toward a comprehensive model of fake news: A new approach to examine the creation and sharing of false information. *Societies, 11*(3). https://doi.org/10.3390/soc11030082.

Chapter 13

Neutralizing the Pathologies of Fake News in Macro Environments

Much has been made of the individual's role and responsibility in the spread of fake news. Some blame ignorance and inattentiveness, while others blame being maliciously or unintentionally duped. In most cases, spreading fake news is seen as a *personal* failing and even a moral transgression akin to lying. Researchers Michel Croce and Tommaso Piazza, perhaps responding in some ways to the failure of people to individually address their shortcomings suggest that *educational approaches* in the area of "public information campaigns [and] changes to school curriculum" may help individuals overcome these personal failings (Millar, 2021). Nevertheless, this advice remains focused on targeting the individual and their interactions with information. On a more forgiving note, though, people often live their lives at the mercy of their individual perspectives, unable to see beyond the scope of their immediate vision, or, as David Lynch describes it, their "golf-ball-sized consciousness" (2006). Life is often spent solely within these limited perspectives, and people can often remain unaware of not only the external influences on their thoughts and actions and the everyday occurrences happening around them but also can remain in the dark about their own personal motivations and character traits. Every so often a person broadens their perspective and sees the world beyond what is in front of their noses, and in expanding their awareness reaches greater understanding.

For all the emphasis on individual agency and personal free will, however, we all confront the reality that many things exist beyond our immediate awareness, despite not being able to visualize or grasp them fully. Many of these things operate beyond human scale, existing as something one individual cannot grasp entirely on their own. Timothy Morton has eloquently described these types of diffuse yet massive entities as "hyperobjects" that extend beyond our normal comprehension, eluding us in their entirety, "time-stretched," as he calls them, "to such as vast extent that they become almost impossible to hold in mind" (2013, p. 58). Morton argues that a number of ubiquitous concepts follow this pattern of existing as if on a different plane (that is, a biosphere, all the plastic humans have ever produced, black holes, the oil industry, etc.) but nonetheless impacting people and their interactions with the natural world despite not consciously grasping them in totality. In describing the Florida Everglades, for example, Morton designates them as a hyperobject because they are "massively distributed in time and space in ways that baffle humans and make interacting with them fascinating, disturbing, problematic, and wondrous" (2013). Hyperobjects, then, are a stand-in for what we might have described loosely in the past as "reality," at least as it is described in terms of the immutable laws of science—for example, gravity or space-time relativity—that we ultimately run smack into despite not being entirely aware of how much they envelop us with their influence. Just because people could not conceive of gravity, hydrogen, or electricity five hundred years ago does not mean these forces did not exist. Much like the *Titanic* running into an iceberg, Morton tells us, modern civilization has now run smack into the hyperobject of global warming.

Whether one accepts Morton's concept or not, one might see the modern internet as a metaphorical "information hyperobject," amassing not only the capital to overcome governments and international borders to effect policy change but also collecting the massive amounts of raw data and information that run the surveillance capitalism machine driving its expansion into all aspects of our private lives. The scale of the endeavor itself is mind-boggling but results in similar reactions that Morton's environmental and physical hyperobjects create, including a "dissolution of the notion of world," the difficulty of "maintaining cynical distance," and new "aesthetic experience and practice" (2013, p. 24). The internet has fully altered how people conceive of their world and environments, irretrievably fragmenting narratives of unity and coherence and subsuming them with its singular but Babel-like immensity. This impacts how people have previously been able to see themselves as outside of a system, like nature, but also as existing within broader so-called information ecosystems. Now, they are fully enmeshed in information technologies that manipulate and utilize their behaviors through data tracking and surveillance, resulting in an inability for people to exist fully beyond their reach. Aesthetically, asymmetry dominates our thinking (p. 22), dousing us in the foreboding sense of imbalance in our comparatively small lives.

With this in mind, the individual's role in information behavior needs to be examined more broadly, investigating the problems of scale and scope—*structural approaches* as Croce and Piazza describe them (Millar, 2021)—that often blur individual results at such extreme margins. While an individual may be seen as unique and unpredictable from a statistical point of view, exceptional as a single data point, in the aggregate patterns emerge as greater numbers of data points are assessed. The wider information world and its impact on individuals necessarily needs to be addressed to better help with minimizing the wider impact of fake news and misinformation.

WIDER INFORMATION WORLDS

Setting aside the world of hyperobjects and large-scale information systems, information behavior research has often tended to focus more on smaller scales, especially individuals and their unique patterns of personal behavior in specific highly identifiable situations. This limited approach, despite many of the successes in the field (especially Chatman's work with poor cohorts) mentioned in chapter 12, nevertheless has its drawbacks. Every person is the sum not only of interior motives, thoughts, and feelings but also of relationships ranging from immediate families and informal friendship groups to the intermediate organizations they may be but a small part of (that is, work or living communities). Beyond that, of course, people are further subject to the macro scales of their regions and national or international communities, which may exert their own pressures and normative values upon people. Personal characteristics show how this micro emphasis can explain individual reasons for the spread of fake news. But, as mentioned, drawbacks to this approach exist and can prevent researchers from seeing the wider issues that affect individual outcomes. Chatman's theories of "life in the round" as well as "small worlds" tend to account for the smaller subcultures within larger cultures, similar to a kind of intersectionality for information behavior, suggesting an inherent limit to any assertions of broad universality associated with these ideas.

Burnett and Jaeger (2011) attempt to link both the small worlds of Chatman's research and the much broader perspectives of researcher Jürgen Habermas (1992), which encompass the totality of a person's experiences and influences. Habermas's research conceptualizes a person's "lifeworld," which is, similar in scope to Morton's hyperobject, a vast collection of influences within a culture that impact a person's perspectives, actions, beliefs, and motives. The lifeworld is described as "that collective information and social environment that weaves together the diverse information resources, voices and perspectives of all of the members of a society" (Burnett and Jaeger, 2011, p. 166). If Chatman's vision is of a life examined in minute detail and small enclosed spaces, Habermas's vision is one of massive influences writ large in the broadest of strokes through the conception of an expansive public sphere.

Burnett and Jaeger, then, propose to reconcile these two approaches with a more novel and encompassing "theory of information worlds" that would supply researchers with "a framework by which to examine the social dimensions and uses of information simultaneously at the immediate and broader social levels" (2011, p. 162). The result of this new approach is an ability to examine how information behavior is impacted by one's immediate influences, the small world in which one consistently interacts with others, and the larger social influences that comprise and inform the culture at large. Notably, they also provide room for the intermediate level that acts as a mediary bridging the small and large worlds they examine. By combining these approaches, the theory would "account for all of these social and structural elements at work in the shaping of information behavior within a society" (p. 167). It results in a far more comprehensive look at the numerous factors influencing any given information user.

Building upon this basic structure of information contexts and influences, Burnett and Jaeger further distinguish between the types of access to information that people are subject to, namely the physical, intellectual, and social. Physical access, which involves a person's ability to find or secure information resources in the physical world or gain internet access to websites tends to be one of the primary subjects studied in LIS research and is linked intimately with the user's sense of personal agency and location. Just as important to this, though, are the intellectual and social aspects of accessing information. Intellectual access focuses on the ability of a person to come to understand the information itself as well as its structure and various critical apparatus used to help contextualize it. People with lower intellectual access may be less educated overall or merely unfamiliar with the various scaffolds and support mechanisms (like indices, tables of contents, search strategies) found in information resources. Information literacy often attempts to surpass the barriers to intellectual access by focusing on the contexts and containers of information itself. Social access, in contrast, is related to the ways in which people come to exchange and receive information from others. The greater role of information technologies and social media have been widely studied, but also represent a new supercharged influence upon the way that people achieve social access to information. These influences depend upon an individual's personal "understanding and acceptance of the social norms and mores surrounding information in a particular social world" (Burnett and Jaeger, 2011, p. 168).

IMPLICATIONS OF EXAMINING
INFORMATION WORLDS

An important distinction in the information worlds proposed by Burnett and Jaeger is that there are a number of interrelated parts that need to be better addressed in the research. These include examining the following: *social norms, social types, information value, information behavior,* and *boundaries* (2011, p. 169). Social norms, for example, define and delineate the ways in which those within a world should behave or present appearances and build identities. In the right-wing Japanese online *Neto-uyo* factions, for example, extremist positions and chronic behaviors of disbelief in mainstream ideas have become normalized by those within their group. The challenge of curtailing misinformation is especially difficult when it has become part of a social group's normative behavior to share and reinforce it. But the information world theory needs to reconcile the individual within not only a small circle of like-minded people who *might* meet in person but also within the context of a larger Japan-wide political movement online that simultaneously ties in with the broader international wave of online right-wing extremism. Being able to examine the individual while seeing the widest context possible is important yet extremely complex to isolate the important variables.

Similarly, social types involve roles that define actors within a social group and how they are perceived within that group. One can surmise that a figure dominant within a group could come to prohibit the sharing of factual information in order to preserve order or to expand power based on a political point. Of the many religious groups in America, fundamentalist groups tend to be more close-minded and willing to accept extreme ideas and conspiracy theories as solutions to unknown information. Umam et al. (2018) find that there is a "link between religious fundamentalism and the need for cognitive closure," which provides a way for people within such groups to be able to settle contentious ideas "once and for all." A person within a group might see their role as one who must be vigilant against any negative outside influences, settling for conspiracies and false information as a way to bolster this self-belief and to preserve the order of roles within a group. Yet social types may morph as groups get larger, and this may yet be a problem for the theory that needs further exploration. Someone currently within a small group might alter the way they see themselves as well as their overall role in it in reaction to growing numbers of new members.

Seeing value in information, a main pillar of information literacy, is described by Burnett and Jaeger as a shared perception of and belief about how important certain ideas or concepts are within a group. It is certainly true that different groups will prioritize different information for various reasons and motives. In the United States, for example, political affiliation often demonstrates differences in priorities or perceptions of problems, such as whether the economy is doing well or poorly, crime is increasing or decreasing, and so on. Indeed, the perception of poor economic performance of one's country is seen by Hornsey et al. (2023, p. 80) as an indicator of belief in conspiracy theories. He writes, "the more strongly people self-reported having conspiracy beliefs, the more positively they reported the economic performance of the country in the past" (p. 85). People who demonstrated such high levels of belief in such a conspiracy were also "characterized by a sense of economic deterioration: things were good once, but not so much now and going forward" (Hornsey et al., 2023). Characteristic of many reactionary groups, the person comes to believe that life was better in the past, unable or unwilling to accept that the current state of things is good, even in the face of overwhelming evidence. It is a kind of curdled nostalgia, a belief in a better, more stable past that was in reality neither stable nor better.

Groups also overemphasize conspiracies based on the current political fortunes of that group. It has often been observed in American politics that those in the opposition party will believe the country is faring poorly when they are out of power and will believe things are not that bad when they are in power. Even the problem of disinformation itself can be filtered through a political lens (Myers and Kang, 2022), with one group believing it to be a problem and another denying it. The result is "a cacophony" of legal and social solutions across states in the United States that may contribute to an increase in information bubbles and further divides on how certain information is prized over others. The value of information, then, is a problematic and complex interplay of expectations, perceptions, and reality that do not always mesh together harmoniously in the mind of not only individuals but also within the shared beliefs and priorities of a group. The group's interaction with meso- and macro-information worlds and the impact this has on the value given to finding truthful information also add compounding complexities to determining these values.

Finally, boundaries represent an important conceptual framework for describing information flow among groups as it helps to identify the areas where differing information worlds might come into contact with each other. Mary Louise Pratt's concept of a "contact zone," which she defines as "social spaces where cultures meet, clash and grapple with each other, often in the contexts of highly asymmetrical relations of power" (2002, p. 4), long a foundational concept in educational theory and praxis, provides a similar understanding of the ways in which differing groups might come into contact with each other and the resulting conflicts, agreements, and reconciliations that occur. But boundaries among micro-, meso-, and macro-information worlds may be impossibly intertwined to fully understand the influences that each make upon any given individual. The problems of scope and scale are inherent to this theory of information worlds. Reconciling all the variables to understand all the levels and all the forces involved may be difficult to achieve.

THE INFLUENCES AND IMPLICATIONS OF FAKE NEWS ON INFORMATION WORLDS

One major point that Habermas makes is that the public sphere should be seen as the great leveler, where equal voices are seen as exchanging information with other voices, resulting in "a conversation among equals" (Burnett and Jaeger, 2011, p. 166) and not a top-down tool for societal control. This basis for our information worlds turns out to be quite important. Without it, societal information pathologies appear to proliferate. But how does the influence of fake news complicate this vision of a public sphere? How does it impact or even ruin the lifeworld or the wider information worlds proposed by Burnett and Jaeger? While they suggest that ideal small worlds will share information among other groups, and that many of our intermediate and large-sized institutions (for example, libraries, schools, government agencies) exist primarily to facilitate this exchange, they also suggest that "other influences serve to constrain the movement of information . . . or constrict socially acceptable perceptions of information" (2011, p. 170). These constraints and constrictions skew or alter the way that information flows among groups of people, defeating any good intentions or motives behind established public entities.

Anecdotally, one sees such impacts in the form of fake stories, lies, misinformation, and general loss of trust overall in public institutions. When lies are spread in the public sphere, it results in a debasement of factual information for the sake of preserving regimes as well as destabilizing enemies, which was hypothesized as a motive for creating fake news in Weiss et al. (2021). The loss of trust in Soviet libraries, for example, is one such good example of how the wider public sphere—or lack of an open one in this case—has impact on the spread of information and the individual's information environment. Yet it also can take merely one lie to undo the truth, no matter how hard fought it was to educate those targeted by misinformation peddlers. As Millar (2021) recounts, researchers have found that reading a statement first about climate change being true can be undercut when a subject next read the false assertion that there was no consensus on its human causes. Imagine, then, the difficulty of combating fake news when the scale is moved beyond an individual and into the massively populated public sphere, with all of its variations in user types and motivations, especially when debasement of true information is so easily accomplished with minimal tampering.

The fake news model proposed in this book addresses those problems of the fake news creator, whose intentions sometimes prove to be malicious and destabilizing. The user becomes unaware, if flooded with misinformation, of the negative effects of the misinformation as it poisons and twists the sense of equality in the public sphere. What happens next is the subversion of the public sphere into the very "hegemonic tool" that it was designed to prevent. Fake news, misinformation, false narratives, and conspiracies help to weaken the public sphere and provide a method for a group to dominate and manipulate those engaged within it. For this reason, understanding how to create larger lifeworld-sized public policy becomes essential.

WIDER IMPACT AND PROPOSALS TO IMPROVE INFORMATION USE/BEHAVIOR

If we can come to a better understanding of how larger-scale entities, including governments, corporations, businesses, political groups, and affiliations, impact personal information behavior, then we might be able to develop successful wider strategies for improving the problems related to fake news and misinformation. There is a need to better understand the role that intermediary entities play in the use and misuse of information and the ways in which information behavior is shaped by them. Ultimately, improving information use is dependent upon a number of factors, including the encouragement of good behaviors on the larger scale, the development of larger-scoped policies that start from the top, and the use of real-world case study evaluations. The ways in which leaders can encourage good behavior interconnects with wider top-down policy that looks at how to scale up desired outcomes across numerous yet disparate personalities. Examining this is linked to case studies that show how the policy—whether regional, national, or international—impacts specific institutions and the people working within them.

The following will examine how different entities of different sizes and impacts might have an effect on curtailing problems of fake news, especially in light of large corporations at the heart of IT and surveillance capitalism itself; government agencies and their past, current, and potential future improvements of public policies; and finally the larger, medium, and smaller societies in which people operate and develop their assumptions about their lives, their thoughts, and their information needs.

IT AND CORPORATE MEASURES AND SOLUTIONS

Corporate measures can provide an important bulwark in curtailing the spread of false information for they "play a key role as intermediary structures" (Selle and Wollebæk, 2015), existing between the larger macro worlds of large-scale societies and the micro worlds of individuals. Working on these intermediate scales, they can exist as go-betweens shaping both the individual in terms of the normative values they impose upon those existing or working within them as well as in terms of the values they attempt to place upon the wider world.

Corporate social responsibility (CSR) has grown out of years of practice within the corporate world focusing on four broad areas that encompass environmental, philanthropic, ethical, and economic responsibility (Stobierski, 2021). Some companies have added specific designations—that is, benefit corporations (B Corps), social purpose corporations (SPCs), and low-profit limited liability companies (L3Cs)—to describe their unique business models and to emphasize the philosophical or social values they wish to espouse. It is seen, in some ways, as "a tactic to preemptively show commitment to society" while allowing the company to "enhance its reputation as a socially responsible company above and beyond what is legally required" (Jeong, et al., 2022).

Within the CSR framework, environmental responsibility, also called stewardship, provides companies with a set of policies and best practices to follow to help avoid unnecessary environmental damage and degradation. Philanthropy and ethics tend to focus on the better treatment of people and the following of standards that improve people's lives. Economic responsibility helps to keep a broader perspective, helping companies see that the improvements in personal lives must coincide with profiteering. To better codify and standardize this approach, the International Standards Organization (ISO) devised ISO 26000 guidelines as way to describe across multiple cultures and countries the requirements for "social responsibility" in corporations that transcend general borders. They believe that these guidelines demonstrate "how businesses and organizations can operate in a socially responsible way, displaying an ethical and transparent behavior that contributes to the health and welfare of society" (ISO, 2016).

However, within these broad areas little is discussed or described about the responsibility of corporations and businesses dealing with the spread and the development of false information. Certainly, ethical responsibility might be an appropriate space to incorporate concepts and issues related to truthfulness and the impact on social well-being. While the issue has been raised much lately, especially in light of certain IT companies' roles in facilitating and speeding up the spread of misinformation, little agreement on responsibility appears to be clearly demarcated. Years earlier, Safieddine et al. (2016) found that the "corporate duty of developers of browsers, social media, and search engines are falling short of the minimum standards of responsibility" and that the spread of fake news and misinformation remained badly enforced through a diminished and poorly implemented sense of corporate social responsibility. Indeed, the failure of X, once known as Twitter, to remain responsible in the face of rising levels of hate speech (one journalist remarks that the platform "is starting to look more and more like an unregulated hate site") is a prime example of how a lack of concern for social responsibility in order to maximize profits poisons the information well (Shah, 2023). New policy at X appears to prioritize the sharing of information regardless of its impact upon others—including the sharing of hate speech and misinformation from right wing content creators—and rewards it by monetizing the amount of sharing and notoriety a piece is given (Nix and Ellison, 2023). As false information and rumors have been shown to move more quickly than factual information and carry far more profit as a result, one can see how upholding standards of truth would decline very quickly.

Complicating matters, however, is the fact that many people seem to have a poor idea about whether corporations are doing enough as it is or whether they even should do something. The Roper Center for Public Opinion Research at Cornell University reports that "Americans do not have fully formed perspectives of corporate social responsibility in the context of dealing with misinformation" (Liu, 2017). The lack of understanding about the responsibilities of platform creators in curtailing misinformation leads to a general sense of quiet acceptance or even general ignorance among social media users. Many blame the creators of the content—especially the trolls pestering comment boards or the cranks spreading conspiracies—rather than the platforms themselves. Still, the decline in the use of some social media platforms that cater to hate speech may suggest that people are reaching their own conclusions about the issue, preferring to abandon an unregulated platform rather than tolerate poor online conditions. Additionally, in an ironic twist, Jeong et al. (2022) find that many users of platforms will lie about themselves in order to protect their identities. This is seen by users as the practical and safe option because obscuring one's identity is sometimes the only way to deal with companies that do not guarantee privacy or make their methods of information handling transparent.

CORPORATE EPISTEMOLOGY

What comes next, then, is the need to develop solutions within the corporate world that help to mitigate the transmission and sharing of misinformation across IT platforms and social media. Lamy and Beyneix (2022) suggest that the problems related to misinformation in the private and public sphere amount to "epistemic pollution." Epistemology concerns itself with the ways in which people create knowledge and the so-called doxastic attitudes (for example, belief, disbelief, or neither) that people express about the world they encounter. Such pollution in the form of misinformation, fake news, lies, and "BS," it is argued, disturbs and distorts the ways in which people are able make new knowledge or commit to a belief in factual information. They argue that companies need to engage in corporate epistemic responsibility (CER), an offshoot of CSR, where the company would "care about the reliability of the information the organization produces" and ultimately hold itself responsible to "account for any possible epistemic faults" it might perpetuate (Beyneix and Lamy, 2021). In other words, CER would commit companies to being purveyors of factual information while also being vigilant protectors of it, providing a place for truth to be fostered and protected from the stain and negative influence of debased information.

Of course, there are issues when using the term "epistemology," as it incorporates multiple perspectives that exist upon a sliding scale ranging from objectivism (for example, meaning exists within an object), constructionism (meaning is created from the interplay of subject and object), and subjectivism (meaning exists solely within the subject). The relationship between misinformation and factual information becomes more difficult to pin down if we are purely examining the world through a subjectivist lens. Essentially, one must assume that Beyneix and Lamy are examining epistemology from a purely objectivist perspective, assuming that truth would be found within objects and therefore easily defined by members of a company. It would follow then that epistemic pollutants stemming from fake news would be easily found and rooted out in this objective perspective.

It becomes more complex, however, when moving into constructionism and subjectivism, with lies and truth being constructed in social or individual contexts. An individual's experience within the world impacts their perception of it, rendering absolute judgments about the veracity of an experience or of a disputed fact that much more difficult to attain. If the corporate structure assumes one thing is true, but its lower-ranking members believe another, strain between two sets of beliefs is bound to occur. As a result, identifying epistemological weaknesses as a main cause of false information being spread through a company might be either difficult, misleading, or a source of conflicting interests within that organization. More pragmatic approaches are needed to explore whether there is validity to this conceptualization. Certainly, the image of "epistemic pollution" is a compelling one, but what one actually believes epistemology to entail needs to be more deeply examined before it can be used as a solution to the incredibly complex interplay of fact, fiction, and belief.

CORPORATE COOPERATION WITH GOVERNMENT AND THE INTERSECTION WITH PUBLIC POLICY

Despite the muddied waters and somewhat ineffective jargon surrounding corporate epistemic responsibility—and the issues of ignoring misinformation within CSR overall—some practical approaches to curtailing fake news across larger organizations and corporations may work. One strategy suggested by Squire (2023) is the so-called deplatforming of websites that spread hate, foment extremism, and traffic in misinformation. Deplatforming entails removing individuals and groups from any online service, including social media platforms, web hosting services, or internet service providers. In one case study, Squire shows the effective impact of deplatforming. After spreading numerous hate speech through its site, white supremacist site *The Daily Stormer* was removed and forced to relocate online seventeen times. The takedowns of their domain spaces resulted in lost audiences and, according to Alexa Domain Rankings, a loss of significant traffic from all users, falling from one of the most trafficked sites to one of the least. Squire concludes from her examination of multiple hate sites (including the notorious 8chan) that "consistent infrastructure-level deplatforming can be crippling, particularly if the domain name is canceled repeatedly before traffic begins to rebuild" (2023).

Such strategies can be helpful, so long as the companies hosting the content work to keep the hate content off their platforms. Yet in the case of X/Twitter, which has been peddling more hate speech since being taken over by Elon Musk, its owner clearly revels in the spread of conspiracies, false information, and various hate-filled tropes. When the owner of such a platform contributes to the spread of false information, there can be little hope of acknowledgment that a problem even exists. For some time, Facebook's Mark Zuckerberg had also taken similar stances toward false information by claiming that it was not Facebook's problem but was entirely the fault of the platform's users. Still, the company made efforts from 2019 onward to improve user interaction with truthful information by "downranking" or diminishing the ability of users to find this false information. Notably, they have attempted to "reduce the spread of posts that made sensationalized health claims" through downranking as well as trying to eliminate access to pages that attempt to sell items or services "based on misrepresented or false health-related claims" (Singh, 2019). For their part, they are doing their little bit to limit the flow of some false and misleading information in the health sphere. However, given that several billion people use Facebook, the amount of false information being spread extends far beyond sensational health claims. In that regard such efforts may wind up being minimal in their impact.

SANTA CLARA PRINCIPLES

In 2018, organizations and social advocates developed the Santa Clara Principles in order to address some of the problems related to information handling in the IT sector, including the use and spread of false information, the disclosure of information to governments, and the need for corporate transparency when removing online content. The principles are designed to provide clear "baseline standards" for businesses to follow in order to describe their own actions and the consequences of removing or altering content online (Santa Clara Principles, 2023). The principles stem in part from the public outrage that occurred some time ago after IT company Yahoo! disclosed the personal information of a journalist to the Chinese government in 2004, resulting in the arrest of political dissidents in that country (Kahn, 2005; Santa Clara Principles, 2021, p. 5). The principles exist now as a call for transparency and responsibility among IT businesses when handling and trading their users' personal information. They are intended to create "meaningful transparency around internet platforms' increasingly aggressive moderation of user-generated content" (Santa Clara Principles, 2021). The principles provide guidelines for several areas, including sharing the number of users or posts taken down by a platform, the need to provide notification of why something has been removed, and the provision of user appeals over decisions to take something down (Santa Clara Principles, 2021, pp. 7–9).

While it is clear that these rules were intended to curtail abuses of power and the limits on free speech imposed by governments and others in power, the principles nevertheless can improve the lives of those harmed by hateful speech and malicious misinformation. The key is not solely that information is kept or removed from platforms, though this is an important issue. Instead the most important aspect is the advocacy for a culture of *transparency* in IT that provides a rationale for why information is handled, examined, and eliminated (or not) from a platform. Issues of free speech notwithstanding, one can argue that being clear on *why* something is removed can go a long way to alleviating the resentment or misunderstanding among groups of people and among individual users. Users who have spread misinformation, for example, may not always be aware it is misinformation, perceiving it instead as something truthful and therefore beneficial for others to receive. Being made aware of this error in judgment and given a rationale for removal may go a long way toward defusing anger while also mitigating the impact of fake news itself.

ANTI-DEFAMATION LEAGUE AND THE
CENTER FOR TECHNOLOGY AND SOCIETY

Similar to the Santa Clara Principles, other organizations have attempted to improve the lives of people interacting with others online. The Anti-Defamation League (ADL) has been a longtime advocate for reducing hate speech and antisemitism. In 2014 it codrafted *Best Practices for Responding to Cyberhate*, which provides online platforms a set of guidelines to help handle and reduce hate messages and similar aggressive behaviors online (ADL, 2014). Subsequently, in 2017 the ADL founded its Center for Technology and Society, an advocacy and research center "focused on fighting hate and harassment on-line" (US Congress, 2020), partnering with various stakeholders in industry, the public sphere, government, and targeted communities (ADL, 2023). The center itself is situated in Silicon Valley and partners with major IT companies including Facebook, Microsoft, and Google with their Cyberhate Problem Solving Lab. X/Twitter is listed by the ADL as also participating in this lab, but its status is unclear given the changes in ownership and direction that X has taken as it becomes looser in the enforcement of policies regarding hate speech on its platform.

In tandem with the Center for Technology and Society, the ADL has given pragmatic suggestions for how to approach solving these difficult information sharing problems, especially rising extremism and hate speech as well as the misinformation that contributes to such a rise in extremist viewpoints. Their emphasis is on a "constantly iterative interdisciplinary approach" (US Congress, 2020, p. 88), which involves ongoing responsive changes in schools, government agencies, NGOs, corporations, and online platform users; it also develops tools, marketing campaigns, litigation, and legislation against hate speech. Some of these suggestions involve the following: strengthening laws against those who spread hate online, advocating for social media to institute "Robust Governance [*sic*]," and improving the training of law enforcement to handle cyber hate crimes (US Congress, 2020). While each of these recommendations speaks directly to issues of hate speech and harassment, misinformation and false narratives also overlap with these pathologies. They can surely be addressed in similar fashion with governments improving laws and the enforcement of regulations against spreading false information.

Further, companies should be urged to apply such policies beyond acts of hate as well. Some of the suggestions from the ADL include enhancing transparency, which should be a universal approach to combating information pathologies and is a major step toward improving accountability. Similarly, organizations need to ensure strong policies against hate and related misinformation by strengthening policy enforcement and reducing the influence and impact of hateful content on individuals. Ultimately, there is the need to expand tools and services for any groups that are typically targeted by hate groups (US Congress, 2020). Each of these suggestions could apply to fighting misinformation as well, especially with the increase in transparency and accountability against perpetrators. Creating tools and services for those who are targeted by fake news creators would also be a worthy endeavor, likely improving conditions for those who are often singled out for their beliefs, ideals, gender, race, or ethnicity.

SOCIETIES AT LARGE: CREATING A "HYPERTOOL" FOR MISINFORMATION MITIGATION

In the end, the question remains how to best amend the societal pathologies and problems exacerbated by fake news, conspiracy theories, misinformation, hate speech, and politicized extremist viewpoints. It becomes clearer, after examining the institutions that have wider impact on societies—for example, governments, IT corporations, third-party nongovernment organizations (NGOs)—that they hold significant responsibility to amend these problems. As larger groups interact and cooperate with each other, they can provide individual users with better environments to share factual information and come to understand and even tolerate alternative perspectives. Selle and Wollebæk (2015) suggest that

> such intersecting organizational networks can lead to increased tolerance and understanding for other people's arguments. If the tension is reduced between organizational members, it can perhaps also have a positive effect on those who stand on the outside. Overlapping and intersecting organizational networks generate knowledge about "the others" and cross-cutting pressure that can counteract escalating conflict between individuals and groups.

It is this intersection of various organizations and the crossing of boundaries that exist between the minds of individuals that can help alleviate the issues surrounding misinformation. The development of such a countermeasure to hate and lies is dependent upon generating familiarity with others outside intolerant groups, but it is imperative to work in tandem with various levels of organizations and to be aware of how these intersect people's lives and impact them whether they are fully aware of them or not.

The ultimate goal, then, is a kind of "social digital responsibility" arising from the interaction of micro-, meso-, and macro-information worlds, tapping into the vast collective mentalities of the society at large, while also respecting individuals in all their complexity and irrational glory. One vision of how this might look examines the various stakeholders in digital responsibility and suggests a series of necessary guidelines to ensure that people understand who is responsible for the ethical sharing and using of information. In other words, we must ask ourselves how we how use digital media, tools, systems, and information-sharing technologies "to create and nurture thriving, productive relationships with employees, customers, communities, and other stakeholders?" (Frick, 2023). While this seems at first glance to be a massive problem beyond comprehension like Merton's hyperobject, it may be helpful to see this as a societal "hypertool," something that harnesses the collective wisdom and crowd-sourced power and wealth of people acting in dedicated ways to solving social problems. Such digital responsibility starts with ourselves, intersects with our local worlds and the intermediate institutions that shape us, and ends with our larger national and international collaborations. The key is insisting upon transparency and demanding agency while igniting imaginations and holding on to hope.

REFERENCES

Anti-Defamation League (ADL). (2014). *Best practices for responding to cyberhate.* ADL. https://www.adl.org/best-practices-responding-cyberhate.

Anti-Defamation League (ADL). (2023). *Center for technology and society.* ADL. https://www.adl.org/research-centers/center-technology-society.

Beyneix, I., and Lamy, E. (2021). Epistemic responsibility: A missing dimension of corporate social responsibility. *ESCP Research Institute of Management (ERIM).* https://academ.escpeurope.eu/pub/IP%202021-45-EN.pdf.

Burnett, G., and Jaeger, P. T. (2011). The theory of information worlds and information behavior. In A. Spink and J. Heinström (eds.), *New directions in information behaviour* (pp. 161–80). Emerald Insight.

Frick, T. (2023). Understanding social digital responsibility. Mightybytes. https://www.mightybytes.com/blog/social-digital-responsibility/.

Habermas, J. (1992). Further reflections on the public sphere. In J. Calhoun (ed.), *The Habermas reader* (pp. 341–65). Cambridge: Polity.

Hornsey, M. J., Pearson, S., Kang, J., Sassenberg, K., Jetten, J., Van Lange, P. A., Medina, L. G., Amiot, C. E., Ausmees, L., Baguma, P., Barry, O., Becker, M., Bilewicz, M., Castelain, T., Costantini, G., Dimdins, G., Espinosa, A., Finchilescu, G., Friese, M., and Bastian, B. (2023). Multinational data show that conspiracy beliefs are associated with the perception (and reality) of poor national economic performance. *European Journal of Social Psychology, 53*(1), pp. 78–89. https://doi .org/10.1002/ejsp.2888.

International Organization for Standardization (ISO). (2016). *Benefits in applying ISO 26000—Selected case studies as a result of the SR MENA Project.* https://www .iso.org/files/live/sites/isoorg/files/archive/pdf/en/srmena_factsheets.pdf.

Jeong, M., Kim, D., Park, H., Zo, H. J., and Ciganek, A. P. (2022). Corporate social responsibility's influence on misinformation in online platforms. *SSRN.* http://dx .doi.org/10.2139/ssrn.4096599.

Kahn, J. (2005). Yahoo helped Chinese to prosecute journalist. *New York Times.* https: //www.nytimes.com/2005/09/08/business/worldbusiness/yahoo-helped-chinese-to -prosecute-journalist.html.

Lamy, E., and Beyneix, I. (2022). Fighting epistemic pollution (fake news, business BS) with extended corporate social responsibility. *LSE Business Review.* https: //blogs.lse.ac.uk/businessreview/2022/03/07/fighting-epistemic-pollution-fake -news-business-bs-with-extended-corporate-social-responsibility/.

Liu, C. (2017). Responsibility, overconfidence, & intervention efforts in the age of fake news. *Roper Center for Public Opinion Research. Cornell University.* https: //ropercenter.cornell.edu/responsibility-overconfidence-intervention-efforts-age -fake-news.

Lynch, D. (2006). *Catching the big fish: meditation, consciousness, and creativity.* Penguin.

Millar, B. (2021). Misinformation and the limits of individual responsibility. *Social Epistemology Review and Reply Collective, 10*(12), pp. 8–21. https://wp.me/ p1Bfg0-6kD.

Morton, T. (2013). *Hyperobjects: Philosophy and ecology after the end of the world.* University of Minnesota Press. https://doi.org/10.5749/j.ctt4cggm7.

Myers, S. L., and Kang, C. (2022). The fight over truth also has a red state, blue state divide. *New York Times.* https://www.nytimes.com/2022/07/10/business/ disinformation-democrats-republicans.html.

Nix, N., and Ellison, S. (2023). Following Musk's lead, YouTube and Facebook are giving up on policing conspiracies. *Washington Post.*

Pratt, M. L. (2002). Arts of the contact zone. In Janice M. Wolff (ed.), *Professing in the contact zone* (pp. 1–20) Urbana, IL.

Safieddine, F., Masri, W., and Pourghomi, P. (2016). Corporate responsibility in combating O-online misinformation. *International Journal of Advanced Computer Science and Applications, 7*(2), pp. 126–32. Doi: 10.14569/IJACSA.2016.070217.

Santa Clara Principles. (2021). *Santa Clara Principles open consultation report. Electronic Frontier Foundation.* https://santaclaraprinciples.org/images/SantaClara _Report.pdf.

Santa Clara Principles. (2023). History. *Electronic Frontier Foundation.* https:// santaclaraprinciples.org/history/.

Selle, P., and Wollebæk, D. (2015). The complex relationship between civil society and trust. *Italian Sociological Review, 5*(3), pp. 273–91. https://doi.org/10.13136/ isr.v5i3.110.

Shah, A. (2023). Experts: Elon Musk offers "economic incentive" to spew "most shocking and hateful" rhetoric on X. *Salon.com*. https://www.salon.com/2023 /08/12/experts-elon-musk-offers-economic-incentive-to-spew-most-shocking-and -hateful-rhetoric-on-x/.

Singh, S. (2019). Rising through the ranks: How algorithms rank and curate content in search results and on news feeds. *New America*. https://www.newamerica.org/ oti/reports/rising-through-ranks/.

Squire, M. (2023). Bad gateway: How deplatforming affects extremist websites. *Anti-Defamation League*. https://www.adl.org/resources/report/bad-gateway-how -deplatforming-affects-extremist-websites.

Stobierski, T. (2021). What is corporate social responsibility? 4 types. *Harvard Business School Online*. https://online.hbs.edu/blog/post/types-of-corporate-social -responsibility.

Umam, A. N., Muluk, H., and Milla, M. N. (2018). The need for cognitive closure and belief in conspiracy theories: An exploration of the role of religious fundamentalism in cognition. In *Diversity in unity: Perspectives from psychology and behavioral sciences* (pp. 629–37). CRC Press. https://doi.org/10.1201/9781315225302–79.

US Congress. House. (2020). Committee on Homeland Security. *Examining social media companies' efforts to counter on-line terror content and misinformation: Hearing before the Committee on Homeland Security, House of Representatives, One Hundred Sixteenth Congress, first session, June 26, 2019*. US Government Publishing Office.

Weiss, A. P., Alwan, A., Garcia, E. P., and Kirakosian, A. T. (2021). Toward a comprehensive model of fake news: A new approach to examine the creation and sharing of false information. *Societies (Basel, Switzerland), 11*(3). https://doi.org/10.3390 /soc11030082.

Afterword

We are living through interesting times, and history unfolds in its own way whether we like it or not. America's culture wars continue; climate change shows wild extremes and anomalous conditions, even as people deny the evidence or concoct conspiracies to rationalize them (Hsu, 2023); distrust of government and different political views remains strong; and our digital lives-in-the-round continue to unfold and morph into something new and unexpected. Yet so much of what seems important now may wind up forgotten, while the things we fail to see currently may wind up in hindsight being the defining characteristics of this era. Those who come after us may chide us for our shortsightedness and our failure to acknowledge what was always right there in front of our faces. Obviously, then, there is a real risk in writing about current technology and how it impacts contemporary society because events and innovations are ongoing and have a way of appearing during writing or, worse, changing the world once everything has been set to paper!

In the case of this book, quite a number of important developments occurred that altered—even if in a tangential way—some of the points made earlier about misinformation and fake news. Certainly, some of these developments merely underscore the points and ideas presented, providing more current examples of ideas already expressed. Some developments, however, may compromise or complicate what has been discussed. As such, this afterword will address a few of these new developments in a cursory fashion so as to point out future developments and potential new directions—though without the benefit of hindsight, a deep-dive examination, or intensive analysis.

One of the major events in the world of information science and academia was the sudden release and widespread adoption of AI in 2023, specifically ChatGPT and other Large Language Models (LLMs) that rely on significant amounts of the digital corpus to conduct machine learning. Notable "weirdness" from some interactions with ChatGPT were shared in the press, ranging from threatening and stalkerish behaviors (Roose, 2023) to outright lying and fabricating information while insisting it was true (Maruf, 2023; Day, 2023).

These events caused quite a lot of public hand wringing and overall surprise. One study in particular has tracked the potential impact of AI on future careers, painting a bleak picture of unemployment in those sectors (Eloundou et al., 2023). This study predicts societal trouble ahead if it is not addressed early on. Economic uncertainty plays a factor in extremism and the spread of misinformation and conspiracy theories, and we should be wary of these developments, but the contribution of LLMs to the general distrust of facts and post-truth apathy—or even nihilism—is largely unexplored. It important to consider whether the impact of this technology will fuel future extremism or contribute to further social unraveling. Already it has been reported that foreign governments are using AI to create and distribute disinformation for the purpose of sowing dissention, further blurring and distorting whatever social and work benefits these technologies might actually provide (Sanger and Myers, 2023).

Of course, it should be noted that LLMs are designed to *satisfy their users* by giving the results and output the user wants. So in that regard it is like a master "bubble maker," a BS-machine, another bendable mirror that relies on what has already been said, giving users the illusion of novelty. LLMs are a powerful reflection into ourselves equipped with near-instant recall and the breadth and depth of human experience recorded in digital texts online. The well-documented (and somewhat sensationalized) tendency of LLMs to "hallucinate" and insist that made-up citations or stories are true is a definite concern (Alkaissi and McFarlane, 2023). The fake news problem may get much worse as a result. But it doesn't necessarily mean it will. So long as users understand the necessary constraints for LLMs and know how to ask the correct questions, LLMs can be controlled by establishing parameters and kept from fabricating things on the spot. Like driving a car, operating an LLM requires knowledge of the rules of the road, so to speak, so it doesn't drive us into a ditch or over a cliff.

What is far more worrisome, however, is the overall urge to anthropomorphize these creations, providing more noise in an already noisy world that blurs fact with fiction, object with subject. We need to remember that no matter what the results, AI output is not the result of cognition. In other words, they are talking but not thinking (Roosen, 2023). Only humanity is at this point capable of the all-important metacognitive functions to self-analyze and reevaluate one's current state of knowledge and ignorance. That anthropomorphized "hallucination" is the result of a program unable to conduct a self-audit of itself using self-awareness and to think about what it is doing. We all know what happens when reality is replaced by fantasy: it only forestalls suffering when the real world comes knocking. In that sense, AI is hardly the direct threat. It is, instead, our own failure to exercise self-awareness of our own ignorance. Socrates was right about what wisdom truly entails: *knowing that you know nothing.* On a note of optimism, though, AI doesn't really lie, it merely recombines what lies (and truths) have already been told by us and has been asked to relay back in new forms to the user. The mirror reveals both truth and lies.

As much as AI and ChatGPT have dominated discussions recently, however, other developments have impacted some of the topics covered in this book, especially in relation to the press and fake news. In April 2023, Dominion Voting Systems settled its lawsuit with Fox News over defamation and the irresponsible assertions that its voting machines had been compromised (Barr et al., 2023). The Great Lie of the stolen 2020 US presidential election is truly one of the more disturbing examples of misinformation and fake news of the past several years. A settlement may have avoided an official ruling on Fox News as a major spreader of right-wing misinformation and propaganda, but a later leak of embarrassing statements made internally at Fox—especially those fretting about losing their audience if they spoke the truth about no evidence of election tampering—expose the fraud that has acted at the heart of their business model (Peters and Robinson, 2023). Their fake news business model represents antijournalism at its worst: a platform for propagandists, antithetical to the standards of objectivity and balance created in the wake of the yellow journalism era, that cater and pander to the false beliefs held by their viewers. The potential dual role of the press as a bulwark against fake news or a facilitator of lies remains as central as ever.

Another story that came out during the writing of this book is the leak of the so-called Discord documents, which were revealed over a gaming chat room by a National Guardsman over a period of several years (Menn, 2023). While the issue is primarily one of national security and the release of classified and sensitive information, some of what was revealed and published in the press involves the extent of misinformation campaigns waged by various governments. In particular, a document describing Russia's Main Scientific Research Computing Center was found that claimed 99 percent of Russian fake profiles in their *Fabrika* misinformation campaign had gone undetected (Menn, 2023). Although this is an ongoing development and such high numbers are not verified, the impact of these campaigns carried out upon an unsuspecting public may be profound. The awareness of such coordinated misinformation campaigns, regardless of their source, is helpful for all of us. The call for transparency among not just IT companies but all governments remains relevant: *we need to know the extent of a problem before we can adequately address it.* Being left in the dark about the success of Russian or other countries' strategic misinformation campaigns only harms us all.

On a final note, a federal judge in July 2023 imposed an injunction against the federal government, limiting its ability to communicate with IT companies and regulate information and expression shared through their online sites (Zakrzewski et al., 2023). While some social media platforms removed right-wing extremists after the January 6, 2021, insurrection against the US Capitol building, Twitter and Facebook have both since reinstated many accounts, including those of former President Donald Trump, who is currently under indictment for instigating the riot. The reframing of hate speech as a primarily First Amendment concern remains troubling, especially in light of growing extremism and lax enforcement against it. While it is too early to say that it will result in more widespread hate speech and related misinformation, it is likely to have an impact on the 2024 election. This is a development that is ongoing yet speaks to the problems outlined in this book and the government policies that need to be bolstered and strengthened to prevent a repeat of the past. One hopes we have learned from our recent past.

Although this is just a small sample of events that have occurred during the writing of this book, they have direct impact on the topics discussed through-out. The struggle to distinguish between falsehood and truth, misinformation and fact is ongoing, from the small world of an individual, the meso information world of a company, and the macro world of a society, nation, or group of nations. At all levels of interaction with information, people are impacted by fake news and misinformation. But in the end, no matter how much falsehood appears to be dominant, no matter how much fake news seems to proliferate among people, so long as we strive for finding truth, reality will always win out.

REFERENCES

Alkaissi, H., and McFarlane, S. I. (2023). Artificial hallucinations in ChatGPT: Implications in scientific writing. *Cureus, 15*(2). https://doi.org/10.7759/cureus.35179.

Barr, J., Farhi, P., Marley, P., and Izadi, E. (2023). Fox News, Dominion settle defamation lawsuit for $787.5 million. *Washington Post.* https://www.washingtonpost.com/media/2023/04/18/fox-news-dominion-settlement/.

Day, T. (2023). A preliminary investigation of fake peer-reviewed citations and references generated by ChatGPT. *The Professional Geographer.* 10.1080/00330124.2023.2190373.

Eloundou, T., Manning, S., Mishkin, P., and Rock, D. (2023). GPTs are GPTs: An early look at the labor market impact potential of Large Language Models. *arXiv.* https://arxiv.org/abs/2303.10130.

Hsu, T. (2023). Falsehoods follow close behind this summer's natural disasters. *New York Times.* https://www.nytimes.com/2023/08/30/business/media/maui-idalia-disinformation-climate-change.html.

Maruf, R. (2023). Lawyer apologizes for fake court citations from ChatGPT. CNN. https://www.cnn.com/2023/05/27/business/chat-gpt-avianca-mata-lawyers/index.html.

Menn, J. (2023). Russians boasted that just 1% of fake social profiles are caught, leak shows. *Washington Post*. https://www.washingtonpost.com/technology/2023/04/16/russia-disinformation-discord-leaked-documents/.

Peters, J. W., and Robinson, K. (2023). Fox stars privately expressed disbelief about election fraud claims. *New York Times*. https://www.nytimes.com/2023/02/16/business/media/fox-dominion-lawsuit.html.

Roose, K. (2023). Why a conversation with Bing's chatbot left me deeply unsettled. *New York Times*. https://www.nytimes.com/2023/02/16/technology/bing-chatbot-microsoft-chatgpt.html.

Roosen, C. (2023). Large Language Models like ChatGPT are writing, but not thinking; and that's an important distinction in the rush toward artificial intelligence. *Adventures in a designed world*. https://www.christopherroosen.com/blog/2023/3/13/chatgpt-writing-not-thinking.

Sanger, D. E., and Myers, S. L. (2023). China sows disinformation about Hawaii fires using new techniques. *New York Times*. https://www.nytimes.com/2023/09/11/us/politics/china-disinformation-ai.html.

Zakrzewski, C., Nix, N., and Menn, J. (2023). Social media injunction unravels plans to protect 2024 elections. *Washington Post*. https://www.washingtonpost.com/technology/2023/07/08/social-media-injunction-doughty-biden-2024-elections/.

Index

About the Author

Andrew Weiss is a digital services librarian at California State University, Northridge, with over fifteen years of experience working in academic libraries. He focuses primarily on scholarly communication issues, especially open access, copyright policy in academia, institutional repositories, and developing better strategies for data curation. He is currently a PhD student with Manchester Metropolitan University in the San Jose State University Gateway program. His current and prior research examines fake news and disinformation; the impact of massive digital libraries such as Google Books, the HathiTrust, and the Internet Archive; the future developments of open access publishing; the impact of "Big Data"; and, last but not least, information ethics. He lives in Los Angeles with his family.

www.ingramcontent.com/pod-product-compliance
Lightning Source LLC
Chambersburg PA
CBHW031411270326
41929CB00010BA/1410